Sin, Grace and Free Will

Volume II

Sin, Grace and Free Will

A Historical Survey of Christian Thought

VOLUME II

From Anselm to the Reformation

Matthew Knell

Ⓒ

James Clarke & Co

For Norm and Donna,
who have taught me what it means to worship God
with all that you are, all that you have and all that you do.

James Clarke & Co
P.O. Box 60
Cambridge
CB1 2NT
United Kingdom

www.jamesclarke.co
publishing@jamesclarke.co

Hardback ISBN: 978 0 227 17607 8
Paperback ISBN: 978 0 227 17655 9

British Library Cataloguing in Publication Data
A record is available from the British Library

First published by James Clarke & Co, 2019

Copyright © Matthew Knell, 2018

Cover vector designed by Garry Killian of Freepik.

Contents

Acknowledgements

The first thanks must go to those writers featured in this book who have wrestled with the revelation of God in their own contexts and in the face of great challenges from culture and philosophy to teach others about the nature of Christian faith concerning sin, grace and free will. I hope that I have treated them honourably in these presentations of their thought and that this work will encourage the wider church, not only those engaged in theological study, to consider these themes from different perspectives to appreciate the riches that are available to us through this great heritage.

For this particular project, I would like to thank all those at the University of Notre Dame that have inspired the writing of these volumes, particularly all those students who have taken the class on sin, grace and free will as they have helped me to process various strands of thought. My thanks also go to the community of the London School of Theology for all the encouragement and support that I receive on a daily basis and especially to Professor Tony Lane for his insight and wise advice as this project developed.

Finally, I am grateful for the patience and love of my family who, given the ongoing work for volumes two and three, are still dealing with the effects of this large-scale research project and who teach me so much about grace through the life we share.

Introduction

I had a difficult but powerful insight as my study of Christianity deepened as I realised that, when reading the Bible, I was finding, even imposing, the theology that I had been taught onto the text. This was not deliberate; the church culture bubble that I grew up in had a very strong influence that was difficult to put to one side in order to allow passages to speak to me and challenge me in fresh ways. The Bible had become, for me, a static text that I would go to with questions in order to find answers, generally ones that gave me comfort. It was no longer the living, breathing word of God. Now, when I read the Bible, I am surprised if it does not subvert ideas that I have of God, humankind and salvation history and convict me to change how I think and how I live my life. It is alive for me once more.

These volumes on sin, grace and free will have taken me on a similar journey through the history of Christian thought. As an undergraduate, one tends to read about the key Christian thinkers of the past, with perhaps excerpts of their writings to illustrate how they approached different concepts. When working at a postgraduate level, one must look far more closely at the sources themselves, although even then secondary sources can play a strong role in research.

The joy of preparing these books has been to seek to throw off the secondary sources, to read the key historical figures' own works, often in their own language (I'm afraid my Greek was not up to working with the early Fathers in the original), and to seek to present these thoughts to the reader. I have tried to keep my voice to a minimum, although it is inevitably present in the choice, organisation and presentation of the material. Throughout, my intention has been to encourage you, the reader, when interested by a thought in these volumes, to go back to the source and decide for yourself what the writer meant.

The results of my research have often been surprising to me. I had not worked heavily on the Reformation period before this book, being more a specialist in the medieval period, and expected a largely popish focus to these writings. That was certainly present, but it was not the sole object of the reformers' writings, which took on Scholastics and fanatics and even each other, often using language that was greatly Catholic in its thought and expression as they sought to reform the faith, rather than restart the faith. It has been pleasing with each thinker presented in the first two volumes to see how greatly each honours Scripture as the prime source of the faith, and how they work with this and the tradition of thought they receive in order to help the Church to understand the faith that it holds. I don't agree with any of them in all they write, but I am struck that these are writers pursuing God as I do within their context and understanding, and, rather than sitting in judgement when I disagree, I am forced to reflect that my own theological matrix probably has many gaps and holes of which I am not aware.

This volume follows the overall method of the previous one in seeking only to present passages that explicitly work with our key themes of sin, grace and free will, although at times there were sections that seemed to scream out for inclusion without any direct references – particularly in areas that discussed the sacraments or the nature of faith. I have stuck to looking at theological works, rather than commentaries on certain portions of Scripture or sermons on specific passages. Occasionally, particularly during the Reformation, there were writers who wrote theological sermons with no set text, rather a set theme, and some of these are included. The volume has been arranged thematically rather than chronologically or by work – except for the short chapter on the Council of Trent that is dealt with by session – in order to bring together different threads of thought on the same issue and show the complexities present in any one thinker's approach to sin, grace or free will.

One change that has been made from Volume One is an attempt to make the language a little more accessible, and so I have sought to modernise the language with my own translations and paraphrases. With good referencing, it is hoped that the task of identifying the precise original passage will not be too hard and this book should be a little more readable. In this regard, I must give great thanks to several current scholars who have allowed me to quote extensively from their translations of the primary sources. Jasper Hopkins has done a wonderful work in translating Anselm of Canterbury into very readable English. He has even made these translations available online for any to access and he very kindly gave me permission to quote from these editions for this work. Professor

Giulio Silano has recently published the first complete translation of Peter Lombard's *Sentences*, a vital work in medieval theology that had a precedence in the study of theology for centuries – far more important in that context than the work of Thomas Aquinas – and I was delighted to receive his permission and that of the Pontifical Institute to use that translation in this volume. Finally, in terms of thanks, Professor Tony Lane and Graham Davies have given me permission to use their work on John Calvin's *On the Bondage and Liberation of the Will* here, the only translation that I know of that work. For the rest, I have sought to work with the original texts, helped of course by available translations, to present readable quotations here for the reader.

The choice of writers to include in this volume was not easy, however, the framework was agreed with the publishers to work from the beginnings of the Scholastic movement with Anselm of Canterbury to the end of the first phase of the Reformation at the Council of Trent. The decision to end at that point controlled things a little, since it seemed to demand the inclusion of Luther, Zwingli, Calvin and Trent itself, which together would produce a sizeable amount of material. Some will have wanted other reforming voices to be included, but the balance of the volume would have been wrong in my opinion.

The balance may still not be right, and as a medievalist I am aware of how many thinkers have been left out in the decision about whom to include. There is a strong domination of early scholastic thinkers from the late eleventh and twelfth centuries. Anselm of Canterbury is a logical inclusion as the father of Scholasticism and the author of the method of 'faith seeking understanding'. Originally, I was going to limit Anselm's contribution to the topic of free will; however, reading through his works again, it seemed important to allow his work on sin, in particular, to feature here as the first major writer on the subject since Augustine. Bernard of Clairvaux could have featured more heavily but, in the end, I decided to focus on his most explicitly relevant work, *On Grace and Free Choice*, partly because of the topic and partly because Bernard is a thinker in the mystical line of medieval thought, while the other choices are more Scholastic in their method. I would have loved to include a full chapter on Peter Abelard, as yet, however, I am unaware of any translations of his great *Theologiae* into English (I know the *Summi Boni* has been translated into German) and to include Abelard would thus break my intention to direct the reader back to the original source – I do not expect you all to learn Latin on the way. Peter Lombard, as stated above, is now available thanks to Professor Silano's work and is a vital voice in medieval theology. Thomas Aquinas had to be included, though only after a deep breath before plunging into the *Summa Theologiae*. I decided not to go outside this work (although there are a few quotations from the Supplement to the *Summa*, which were collected from Aquinas' other writings), given that it runs to many thousands of pages in itself, and hope that you will not judge me for limiting your access to Aquinas. There were many other writers in the medieval period who could justly be included – I nearly put in a chapter on Duns Scotus and his views on free will – but there was not sufficient space to include any more and I seek the pardon of those with specific interests that are not represented here.

The inspiration for this series was a perceived gap in the presentation of the Church's thought on sin, grace and free will, combined with a desire to allow readers to meet key historical figures directly rather than purely through the thoughts of secondary scholars. Most of the writings looked at in the first volume felt a little chaotic when looking particularly for these themes, but this was because their major motivation was establishing the foundations of the Christian faith in light of diverse thought and under great political pressure. In this second volume, the thinkers under study present works on particular subjects that makes access to and presentation of their thought generally a little easier, although Martin Luther was a struggle on this level as he was writing in reaction to so many different views – he felt much more like an Early Church thinker than a late medieval one in this regard. What continues to come across strongly as this research progresses is that there is a level of commonality across the Church on some aspects – the priority of grace, the effects of original sin, the limitations of the human will; however, the complexities present in the concepts themselves, in how different thought patterns mould writers' approaches and, most importantly, in the various parts of the Bible that speak about these concepts, lead to a wide variety in ways of thinking that stretches our minds well beyond any automatic understanding.

We shall begin with Anselm and, for those continuing from Volume One – I can't think many have been anxiously awaiting this next instalment in Harry Potter-like frenzy – we move out of the Dark Ages with its limited novel thinking into a new renaissance period. Erigena, featured in the Epilogue to Volume One, lived at the time of the Carolingian Renaissance under the Emperor Charlemagne, a brief revival of learning but not one that transformed Western thought. Augustine's writings remained supreme as the theological tool to work with Scripture and faith, and in many ways this continues through the medieval and modern periods. The difference is that there is not an unswerving devotion to his thought, rather an appreciation of his wisdom while recognising that it is not the final, complete word on our understanding of God, humankind and all that exists. The twelfth-century renaissance (not a catchy title, I know) ushered in the movement known as Scholasticism in which, on the basis of the authority of Scripture and the faith determined by the Church Fathers, people sought to engage the various forms of revelation more deeply with their reason. The Father of this movement was Anselm of Canterbury.

I.

Anselm of Canterbury

As the introduction indicated, Anselm of Canterbury (c.1033-1109) ushers in a new phase in the history of Christian thought in the movement known as Scholasticism. His title would seem to give Anselm a very English identity, but this is misleading. Born in Aosta in Italy, he travelled to Bec in Normandy to study under Lanfranc (c.1005/1010-1089), who was then gaining fame for his teaching. Anselm succeeded Lanfranc both as the abbot of the monastery at Bec and then as Archbishop of Canterbury as part of the Norman development of England. His method is best exemplified in his phrase 'faith seeking understanding', built upon a sentence that Augustine of Hippo had highlighted from the book of Isaiah: 'For I do not seek to understand so that I may believe; but I believe that I might understand.'[1]

For first-time readers of Anselm, he can appear to be a pure philosopher-theologian, given the paucity of references in many works to either Scripture or the Church Fathers, but this would be to misunderstand his context and purpose. Anselm's writings were largely developments from discussions with his student monks and intended for reading by other schooled members of the Church. They were thus not 'Apologetics' in any modern sense of a rational exploration of the Christian faith that might be accepted by someone outside the Church; rather, a right faith built upon Scripture and accepting the traditional teaching of the Church was assumed, and Anselm sought with the use of reason to build on this through a rational engagement with the revelation of God in all its forms.

---

1. Anselm, *Proslogion*, 1. The quotation does not marry up with a modern translation of Isaiah 7:9, and is even an extension from Jerome's Latin translation that would more naturally become 'if you will not believe, you will not be steadfast' (the last word in Latin is *'permanebitis'*, from which we get the word 'permanent'). Augustine's work with this verse made the concept of understanding accepted by Anselm's time.

A classic example of this would be his ontological argument for the existence of God, in which Anselm seeks to demonstrate that the concept of a supreme being necessitates the existence of that being because otherwise the idea itself is wrong.[1] Anselm's case is internally logically consistent and is an interesting study for someone inside the Church wanting to wrestle with God's existence. However, as Immanuel Kant (1724-1804) first conclusively showed, it carries no authority outside the faith – as if a good enough argument would force God to pop into existence. In recent years, the ontological argument has resurfaced as a tool aimed at convincing those without faith, which seems neither to honour Anselm's intent in his writing nor the audience, given that the argument presupposes faith.

Anselm's most famous works are the *Proslogion* and *Cur Deus Homo* (Why God Became Man). The *Proslogion* is the source used for his method and the ontological argument, and is an exploration of God, with little on themes relevant to this book. It exemplifies how Anselm was tied to the teaching he had received, most notably in the construction of a Trinitarian God from 'pure' rational principles that inevitably results in an Augustinian analogy of mind, knowledge and love; the rational exploration is controlled by the faith of the Church. The *Cur Deus Homo* is a crucial work for those interested in the doctrine of salvation, and thus does have material on sin and on salvific grace, but these are not as clearly developed as they appear in other works that will be presented here. This chapter will begin by looking at two works by Anselm that deal with sin, firstly, looking at the origin of sin and evil itself in the book *On the Fall of the Devil* and, then, looking at sin and humankind in *On the Virgin Conception and Original Sin*. The second part of the chapter will move to Anselm's writing on free will, which is closely related to themes of sin and grace, in two books – *On Free Will* and the *De Concordia* – which examine human free will, the latter in relation to of the concepts of foreknowledge, predestination and grace.

On the Fall of the Devil

On the Fall of the Devil (*De Casu Diaboli*) takes the form of a conversation between teacher and student, a common approach for Anselm and one most famously associated with Plato. The style can help the writer to

---

1. Anselm, *Proslogion*, 2. This is the briefest introduction to the case, which in classic Anselmian fashion repeats similar concepts multiple times in any given paragraph that seems almost designed to confuse the reader – examples of this will be found later in this chapter.

consider a subject from an opposing viewpoint, although often questions one might wish to raise are not dealt with, while others are answered briefly with the student responding along the lines of, 'I cannot see anything wrong with that', where the modern reader may be thinking, 'I can'.

The book begins with standard ideas on God from the Early Church, that he is good in his essence and therefore cannot be the cause of evil. Related to this is the concept of being, and since God is the fount of all being, all that truly has existence is good and sin or evil is therefore the opposite of this, the negation of being. Enter Anselm of Canterbury with a characteristically repetitive statement:

> In this [improper] mode God is said to cause many things which he does not cause. For example, he is said to lead into temptation because he does not keep from temptation, although he is able [to keep from temptation]. And [he is said] to cause what-is-not not to be because he does not cause it to be, although he is able [to cause it to be].[1]

Anselm then moves on to the devil and why, unlike other angels, the devil was not given persevering grace to retain his created, blessed state. The student proposes that, had God given the devil persevering grace, he could not have fallen and would not then have tempted humanity. In responding to this, Anselm distinguishes between the gift of perseverance, the ability to receive it and the will to receive it, clarifying this by an example from the student's experience:

Teacher. God did give him the ability and the will to receive perseverance.

Student. Then, he received what God gave, and he had what he received.

T. Yes, he received it and had it.

S. Therefore, he received and had perseverance.

T. No, he did not receive it; and so, he did not have it.

S. But did you not say that God gave to him, and he received, the ability and the will to receive perseverance?

T. I said it. But I did not say that God gave him the receiving of perseverance. [I said] only [that God granted him] to be able to, and to will to, receive perseverance.

S. So if he was able [to receive perseverance] and willed [to receive it], then he did receive it.

---

1. Anselm, *On the Fall of the Devil*, 1.

T.   This inference does not necessarily follow.

S.   Unless you show me, I fail to see why not.

T.   Have you ever begun something with the ability and the will to complete it, but nevertheless failed to complete it because your will was changed before the completion of the thing?

S.   Often.

T.   So you willed to, and were able to, persevere in what you did not persevere.

S.   To be sure, I willed [to persevere]; but I did not persevere in willing, and thus I did not persevere in the action.[1]

From this, the teacher seeks to show that, while the devil had the ability and the will to receive perseverance, yet his part in willing to receive it was not complete. Anselm states: 'It is not the case that he did not receive it because God did not give it; rather, God did not give it because he did not receive it.'[2] He continues:

> [The Devil] freely lost the will which he had. And just as he received the possession of it for as long as he had it, so he was able to receive the permanent keeping of what he deserted. But because he deserted, he did not receive. Therefore, that which he did not receive to keep because he deserted it, he did not receive not because God did not give it, but, rather, God did not give it because he did not receive it.[3]

The responsibility for the fall into evil is thus wholly laid at the door of the devil:

> Therefore, I say that the reason [the Devil] did not will when and what he ought to have willed is not that his will had a deficiency which resulted from God's failure to give; rather, [he did not will when and what he ought to have willed] because by willing what he ought not to have willed, he expelled his good will in consequence of a supervening evil will. Accordingly, it is not the case that he did not have, or did not receive, a good persevering will because God did not give it; rather, God did not give it because he deserted it by willing what he ought not to have willed; and by deserting it he did not keep it.[4]

---

1. Ibid., 3.
2. Ibid.
3. Ibid.
4. Ibid.

Anselm still has the issue of the very existence of evil to deal with: how could anything created by the good source of being will something evil? Anselm does not want to place the blame in the will, and therefore brings in the concept of injustice as the essence of evil.

> We ought to believe that justice is the good in virtue of which men and angels are good, or just, and in virtue of which the will is called good, or just. But we ought to believe that injustice is the evil which makes both the will and [men and angels] evil and which we call nothing other than the privation of the good; and so, we maintain that this very injustice is nothing other than a privation of justice. For when a will was first given to rational nature, it was – at the moment of giving – turned by the Giver towards what it was supposed to will; or better, it was not turned but was created upright. As long as the will stood fast in this uprightness (which we call truth or justice) in which it was created, it was just. But when it turned itself away from what it was supposed [to will] and turned towards that which it ought not to have [willed], it did not stand fast in the 'original' uprightness, so to speak, in which it was created. When [the will] deserted this original uprightness, it lost something great and received nothing in its place except its privation, which has no being and which we call injustice.[1]

The student does react against this in the following chapter, arguing that evil does seem to have existence since it does have an influence or power. The teacher replies to this that evil appears to have existence, but the fact that we identify anything as a thing or having effects does not mean that it actually exists.

> Therefore, it is not necessary that nothing be something simply because its name somehow or other signifies something. Rather, it is necessary that nothing be nothing, because its name signifies something in the aforementioned way. And so, in this aforementioned way the fact that evil is nothing is not opposed to the fact that the name 'evil' is significative – provided that 'evil' signifies something by destroying [i.e. by negating] it and, thus, is constitutive of no thing.[2]

For the most part, the remainder of this book works through the ideas presented here to greater depth – the will of the devil or of angels, what justice and injustice are. For the purpose of our current study, there is

---

1. Ibid., 9.
2. Ibid., 11.

one other quotation highly worthy of note since it hints towards the whole paradigm of God and time that will be key to understanding foreknowledge and predestination in Anselm's work. It comes in a section comparing God's foreknowledge with the devil's, the latter being incomplete but sufficient to know that punishment would result from a wrong use of the will. Anselm notes at this point that God's foreknowledge needs to be understood within a wider concept of his being, an area that he will develop significantly in the *De Concordia*.

God's foreknowledge is not properly called foreknowledge. For the one to whom all things are always present does not have foreknowledge of future things; rather he has knowledge of present things. Therefore, since foreknowledge of a future event is a different notion from knowledge of a present event, divine 'foreknowledge' and the foreknowledge about which we are asking need not have the same consequence.[1]

Foreknowledge, in relation to God, is thus a misnomer in Anselm's opinion, since God at all times and in all places simply has knowledge of all that was and is and will be. We shall return to this when investigating Anselm's thought on free will and grace.

On the Virgin Conception and Original Sin

This book (in Latin *De Conceptu Virginali*) expands on an aspect of an issue that Anselm raised in his book on why God became man (*Cur Deus Homo*). The question concerns how Christ could be conceived and born of a human (the prologue uses the phrase 'the sinful mass of the human race'[2]) since this would imply that Christ inherits original sin and the punishment that that entails. This is a major issue that results from a late Augustinian understanding of sin, and causes Anselm to investigate the nature and transmission of sin under his higher purpose of defending the purity of Christ, in order that he might be able to die for the sins of the whole world, rather than for the sin that he himself inherits from Adam.

Before delving into Anselm's construction of original sin, we shall look first at what Anselm considers sin to be in the relevant sections; this presentation will then look at original sin, sin in infants, their relation to Adam and the effects of baptism. Finally, some of the sections on Christ's relationship to Adam will be mentioned, although these will be limited since they are not at the core of this project.

---

1. Ibid., 21.
2. Anselm, *On the Virgin Conception and Original Sin*, Prologue.

Anselm makes two interesting statements on the nature of sin in chapters four and five. Firstly, he states that sin is fundamentally related to the will rather than to the action.

> As for my having said that an action is called unjust not in itself but on account of an unjust will . . . Now, if the action were a sin, then when the action passed away so that it no longer existed, the sin would likewise pass away and no longer exist. Or [if the work were a sin, then] as long as the work [*e.g.* the letters] remained, the sin would not be removed. But we often see cases in which sins are not removed even though the action ceases, as well as cases in which sins are removed even though the work remains. Therefore, neither the action (which passes away) nor the work (which remains) is ever [itself] a sin.[1]

This will be important when relating original sin to infants. Secondly, related to some of the teaching in *On the Fall of the Devil*, sin is linked to injustice and a lack of being:

> By comparison, when an evil man rages and is driven into various dangers to his soul, *viz.* evil deeds, we declare that injustice causes these deeds. [We say this] not because injustice is a being or does something but because the will (to which all the voluntary movements of the entire man are submitted), lacking justice, driven on by various appetites, being inconstant, unrestrained, and uncontrolled, plunges itself and everything under its control into manifold evils – all of which justice, had it been present, would have prevented from happening. From these considerations, then, we easily recognize that injustice has no being, even though we are accustomed to give the name 'injustice' to an unjust will's affections and acts, which, considered in themselves, are something. By this line of reasoning we understand evil to be nothing. For even as injustice is only the absence of required justice, so evil is only the absence of required good. But no being – even if it is called evil – is nothing; and for it to be evil is not the same thing as for it to be something. Indeed, for any being to be evil is simply for it to lack the good which it ought to have. But to lack the good which ought to be present is not the same as to be something.[2]

This concept of justice is important in Anselm's ideas of original sin going back to Adam and Eve as the essence of the effects of sin:

---

1. Ibid., 4.
2. Ibid., 5.

Therefore, if Adam and Eve had kept their original justice, those who were to be born of them would originally have been just, even as were Adam and Eve. But because Adam and Eve sinned personally – sinned even though originally they were strong and uncorrupted and had the ability always easily to keep justice – their whole being became weakened and corrupted. Indeed, the body [became weakened and corrupted] because after their sin it became like the bodies of brute animals, *viz.* subject to corruption and to carnal appetites. And the soul [became weakened and corrupted] because as a result of the bodily corruption and the carnal appetites, as well as on account of its need for the goods which it had lost, it became infected with carnal desires. And because the whole of human nature was in Adam and Eve, none of it being outside of them, human nature as a whole was weakened and corrupted.[1]

While Anselm here talks of the defects in human nature that resulted from the first sin, in the opening chapter he is careful to make a distinction in defining original sin that this is found in the origin of each person rather than the origin of human nature itself.

Indeed, there is no doubt that the word 'original' is derived from the word 'origin'. Hence, if original sin is present only in man, it seems to take its name either (1) from reference to the origin of human nature (*i.e.* from the beginning of human nature) – original in that this sin is contracted at human nature's origin – or else (2) from reference to the origin (*i.e.* to the beginning) of each person, because this sin is contracted at each person's origin. But this sin is seen not to stem from the beginning of human nature, since human nature's origin was just, for our first parents were created just and altogether sinless. Therefore, original sin seems to take the name 'original' from reference to the origin of each human person. Yet, if anyone says that original sin is called original because of the fact that individuals acquire it from those from whom they received the origin of their nature, I will not object – provided he does not deny that original sin is contracted at the time of the origin of each person.[2]

This will be vital to his overall thesis in this book, because, if the entirety of human nature has been corrupted, then the nature of Christ seems to become bound to sin and the efficacy of the Incarnation is called

1. Ibid., 2.
2. Ibid., 1.

into question. In this area of the origin of the person, Anselm discusses at what point original sin, which he equates with injustice, is present and concludes that it can only be present when there is rationality:

> I think that original sin can in no way be asserted [to] be in an infant before he has a rational soul – even as justice [cannot be said] to have been in Adam before he became a rational man. Now, if, while remaining sinless, Adam and Eve had begotten offspring, justice would not and could not have been in the seed prior to the seed's having been formed into a living human being. Therefore, if the seed of a human being cannot admit of justice before becoming a human being, then the seed cannot be subject to original sin before becoming a human being.
>
> But, if justice is uprightness-of-will which is kept for its own sake and if this uprightness can be present only in a rational nature, then it follows that even as no nature except a rational nature can admit of justice, so no nature except a rational nature ought to have justice. Therefore, since injustice can be present only where there ought to be justice, original sin – which is injustice – is present only in a rational nature. But only God, angels, and the human soul (by virtue of which a man is called rational, and without which he is not a man) are rational natures. Therefore, since original sin is not present in God or in an angel, it is present only in the rational soul of a man.[1]

Anselm is left with a dilemma in that he holds that sin begins when a will is formed, rather than at conception, but he must bear in mind scriptural references to sinfulness from conception. In seeking to honour both positions, he responds by stating that there is a necessity of sinning when the will is formed, but not sin itself present.

> From the things already said it is now clear, I believe, that sin and injustice are nothing, that they are present only in a rational will, and that no being except a will is properly called unjust. Hence, an alternative seems to follow: either from the very moment of his conception an infant has a rational soul (without which he cannot have a rational will), or else at the moment of his conception he has no original sin. But no human intellect accepts the view that an infant has a rational soul from the moment of his conception. For [from this view] it would follow that whenever – even at the very moment of reception – the human seed which was received

---

1. Ibid., 3.

perished before attaining a human form, the [alleged] human soul
in this seed would be condemned, since it would not be reconciled
through Christ – a consequence which is utterly absurd. Thus,
this half of the alternative must be completely excluded.

[Scriptures are then quoted regarding sin and conception and
sin through Adam.] We can understand in a similar manner [the
statement] that a man is conceived from unclean seed and in
iniquities and sins, *i.e.* not in the sense that in the seed there is
iniquity or sin or the uncleanness of sin, but in the sense that
from the seed and from the conception from which a man begins
to exist he receives the necessity that when he comes to possess a
rational soul, he will have the uncleanness-of-sin, which is nothing
other than sin and iniquity. For even if an infant be begotten by
a corrupt concupiscence, there is no more fault in the seed than
there is in the spittle or the blood should someone malevolently
expectorate or malevolently shed some of his own blood. For what
is at fault is not the spittle or the blood but the evil will. Therefore,
it is clear both how there is no sin in infants from the moment of
their conception and how those statements that I adduced from
divine Scripture are true. Indeed, there is no sin in those infants,
for they do not have a will, which is a necessary condition for the
presence of sin. Nevertheless, sin is said to be in them, since in the
seed they contract the necessity of sinning at the time when they
will become human beings.[1]

Later, Anselm covers this ground again by stating that it is not because
of the human nature that a person is sinful, but he becomes sinful via
Adam himself, thus not by created nature but by the reproduction of a
sinful nature.

Indeed, every descendant of Adam is human by virtue of his
creation and is Adam by virtue of his propagation and is a person
by virtue of the individuation by which he is distinguished from
others. Now, he has his humanity through Adam but not on
account of Adam. For just as Adam did not make himself human,
so he did not create in himself a reproductive nature; rather, God,
who created him human, created this reproductive nature in him
so that human beings might be propagated from him. But there
is no doubt about why each of us is bound by the obligation we
are discussing. The reason is not that each of us is human or
that each of us is a person. For if each one were bound by this

---

1. Ibid., 7.

obligation because he is human or is a person, then it would have been necessary for Adam to have been bound by this obligation even before he sinned, since he was then both human and a person. But this consequence is utterly absurd. Hence, the remaining alternative is that each one is under this obligation only by virtue of the fact that he is Adam – yet, not simply by virtue of his being Adam, but rather by virtue of his being Adam the sinner. [For were it simply by virtue of being Adam], then, assuredly, it would follow that if Adam had never sinned, those propagated from him would nevertheless be born with this debt – an impious consequence. . . . But since Adam was unwilling to be subject to the will of God, his reproductive nature, although not destroyed, was not subject to his will as it would have been had he not sinned. Moreover, he lost the grace which he was able to keep for those to be propagated from him; and all who are propagated by the operation of the nature that Adam had received are born obligated by his debt. Accordingly, since human nature (which as a whole was so present in Adam that none of it was present outside of him) dishonored God by uncoerced sinning and thus was unable to make satisfaction by itself, human nature lost the grace which it had received and which it was able always to keep for those to be propagated from it; and each time it is propagated by the bestowed reproductive nature, it contracts sin together with the accompanying penalty for sin.[1]

On the Virgin Conception and Original Sin remains concentrated on the nature of humanity and original sin, particularly with regard to infants, since the application is ultimately directed towards the human nature of Christ and how Christ could be sinless in that which he received from Mary. In building his case, Anselm makes a differentiation between the sin of Adam and the sin that is in infants.

Although, because of Adam's sin it happened that no infant can be born without sin, which is followed by condemnation, I do not think that Adam's sin passes down to infants in such way that they ought so to be punished for it as if each one of them had committed it personally, as did Adam.[2]

In developing this, Anselm makes a distinction between the fact that all people are in Adam as his seed, yet every individual has his own personhood in addition to the nature that is received.

---

1. Ibid., 10.
2. Ibid., 22.

However, unless we understand why and how [sin] is present, we do not know why it is less [in them than in Adam]. Although I have discussed this point above to the extent required by my investigation, it will not be superfluous to repeat it briefly here. Assuredly, one cannot deny that infants existed in Adam when he sinned. Now, in him they existed causally or materially as in a seed; but in themselves they exist personally. For in him they were his very seed; but in themselves they are individual and distinct persons. In him they were not distinct from him; but in themselves they are distinguished from him. In him they were himself; but in themselves they are themselves. Therefore, they existed in him, but not as themselves, since they did not yet exist as themselves.

As I have said, there is a sin which derives from a nature, and there is a sin which derives from a person. Thus, the sin which derives from a person can be called personal sin; and the sin which derives from a nature can be called natural sin. (It is also called original sin.) Now, just as the personal sin passes over to the nature, so the natural sin passes over to the person. For example, Adam's nature required that he eat, because his nature was created in such way as to have this need. But that he ate from the forbidden tree was the doing not of his natural will but of his personal will – *i.e.* of his own will. Nevertheless, that which was done by the person was not done without the nature. For the person was what was called Adam; and the nature was what was called man. Therefore, the person made the nature sinful, because when Adam sinned, the man [*i.e.* the nature] sinned. Indeed, it was not because he was a man that he was impelled to partake of what was forbidden; rather, he was drawn to this by his own act-of-will, which his nature did not require but which the person fancied.

A converse but similar thing happens in the case of infants. Assuredly, the fact that the justice which they should have is not in them does not result from their personal willing, as it did in Adam's case, but results from a natural deprivation which their nature has received from Adam. For in Adam, outside of whom no part of [human] nature existed, [human] nature was stripped of the justice which it possessed; and it always lacks justice unless assisted [to regain it]. Accordingly, since [human] nature exists in persons and since persons do not exist without a nature, the nature makes the persons of infants sinful. Thus, in Adam the person deprived the nature of the good of justice; and the nature, having become impoverished, causes all the persons whom it

procreates from itself to be sinful and unjust because of the lack
of justice. In this way, the personal sin of Adam passes over to all
who are naturally propagated from him; and in them it is natural,
or original, sin.[1]

This allows for a common position of all humanity, outside the
kingdom of God, due to the fact of sin, but an inequality in the presence
and impact of sin:

But clearly there is a great difference between Adam's sin and
infants' sin. For Adam sinned of his own will, but his progeny sin
by the natural necessity which his own personal will has merited.
Although no one thinks that equal punishment follows unequal
sins, nevertheless the condemnation of personal and of original
sin is alike in that no one is admitted to the Kingdom of God (for
which man was made) except by means of the death of Christ,
without which the debt for Adam's sin is not paid. Yet, not all
individuals deserve to be tormented in Hell in equal degree. Now,
after the Day of Judgment every angel and every man will be either
in the Kingdom of God or in Hell, so, then, the sin of infants is
less than the sin of Adam; and yet, no one is saved without the
universal satisfaction through which sin, both great and small, is
forgiven.[2]

Recognising the personal dimension of sin in addition to the natural
allows Anselm to move on to a fascinating development in the effects of
sin and grace on succeeding generations. As sin increases corruption and
grace restores a person, so the level of corruption that is received differs
from person to person.

But someone may say: Unjust ancestors do not add [numerically]
any injustice to their own infant offspring, from whom they are not
able to remove any justice. However, these ancestors do aggravate
the original injustice which their infant offspring have from Adam.
So also, then, just ancestors mitigate the original injustice in their
infant offspring. Consequently, if the infant offspring of just
ancestors are less unjust than those of unjust ancestors, the former
ought to be condemned less than the latter. Let him say this who
dares to and who can prove it. But I do not dare to, since I see that
a mixture of infants of just and unjust ancestors is elected to and
reprobated from the grace of baptism. Still, even were someone to

1. Ibid., 23.
2. Ibid.

make the above claim, he could not prove it. Indeed, even as only someone who more resolutely desires or avoids what he ought to is thereby more just than someone else who is just, so only someone who more intensely loves or despises what he ought not to is more unjust than someone else who is unjust. Therefore, if it cannot be shown that once infants have souls the one in greater or lesser degree wills what he ought to or what he ought not to, then no one can prove that in the case of infants one infant is born more just or more unjust than another. It seems equally true, then, that just ancestors by means of their justice do not mitigate the original injustice in their infant offspring and that unjust ancestors by their injustice do not aggravate the original injustice in their infant offspring. Hence, if by their own sinfulness unjust ancestors are not able to increase, either in number or in magnitude, original sin in their infant prodigy, then it seems to me that the sins of ancestors since Adam are not reckoned in the original sin of their infant prodigy.[1]

He continues this teaching in the following chapter:

But if the sins of ancestors sometimes harm the souls of their descendants, then I think that this happens, rather, in the following manner: It is not that God imputes these sins to them or that on account of their ancestors he leads them into any transgressions but rather that even as God often rescues from sin the descendants of the just because of the merits of their ancestors, so he sometimes leaves in their sins the descendants of the unjust because of the demerits of their ancestors. For since no one is free from sin unless God sets him free, when God does not set him free from sin, he is said to lead him into it; and when he does not soften, he is said to harden. For it seems much more acceptable that on account of the sins of ancestors God leaves a sinful soul (to which He owes nothing except punishment) in its own sins, so that it is punished for its own sins, than that he burdens it with others' sins, so that it is tormented for their sins. Thus, then, the following statements are consistent with one another: Original sin is the same in all individuals, and 'the son shall not bear the iniquity of the father', and 'each one shall bear his own burden', and each one shall receive 'according as he has done' in the body, 'whether it be good or evil', and 'unto the third and fourth generation' God visits the sins of the parents on their children (even if this occurs with respect to their

---

1. Ibid., 24.

souls), and whatever else we read which is seen to signify that the sins of ancestors harm the souls of their descendants. Indeed, the soul of the son dies not because of the sin of the father but because of its own sin. And when anyone is left in his own iniquity, he bears his own iniquity, not the iniquity of his father; and he bears his own burden, not another's burden. And he receives according as he has done in the body, not according as his father has done. But since on account of the sins of his ancestors he is not set free from his own iniquities, the iniquities which he bears are ascribed to the sins of his ancestors.[1]

At this point, Anselm recognises that there seems to be an intermediary sin between the original sin that is derived from Adam and the personal sin of each person. He counters this idea by stating that our ancestors never received original justice, as Adam did, and therefore do not directly affect the status of a person:

Perhaps someone may argue that all who are not saved by faith in Christ bear the iniquity and burden of Adam, but may so argue with the intent of proving thereby that either infants ought likewise to bear the iniquity of their other ancestors or else they ought not to bear Adam's iniquity. But let this objector consider carefully that infants bear their own sin, not Adam's sin. For Adam's sin was one thing, and infants' sin is another thing, because these sins differ, as was stated. For the former was a cause, whereas the latter is an effect. Adam was deprived of required justice because he himself (and not because someone else) deserted it; but infants are deprived because someone else (and not because they themselves) deserted it. Therefore, Adam's sin and infants' sin are not the same thing. Moreover, when the apostle says (as I mentioned above) that 'death reigned from Adam to Moses, even over those who did not sin according to the likeness of Adam's transgression', just as he signifies that the sin of infants is less than the sin of Adam, so he indicates clearly that the sin of infants is distinct from the sin of Adam.

Accordingly, when an infant is condemned on account of original sin, he is condemned not on account of Adam's sin but on account of his own. For if he did not have sin of his own, he would not be condemned. So, then, he bears his own iniquity and not Adam's, even though he is said to bear Adam's iniquity because the iniquity of Adam was the cause of his own sin. However, this cause of infants' being born in sin – a cause which was in Adam –

1. Ibid., 25.

is not in the other ancestors, because human nature in them does not have the power (as I said) to propagate descendants who are just. Hence, it does not follow that sin is in infants because of the sin of their ancestors, as [it does follow that it is there] because of the sin of Adam.[1]

From all of this, Anselm moves back to his definition of original sin, which is in all infants once they have a rational soul.

Therefore, I understand original sin to be nothing other than that sin which is in an infant as soon as he has a rational soul – irrespective of what may have happened to his body (*e.g.* the corruption of its members) before it was thus animated, or irrespective of what may happen to either his body or his soul afterwards. And on the basis of the aforegiven reasons I think that in all infants who are naturally propagated original sin is equal and that all who die with only this sin are equally condemned. Indeed, whatever sin accrues to a man over and above original sin is personal sin. And just as the person is born sinful because of the nature, so the nature is made more sinful because of the person, since when any person sins, his human nature (*homo*) sins.[2]

For all people, there is thus a need for baptism in Anselm's view to overcome the effects of the original sin, although he has removed it one stage from conception. The fact that personal sin is a later development additional to the original sin received in no way removes the infant from the state of injustice.

There are those whose mind resists accepting [the view] that infants dying unbaptized ought to be condemned solely on account of the injustice of which I have spoken. Their reasons are (1) that no man judges infants to be blameworthy as the result of another person's sin, (2) that in such a state infants are not yet just and discerning, and (3) that God (so they think) ought not to judge innocent infants more severely than men judge them. These people must be told that God ought to act toward infants in one way and man [ought to act toward them] in another way. For man ought not to demand from a nature what he has not bestowed and what is not owed to him. Nor does one man justly reproach another man for being born with a fault with which he himself is born and from which he himself is healed only by someone else.

1. Ibid., 26.
2. Ibid., 27.

But God does rightly demand from a nature what He bestowed on it and what is rightly owed to him.

But if we consider the matter, even this judgment by which infants are condemned is not much different from the judgment of men. For take the case of a man and his wife who not by their own merit but by favor alone (*gratia sola*) have been elevated to some great dignity and estate, and who together commit an unpardonably serious crime, and who on account of this crime are justly cast down and reduced to servitude. Who will say that the children whom they beget after their condemnation ought not to be subject to the same servitude but ought rather to be gratuitously restored to the goods which their parents rightfully lost? Such is the case with our first parents and with the descendants whom they — justly sentenced because of their own fault to [be cast down] from happiness into misery — beget into their own exile. Therefore, there ought to be like judgment for like cases; but in the case of our first parents the more reprehensible their crime can be shown to be, the more severely [it ought to be judged].[1]

Anselm therefore follows Augustine's high view of the effects of baptism on original sin and thus on the state of infants:

I have said that the inability to have justice does not excuse the injustice of infants. Perhaps, then, someone will ask: If there is sin, *i.e.* injustice, in an infant before his baptism, and if (as you say) the inability to have justice is no excuse, and if in baptism only sin which was prior thereto is remitted, then since after baptism an infant, for as long as he is an infant, lacks justice and cannot even understand the justice which he should keep (if indeed justice is uprightness-of-will kept for its own sake), why is he not also unjust after having been baptized? Thus, if a baptized infant dies in infancy (though not immediately after baptism) before he knows how to repent, then since he does not have the required justice, and since his inability does not excuse him, he passes from this life unjust (even as he would have done before his baptism), and he is not admitted into the Kingdom of God, into which no one who is unjust is received. But the Catholic Church does not hold to this view. Now, if in baptism a subsequent sin within infancy is remitted to infants, then why [are] not also those sins which are committed at a later stage of development [forgiven at the time of baptism]?

1. Ibid., 28.

To this question, I give the following answer. In baptism the sins which were present before baptism are completely blotted out. Accordingly, the original inability to have justice is not reckoned as sin in the case of those who have already been baptized – as [it is reckoned to them] prior [to their baptism]. Hence, just as prior to their baptism this inability could not excuse the absence of justice, since the inability was culpable, so after their baptism the inability completely excuses the absence of justice, because although the inability remains it is without any culpability. Thus it happens that the justice which before their baptism was required of infants, without any excuse on their part, is after their baptism not demanded of them as their requirement. Therefore, as long as it is only because of the original inability that they do not have justice, they are not unjust, since there is no absence in them of required justice. For what is both impossible and free of all culpability is not required. Therefore, if infants die in such a condition, then because they are not unjust they are not condemned; rather, by the justice of Christ, who gave Himself for them, and by the justice of faith on the part of the Church, their mother, which believes on their behalf, they are saved, [being reckoned] as just.[1]

Throughout this book, it is important to keep in mind Anselm's greater purpose, which is to defend Christ as one born of a human and yet not stained by original sin. He believes that his approach is honourable in this, yet does note that it may not be right:

I do not deny that in addition to the argument presented here and the other one presented elsewhere there may be some other deeper rationale for how it was possible for God to assume a sinless human nature from the sinful mass, as something unleavened is taken from something leavened. If this other rationale is shown to me, I will gladly accept it; and if my accounts can be shown to be opposed to the truth – which I do not think they can be – I will abandon them.[2]

The fact that original sin takes hold from time of rationality allows Anselm to distinguish Christ's assumed human nature from the 'sinful mass':

So if these conclusions are true, as I think they are, then because that which is taken into an offspring from a parent has no will, it has no sin. Hence, it is clear that the stain of sin could not at all have been present in that which the Son of God took into His

---

1. Ibid., 29.
2. Ibid., 21.

own person from the Virgin. But I stated that the seed contracted from parents is contracted with the necessity for sin at that future time when the seed will be enlivened by a rational soul. The only reasons for this necessity are the following: Human nature is born in infants, as I said, with the obligation to make satisfaction for the sin of Adam and (in accordance with what I supposed) of recent ancestors; but it cannot at all make this satisfaction, and as long as it does not do so it is sinning. Furthermore, human nature is not able by itself to re-acquire the justice which it deserted; and the soul, which is burdened by the corrupted body, is not able even to understand justice, which can be neither kept nor possessed without first being understood. Consequently, if the seed taken from the Virgin can be shown to be free of these constraints, we shall see clearly that it did not at all contract the necessity for sin.

If first we repel [from that seed] the necessity by which human nature seems to be obliged to make satisfaction for the sins of both its first and its recent ancestors, then because the assuming and the assumed natures are a oneness of person, we can readily show that the following necessities are foreign to that seed: the necessity by which human nature is unable by itself to recover justice, and the necessity by which the corrupted body so burdens the soul that in the completely formed human being the soul is unable without the assistance of grace to keep justice were it received, and in infants is unable even to understand justice. Now, if that seed can be understood to be free from the obligation of our first parents, then there will be no doubt about the fact that it incurs no obligation from its more recent ancestors.[1]

Although this would not seem then to require that the blessedness of Mary be elevated as was common in the medieval period, Anselm does believe that her relational status required a certain purity:

Although, then, the Son of God was most truly conceived from a most pure virgin, nevertheless this was done not of necessity, as if it were rationally impossible for a just offspring to be begotten from a sinful parent by this kind of propagation. But [it was done] because it was fitting that the conception of that man be accomplished from a most pure mother. Assuredly, it was fitting that the Virgin be beautified with a purity than which a greater cannot be conceived, except for God's. For, toward her, God the Father was so disposed to give his only Son – whom he begot as

1. Ibid., 8.

equal with himself and whom from his own heart He loved as
Himself – that the Son was naturally one and the same common
Son of God the Father and of the Virgin. And she was the one
whom the Son chose to make substantially His mother. And with
respect to her the Holy Spirit willed, and from her he was going
to accomplish, that the very one from whom he himself proceeded
would be conceived and begotten. Now, I have already spoken of
how the Virgin was cleansed by faith before this conception; but
there I presented a different argument concerning the topic being
discussed here.[1]

It is clear, however, that the focus is not on the status of Mary but on
the nature of the Christ child and his relation to original sin:

Now, regarding original sin, I think that I have adequately shown,
just as I proposed to, how this sin could not in any respect be
passed down from his ancestors to the man conceived from the
Virgin but how, instead, he ought to have been made just and
happy, as reason requires. Therefore, since from a just Father with
respect to His divine nature and from a just mother with respect
to his human nature he was born just from the time of His very
'origin', so to speak, it is not unfitting that He should be said to
have original justice in place of the original injustice which all
other sons of Adam have from the time of their origin.[2]

This has been a rather lengthy treatment of Anselm's book on original
sin, and this is largely due to Anselm's position in the history of Western
thought as the Father of Scholasticism and as the first major thinker since
Augustine, giving us the opportunity to see how Augustine's thought on
original sin is received after it has settled over the intervening 600 years. We
now move on to another key area in Augustine's late work, grace, and its
impact on the human will, in two works of Anselm of Canterbury. The first
is *On Free Will* and the second, written over 20 years later, is *De Concordia*.

On Free Will

This short treatise (in Latin *De Libertate Arbitrii*) is classic Anselm in
the lack of Scripture references (there is one to the gospel of John) or
explicit teachings of the Church Fathers, but a sense throughout that
these underpin the discussion between teacher and student. This is made

1. Ibid., 18.
2. Ibid., 20.

clear from the beginning in discussion about the nature of free will, which is not libertarian (*i.e.* that a will is free to choose whatever it wants) but a will that is able to do that which it ought to do (as Augustine taught).

> Student. Since free choice seems to be opposed to the grace, predestination, and foreknowledge of God, I desire to know what freedom of choice is and whether we always have it. For if freedom of choice consists in being able to sin and not to sin (as some persons are accustomed to say) and if we always have this ability, how is it that we sometimes need grace? But if we do not always have this ability, why is sin imputed to us when we sin without a free choice?
>
> Teacher. I do not think that freedom of choice is the ability to sin and not to sin. Indeed, if this were its definition, then neither God nor the angels who are not able to sin would have free choice – a blasphemous thing to say.
>
> S. What if we say that the free choice of God and of the good angels is different from ours?
>
> T. Although the free choice of men differs from that of God and of the good angels, nevertheless, the definition of this freedom ought to be the same in both cases, in accordance with the name 'freedom'. For example, although one animal differs from another either substantially or accidentally, the definition [of 'animal'] is the same for all animals, in accordance with the name 'animal'. Hence, it is necessary to give such a definition of 'freedom of choice' – a definition which contains neither more nor less than freedom does. Therefore, since the free choice of God and of the good angels is not able to sin, 'to be able to sin' does not pertain to the definition of 'freedom of choice'. In fact, the ability to sin does not constitute either freedom or a part of freedom.[1]

There is a sense in this of the previous concepts of being and goodness as having true existence, with their opposites in fact not existing despite their apparent strength. The discussion continues later in this chapter:

> T. Don't you see that someone who so possesses what is fitting and advantageous that he cannot lose it is more free than someone else who possesses the same thing

---

1. Anselm, *On Free Will*, 1.

	in such a way that he can lose it and can be induced to
	what is unfitting and disadvantageous?
S.	I think that no one doubts this.
T.	Will you admit that it is equally certain that sinning is
	always unfitting and harmful?
S.	No one of sound mind thinks otherwise.
T.	Then, the will which is not able to turn away from the
	uprightness of not sinning is more free than the will
	which is able to desert uprightness.
S.	Nothing can more reasonably be asserted, it seems to me.
T.	Do you think that something which if added decreases
	freedom and if subtracted increases it is either freedom
	or a part of freedom?
S.	I am not able to think this.
T.	Then, the ability to sin, which if added to the will decreases
	the will's freedom and if subtracted from the will increases
	its freedom, is neither freedom nor a part of freedom.
S.	Nothing follows more logically.[1]

Overlooking the sycophantic contributions of the student here, Anselm is setting up a definition of free will that follows Augustine closely: a truly free will is one that is not contaminated by sin in any way. In applying this to Adam (and to the devil), Anselm can defend their responsibility for their sins; in then looking at the case of humanity after the Fall, there seem to be greater issues in holding to continuing free will. The first stage is to look at Adam:

> The apostate angel [Satan] and the first man [Adam] sinned by free choice, for [each] sinned by his own choice, which was so free that it could not be compelled by any other thing to sin. Therefore, [each of them] is justly blamed because in spite of having this freedom of choice, each sinned freely and out of no necessity and without being compelled by anything else. However, each sinned by his own choice, which was free; but neither sinned by means of that in virtue of which his choice was free. That is, [neither sinned] by means of the ability in virtue of which he was able not to sin and not to serve sin; but [each sinned] by means of his ability to sin; and by means of this ability he was neither helped towards the freedom not to sin nor compelled into the service of sin.[2]

---

1. Ibid.
2. Ibid., 2.

The work then turns to whether there was any freedom of the will after Adam entered the service of sin.

S.   You have convinced me that, before sin, nothing indeed prevented this [*i.e.*, prevented Satan's and Adam's having had free choice]. But after they made themselves servants of sin, how is it that they were able to keep free choice?

T.   Although they had subjected themselves to sin, they were not able to destroy their natural freedom of choice. However, they were able to cause themselves no longer to be able to use this freedom without a grace different from the grace they had originally possessed.[1]

The nature of the will that is retained is still questionable, since a righteousness is now received rather than inherent. The freedom that is being explored remains linked to the original definition:

T.   Accordingly, since all freedom is ability, that freedom of choice is the ability to keep uprightness-of-will for the sake of this uprightness itself.

S.   It cannot be anything else.

T.   So it is now clear that a free choice is nothing other than a choice which is able to keep uprightness-of-will for the sake of this uprightness itself.[2]

At this point in Anselm's argument there is a subtle distinction made between the ability of the free will in humankind and the state of humankind:

Therefore, if there is no object nearby to be seen and if when we are placed in darkness and have our eyes closed or covered, we still have within us the ability to see any visible thing whatsoever, what prevents our having the ability to keep uprightness-of-will for the sake of this uprightness itself – even in the absence of this uprightness – as long as within us we have reason, by which to recognize it, and will, by which to hold it fast? For the previously mentioned freedom of choice consists of both of these.[3]

The absence of substantial discussion on grace in *On Free Will* seems to leave this tension for much of the rest of the work, that there is an

1. Ibid., 3.
2. Ibid.
3. Ibid., 4.

ability to maintain righteousness but not necessarily any righteousness to maintain. Anselm's next step is to guard against any power being given to temptation to dominate over a person's will.

S.   But in what way is the choice of the human will free by virtue of this ability, since oftentimes a man who has an upright will deserts this uprightness against his will because of the pressure of temptation?

T.   No one deserts this uprightness except by willing to. So if 'against one's will' means 'unwillingly', then no one deserts uprightness against his will. For a man can be bound against his will, because he can be bound when he is unwilling to be bound; a man can be tortured against his will, because he can be tortured when he is unwilling to be tortured; a man can be killed against his will, because he can be killed when he is unwilling to be killed. But a man cannot will against his will, because he cannot will if he is unwilling to will. For everyone-who-wills wills that he will.[1]

Anselm develops his discussion on temptation at some length, even to the extent of stating that God cannot remove uprightness-of-will because this would go against his desires for a person. Rather God's work is to restore a right will (as Anselm understands this) and this is described as a greater miracle than bringing the dead to life. The uprightness of the will, however, does not directly affect its freedom:

T.   Therefore, a rational nature always has free choice since it always has the ability to keep (although sometimes with difficulty) uprightness-of-will for the sake of uprightness itself. But when free will deserts uprightness because of the difficulty of keeping it, then, assuredly, free will subsequently serves sin because of the impossibility of recovering uprightness through its own efforts. So, then, it becomes 'a wind that goes out and does not return', since 'he who commits sin is the servant of sin'. Indeed, just as before having uprightness, no will was able to take it without God's giving it, so upon deserting the uprightness which has been received, the will is unable to recover it unless God gives it again.[2]

---

1. Ibid., 5.
2. Ibid., 10.

What results can seem to be a concentration more on a right will than on a free will, the lack of importance of the latter being best exemplified in the last section of this quote:

> T.   If you distinguish clearly, [you will see how] a man is both servant and free, without contradiction, when he does not have the uprightness we have been discussing. For he never has the ability to acquire uprightness when he does not have uprightness; but he always has the ability to keep uprightness when he does have it. With respect to the fact that he cannot return from sin, he is a servant; with respect to the fact that he cannot [forcibly] be drawn away from uprightness, he is free. Now, he can be turned away from sin and from servitude-to-sin only by someone else; but he can be turned away from uprightness only by himself; and he cannot be deprived of his freedom either by himself or by anyone else. For he is always naturally free for keeping uprightness if he has it, and even when he does not have any to keep.[1]

After the Fall, humankind has a free will, which involves the ability to maintain a righteous state even when we do not have such a state. As indicated above, what is lacking in this work is serious engagement with the nature and role of grace, something that is included in the later work on this issue, the *De Concordia*.

De Concordia

This book that seeks a harmony of the concepts of free choice, foreknowledge, predestination and grace is much more clearly structured than *On Free Will* and this, together with a mature Anselm, results in a greater purpose to the discussion. The work is also manifestly theological in nature, where the earlier work often feels more philosophical, and thus the application to the concepts being studied in this project is clearer. The concept of free choice as meaning to be able to do what one ought, received from Augustine and foundational to the earlier work, is retained, but Anselm does not start with this but engages directly with his major themes. His definition continues to underpin the whole argument, but often subtly and implicitly. The brief introduction sets up the work in three sections dealing respectively with free choice and foreknowledge, free choice and predestination, and free choice and grace.

1. Ibid., 11.

Each section starts with an acknowledgement of apparent contradiction in the concepts being discussed, so the first begins as follows:

> Admittedly, free choice and the foreknowledge of God seem incompatible; for it is necessary that the things foreknown by God be going to occur, whereas the things done by free choice occur without any necessity. Now, if these two are incompatible, then it is impossible that God's all-foreseeing foreknowledge should coexist with something's being done by freedom of choice.[1]

Anselm then sets himself the challenge of discerning whether the two can coexist, focusing on the concept of necessity:

> Now, if something is going to occur without necessity, God foreknows this, since he foreknows all future events. And that which is foreknown by God is, necessarily, going to occur, as is foreknown. Therefore, it is necessary that something be going to occur without necessity. Hence, the foreknowledge from which necessity follows and the freedom of choice from which necessity is absent are here seen (for one who rightly understands it) to be not at all incompatible. For, on the one hand, it is necessary that what is foreknown by God be going to occur; and, on the other hand, God foreknows that something is going to occur without any necessity.[2]

The main point of the examination is then made clear in its application to sin and whether there can be true responsibility for sin with an understanding of God's complete foreknowledge.

> But you will say to me: 'You still do not remove from me the necessity of sinning or the necessity of not sinning. For God foreknows that I am going to sin or foreknows that I am not going to sin. And so, if I sin, it is necessary that I sin; or if I do not sin, it is necessary that I do not sin.' To this claim I reply: you ought to say not merely 'God foreknows that I am going to sin' or 'God foreknows that I am not going to sin' but 'God foreknows that it is without necessity that I am going to sin' or 'God foreknows that it is without necessity that I am not going to sin.'[3]

In Anselm's view, a choice is free if it is neither coerced nor restrained, and the fact of foreknowledge does not seem to involve either of these.

---

1. Anselm, *De Concordia*, 1.1.
2. Ibid.
3. Ibid.

For God, who foresees that some action is going to occur voluntarily, foreknows the very fact that the will is neither compelled nor prevented by anything. Hence, what is done voluntarily is done freely.[1]

Rather, the foreknowledge of God seems at this stage only to establish what might be termed Anselm's '*Que Será, Será*' theology:

Indeed, if it were not necessary that everything which is going to happen were going to happen, then something which is going to happen would not be going to happen – a contradiction. Therefore, necessarily, everything which is going to happen is going to happen; and if it is going to happen, it is going to happen. (For we are saying of what is going to happen that it is going to happen.) But ['necessarily' here signifies] subsequent necessity, which does not compel anything to be.[2]

While this may appear rather tautological, it is a crucial point in Anselm's overall concept of God and time and seems to allow a balance in the tension between God's transcendence and immanence, that God does not engage as one completely outside of time but as one who is present at all times and therefore is present in what has happened, what is happening and what will happen.

Therefore, when of what God foreknows to be going to occur we say that it is necessary that it be going to occur, we are not in every case asserting that the event is going to occur by necessity; rather, we are asserting that an event which is going to occur is, necessarily, going to occur. For something which is going to occur cannot at the same time be not going to occur. The meaning is the same when we say, 'If God foreknows such-and-such an event' – without adding 'which is going to occur'. For in the verb 'to foreknow' the notion of future occurrence is included, since to foreknow is nothing other than to know the future; and so, if God foreknows some event, it is necessary that this event be going to occur. Therefore, from the fact of God's foreknowledge it does not in every case follow that an event is going to occur by necessity. For although God foreknows all future events, he does not foreknow that all of them are going to occur by necessity. Rather, he foreknows that some of them will occur as the result of the free will of a rational creature.[3]

1. Ibid., 1.2.
2. Ibid.
3. Ibid., 1.3.

This is then applied again to the core topic of sin:

> Now, with respect to the human will's sin when it wills to sin: if someone
> asks whether this sin occurs by necessity, then he must be told that just
> as the will does not will by necessity, so the will's sin does not occur by
> necessity. Nor does the human will act by necessity; for if it did not
> will freely, it would not act – even though what it wills must come to
> pass, as I have just said. For since, in the present case, to sin is nothing
> other than to will what ought not [to be willed]: just as willing is not
> necessary, so sinful willing is not necessary. Nevertheless, it is true that
> if a man wills to sin, it is necessary that he sin – in terms, that is, of that
> necessity which (as I have said) neither compels nor prevents anything.[1]

Anselm then gets slightly ahead of himself in continuing this thought
in relation to predestination, which will be the theme of his next section.
However, one key scriptural reference to foreknowledge, in Romans 8:28-
9, is connected to predestination and deserves consideration at this point.

> This is also what the Apostle Paul says about those who, in accordance
> with [God's] purpose, are called to be saints: 'Whom he foreknew He
> predestined to become conformed to the image of His Son, so that
> His Son would be the firstborn among many brethren. And whom
> he predestined, these he also called. And whom he called, these he
> also justified. And whom he justified, these he also glorified.' Indeed,
> within eternity (in which there is no past or future but is only a present)
> this purpose, in accordance with which they have been called to be
> saints, is immutable. But in these men this purpose is at some time
> mutable because of freedom of choice. For within eternity a thing has
> no past or future but only a present; and yet, without inconsistency, in
> the dimension of time this thing was and will be. Similarly, that which
> within eternity is not able to be changed is proved to be, without
> inconsistency, changeable by free will at some point in time before
> it occurs. However, although within eternity there is only a present,
> nonetheless it is not the temporal present, as is ours, but is an eternal
> present in which the whole of time is contained. For, indeed, just as
> present time encompasses every place and whatever is in any place,
> so in the eternal present the whole of time is encompassed at once,
> as well as whatever occurs at any time. Therefore, when the apostle
> says that God foreknew, predestined, called, justified, and glorified
> His saints, none of these actions is earlier or later for God; rather
> everything must be understood to exist at once in an eternal present.

---

1. Ibid.

For eternity has its own 'simultaneity' wherein exist all things that occur at the same time and place and that occur at different times and places.[1]

On this basis, Anselm argues that Scripture speaks in different passages from separate temporal viewpoints:

In this manner, then, whenever Sacred Scripture speaks as if things done by free choice were necessary, it speaks in accordance with eternity, in which is present immutably all truth and only truth. Scripture is not speaking in accordance with the temporal order, wherein our volitions and actions do not exist forever.[2]

In the last parts of this section, Anselm moves on to look at salvation and the place of free choice. Again, he seems to be slightly ahead of himself, since there are references to the work of grace in relation to uprightness-of-will, although that topic is the last to be discussed in *De Concordia*. Anselm notes a concern that he has found in some people that they play no role in either salvation or condemnation because of their understanding of God's foreknowledge.

However, the present investigation is being conducted only with respect to that choice and that freedom without which a man, after once being able to use them, cannot be saved. For many people lament because they believe that free choice is of no avail for salvation or condemnation but that, as a result of God's foreknowledge, only necessity [determines salvation or condemnation]. Therefore, since after a human being has reached the age of understanding, he is not saved apart from being just: the choice and the freedom which are under discussion must be dealt with in terms of where the seat of justice is. Accordingly, first justice must be exhibited and, next, this freedom and this choice. Indeed, any justice whatever (whether great or small) is uprightness-of-will kept for its own sake. And the freedom [which is under discussion] is the ability to keep uprightness-of-will for its own sake.[3]

Behind these ideas, it is vital to understand that Anselm has a high view of baptismal grace, so that the effects of original sin have been overcome, in line with Augustine's thought, thus establishing the conditions for

---

1. Ibid., 1.5.
2. Ibid.
3. Ibid., 1.6.

an upright will to exist.[1] Since this is established in baptism, Anselm argues that it is not within God's character to remove this upright will if a person wants to retain it:

> Now, since it is evident that the justice by which someone is just is uprightness-of-will, which (as I have said) is present in someone only when he wills what God wills for him to will: it is evident that God is not able to remove this uprightness from him against his will; for God cannot will this removal. Moreover, neither can God will for one who possesses uprightness to desert it unwillingly as the result of some compelling force. (Indeed, [were that the case] God would will for him not to will that which He wills for him to will – which is impossible). Therefore, it follows that in this manner God wills that an upright will be free for willing rightly and for keeping this uprightness. And when the upright will is able [to do] what it wills, it does freely what it does. Hence, we can also recognize very clearly that both a will and its action are free – without its being the case that God's foreknowledge is incompatible therewith, as was demonstrated above.[2]

The final stage of this first section looks at the root cause of all things, whether in the free choice or in the knowledge and therefore being of God.

> Since God is believed to foreknow or know all things, we are now left to consider whether his knowledge derives from things or whether things derive their existence from his knowledge. For if God derives his knowledge from things, it follows that they exist prior to his knowledge and, hence, do not derive their existence from him, from whom they are not able to exist except through his knowledge. On the other hand, if all existing things derive their existence from God's knowledge, God is the creator and the author of evil works and, hence, is unjust in punishing evil creatures – a view we do not accept.[3]

---

1. Baptism is left until very late in *De Concordia*: 'But as regards those to whom the grace of Christian faith is given: just as in baptism the original injustice with which they are born is forgiven them, so [in baptism] there is forgiven all guilt of inability and of all the corruption which they incurred because of the sin of our first parent – corruption through which God is dishonored. For after baptism, they are not blamed for any of the guilt which was in them before baptism even though the corruption and the appetites which are the penalty for sin are not immediately blotted out in baptism.' (Ibid., 3.8.)
2. Ibid., 1.6.
3. Ibid., 1.7.

Anselm here refers to his earlier works *On the Fall of the Devil* and *On the Virgin Conception and Original Sin*, examined above, to understand the nature of evil and the relation of this to God as the source of all that is:

> For injustice is neither a quality nor an action nor a being but is only the absence of required justice and is present only in the will, where justice ought to be. And every rational nature as well as any of its actions is called just or unjust in accordance with a just or an unjust will. Indeed, every quality and every action and whatever has any being comes from God, from whom all justice and no injustice is derived. Therefore, God causes all the things which are done by a just or an unjust will, *viz.* all good and evil deeds. Indeed, in the case of good deeds he causes what they are [essentially] and the fact that they are good; but in the case of evil deeds he causes what they are [essentially] but not the fact that they are evil.[1]

Moving on to predestination as the main topic (a comparatively very brief section), Anselm again shows the apparent contradiction that such a notion entails:

> Predestination is seen to be the same thing as foreordination or predetermination. And so, that which God is said to predestine, he is recognized to foreordain – *i.e.* to determine to be going to occur. But what God determines to be going to occur must, it seems, be going to occur. Therefore, it is necessary that whatever God predestines be going to occur. Hence, if God predestines the good and the evil actions which are done, nothing is done by free choice but everything occurs of necessity. On the other hand, if He predestines only good actions, only good actions occur of necessity, and there is free choice only with respect to evil actions – a consequence which is utterly absurd. Therefore, it is not the case that God predestines only good actions. But if free choice does any good works through which men are justified apart from predestination, then God does not predestine all the good works which justify men. Accordingly, he did not [predestine] those men who are justified by virtue of the works of free choice. Therefore, it would not be the case that God foreknew these men, since 'whom He foreknew, these He also predestined'. But it is false that there are some good works or just men that God does not foreknow. Therefore, it is not the case that some good works of free choice alone are justificatory; instead, only those good works which God predestines are justificatory.[2]

---

1. Ibid.
2. Ibid., 2.1.

It is good to restate the underlying, unstated role of baptismal grace, since without this Anselm could be read as implying a very strong works-justification. In responding to the quandary, Anselm's first step is to clarify that Scripture applies predestination to both good and evil, although for the latter he believes in permission rather than active causation.

> At the outset, then, and before settling the main issue, we must notice that predestination can be said [to apply] not only to good men but also to evil men – even as God is said to cause (because he permits) evils which He does not cause. For He is said to harden a man when he does not soften him, and to lead him into temptation when he does not deliver him. Hence, it is not inappropriate if in this manner we say that God predestines evil men and their evil works when he does not correct them and their evil works. But he is more properly said to foreknow and to predestine good works, because in them he causes both what they are [essentially] and the fact that they are good. But in evil deeds he causes only what they are essentially; he does not cause the fact that they are evil – as I have already said above. We must also realize that just as foreknowledge is not properly said to be found in God, so predestination is not either. For nothing is present to God either earlier or later, but all things are present to him at once.[1]

In seeking to resolve free choice and predestination, Anselm builds directly on his first section on God's foreknowledge and sees this as foundational to his predestination: 'Surely, we ought not to doubt that God's foreknowledge and predestination do not conflict. Instead, just as he foreknows, so also He predestines.'[2] This could seem to involve a very low view of God's engagement with the world, were it not for a clarification that all good works do stem from a work of grace:

> For although God predestines these things, he causes them not by constraining or restraining the will but by leaving the will to its own power. But although the will uses its own power, it does nothing which God does not cause – in good works by His grace, in evil works not through any fault of His but through the will's fault. (As I promised, this shall become clearer when I shall speak about grace.) And just as foreknowledge, which is not mistaken, foreknows only the real thing as it will occur – either necessarily or freely – so predestination, which is not altered, predestines

---

1. Ibid., 2.2.
2. Ibid., 2.3.

only as the thing exists in foreknowledge. And although what is foreknown is immutable in eternity, it can nevertheless be changed in the temporal order at some point before it occurs. Similarly, the case is in every respect the same for predestination.[1]

The role of grace is thus indicated, but Anselm's argument on predestination is rather unsatisfying until this is developed in the last section on grace and free will. In stating the contradiction, Anselm has an extended presentation of relevant Scriptures, firstly, those that indicate that grace alone is necessary for salvation and, secondly, those that seem to speak 'as if our entire salvation were dependent upon our free will'.[2] Anselm gives himself the task of honouring both, against those who would advocate following either one or other set:

> Therefore, since we find in Sacred Scripture certain passages which seem to favor grace alone and certain passages which are believed to establish free choice alone, apart from grace: there have been certain arrogant individuals who have thought that the whole efficacy of the virtues depends only upon freedom of choice; and in our day there are many who have completely given up on the idea that there is any freedom of choice. Therefore, in regard to this dispute, my intention will be to show that free choice coexists with grace and cooperates with it in many respects – just as we found it to be compatible with foreknowledge and with predestination.[3]

Anselm clarifies that he will concentrate on grace and free choice as they concern salvation, rather than these concepts more generally:

> We must recognize that just as this controversy (as I have said above) concerns no other free choice than that without which no one (after he has reached the age of understanding) merits salvation, so it concerns no other grace than that without which no man is saved. For every creature exists by grace, because by grace he was created; moreover, by grace God gives in this life many goods without which a human being can still be saved. Indeed, in the case of infants who die, baptized, before they are able to use their free choice, the harmony which we are seeking does not appear. For in their case grace alone accomplishes salvation apart from their free choice. For the following fact occurs by grace:

1. Ibid.
2. Ibid., 3.1.
3. Ibid.

viz. that to others is given the will to assist, by their faith, these infants. Therefore, the solution we are seeking must be exhibited with regard to those who have reached the age of understanding, because the controversy concerns them alone.[1]

He develops these ideas by advocating a cooperation of grace and free choice, albeit with a first movement of grace:

Thus, it follows that only by the grace of God does a creature have the uprightness which I have called uprightness-of-will. Now, I have shown that uprightness-of-will can be kept by free choice (as I stated above). Therefore, by the gift of God we have found that His grace harmonizes with free choice in order to save human beings. Thus, as happens in the case of infants, grace alone can save a human being when his free choice can do nothing; and in the case of those with understanding, grace always assists the natural free choice (which apart from grace is of no avail to salvation) by giving to the will the uprightness which it can keep by free choice.[2]

Anselm develops this idea further in the next section:

Assuredly, no one keeps this received uprightness except by willing it. But no one can will it unless he possesses it. And he cannot at all possess it except by means of grace. Therefore, just as no one receives uprightness except by means of grace preceding, so no one keeps uprightness except by means of this same grace following. Assuredly, even though uprightness is kept by free choice, still its being kept must be imputed not so much to free choice as to grace; for free choice possesses and keeps uprightness only by means of prevenient and of subsequent grace.

However, grace so follows its own gift that the only time grace ever fails to bestow this gift – whether it is something large or something small – is when free choice by willing something else forsakes the uprightness it has received. For this uprightness is never separated from the will except when the will wills something else which is incompatible with this uprightness – as when someone receives the uprightness of willing sobriety and rejects it by willing the immoderate pleasure of drinking. When a man does this, it is by his own will; and so, through his own fault he loses the grace which he received.[3]

1. Ibid., 3.2.
2. Ibid., 3.3.
3. Ibid., 3.4.

The resolution is thus that both grace and free choice need to be recognised in dealing with scriptural references to salvation:

> If the points which have been made are considered carefully, one recognizes clearly that when Sacred Scripture says something in favor of grace, it does not completely do away with free choice; and when it speaks in favor of free choice, it does not exclude grace. The case is not as if grace alone or free choice alone sufficed to save a man (as it seems to those who are the cause of the present controversy). Indeed, the divine sayings ought to be construed in such way that, with the exception of what I said about infants, neither grace alone nor free choice alone accomplishes man's salvation.[1]

Conclusion

Anselm of Canterbury is a fascinating thinker both in himself and in his context in the history of Christian thought as the first major writer since St Augustine. Throughout these texts, it is clear that Augustine's notions of original sin and necessary grace are well rooted in the thought of the Western Church with an awareness of the implications for the nature of humanity, and the will, in particular. However, Augustine's teaching on the effects of baptismal grace in relation to original sin similarly has a major role that allows humanity to play an active part in people's lives and even in their salvation as free will and grace cooperate, always on the back of prevenient grace, in Christian faith and life. Anselm shows an awareness of issues that Scriptural passages raise that seem contradictory and his approach is largely to allow the tensions to exist rather than to solve any questions absolutely one way or the other.

As stated in the introduction, I am greatly in debt to Jasper Hopkins for his permission to use his translations of Anselm's works in this chapter, saving me many hours working through the Latin. He has very kindly made available online his translations of most of the major books at http://jasper-hopkins.info. Brian Davies and G.R. Evans have also edited a collection of translations with an excellent introduction, in a book entitled *Anselm of Canterbury: the Major Works* (Oxford: OUP, 1998).

---

1. Ibid., 3.5.

2.

Bernard of Clairvaux

The second figure chosen for the medieval period is St Bernard of Clairvaux (1090-1153). Some may query why Bernard should be included ahead of other medieval figures, however, I believe there are good reasons why he merits attention. Before introducing the man, his life and his place in the Church of the early twelfth century, it is worth noting that the only work that will be presented here is his *On Grace and Free Choice*, chosen because Bernard is an important strand in the continuation of thought in these areas in the development of Augustine's teaching.

Bernard is a fascinating figure who was important in many different areas of the Church. To start with, he was involved in a renewal and revival of the monastic system that had begun in the eleventh century. Prior to this, the dominating standard form of monasticism in the West was Benedictine, following the Rule of St Benedict, but as Europe began to stabilise, forms of monasticism with different core concentrations were approved and grew, for example, the eremitical (hermit-like) Carthusians, the very practical Canons Regular or Augustinian Canons and the Cistercians, who sought a stricter rule and a more isolated community than was generally the case for a Benedictine monastery.

Bernard was the driving force behind the popularity of the Cistercian Order, which grew incredibly quickly during the twelfth century in terms of numbers of monasteries and monks. Central to this were Bernard's writings, which led to him being hailed as *Doctor Mellifluus* (the honey-sweet teacher) by Pope Pius XII in 1953. Among his most famous works are his treatise *On Loving God* and his set of 86 sermons on the Song of Songs.

When contemplating God, there is a wonderful humility that pervades Bernard's writing, and this sets him apart from other streams of thought and merits his inclusion in this volume. Bernard was wary of the growing role of reason in Christian writing that was developing from Anselm of Canterbury's foundations. Where Anselm had clearly laid faith at the base of all understanding, the early progress of Scholasticism was already tending to elevate reason, exemplified in the work of Peter Abelard (about whom there is an appendix to this chapter). Abelard wrote three great *Theologia* (studies of God) discussing the faith, but the presumption of studying God seemed impertinent to Bernard who referred to the practice as *Stultilogia* (studies of stupidity). Bernard is thus included here as part of a more mystical stream of thought that continued throughout the medieval period, in contrast with Lombard and, to a greater extent, Aquinas, who were more rational, and whose works will be discussed in the next two chapters.

Monastic development and writing were not the full extent of Bernard's influence. He was important in the politics of the Church, and therefore of Europe: his voice proved decisive in the eventual victory of Innocent II in the disputed papal election of 1130; in 1145 one of his pupils was elected to the papal throne as Eugenius III, the first Pope to come from the Cistercian order. He even touched military affairs: Eugenius commissioned him to whip up support for the Second Crusade after the loss of the County of Edessa; and he wrote a book encouraging a new military monastic order, the Knights Templar, entitled *In Praise of the New Knighthood*. Finally, it is worth noting his influence on the Protestant reformers, particularly John Calvin, who quoted extensively from Bernard as a right receiver of the interpretive tradition of the Church.

On Grace and Free Choice

This book (in Latin *De Gratia et Libero Arbitrio*) was written around 1128, and works largely (although not exclusively) with the book of Romans as Bernard seeks to understand the relationship in Paul's writing between the power of grace and the responsibility of people. It is perhaps most noteworthy, as shall be shown, for the repositioning of free choice in a wider set of freedoms that Bernard sees created in people and experienced through sin and grace. Bernard begins the work with a story of his own experience of grace and will working together as he sought holiness, and a discussion that resulted from this in which Bernard asserted the prime role of the Spirit and therefore grace:

> On one occasion, I chanced in conversation to mention my experience of God's grace, how I had recognised that I was impelled to do good through its prevenient action, felt that I was being

carried along by grace and given aid by it to find perfection. 'What part do you play, then,' asked someone standing by, 'or what reward or prize are you hoping for, if everything is God's work?' 'What do you think?' I replied. 'To glorify God,' he replied, 'who freely went before you, aroused you and set you in motion; after this, to live a worthy life that proves your gratitude for the kindnesses you have received and your suitability for receiving more.' 'That seems to be sound advice,' I observed, 'if only you would give me the ability to carry it out. Indeed, it is easier to know what it is that one ought to do than it is to do it, because it is one thing to lead a blind person but another to provide a vehicle for the weary. . . . You certainly give good teachings for my ignorance, but unless the Apostle is mistaken, the Spirit helps us in our weakness. Indeed, whoever advises me in your words must also help me through God's Spirit so that I can do as you advise. It is already partly because of this help that I can will what is right but, as yet, I cannot do it. However, I would have no basis for believing that I could one day manage to do what is right if not for the fact that he who has allowed me to will shall also enable me to accomplish this on account of my good will.' To this he replied, 'Then where are our merits or our hope?' 'Listen,' I told him. 'He did not save us because of any deeds done by us in righteousness, but because of His own mercy.'[1]

This seems to raise a concern that free choice plays no role in salvation and would lead to a very deterministic position. However, while asserting the prime movement in grace, Bernard does not believe that a person is merely passive in salvation but that, once grace has operated to create freedom, it is then the responsibility of the person to use that freedom to consent to the ongoing work of grace.

Perhaps you are asking what part free choice plays? I'll answer you in one word: it is saved [salvatur]. Remove free choice and there will be nothing to be saved; remove grace and there will be nothing under which we may be saved. Without the two together, this work cannot be accomplished: one as the operating principle, the other as the object to which or in which it is done. God is the author of salvation; the faculty of free will that which is capable of receiving it. Only God can give it, and nothing but free choice can receive it. Therefore, what is given by God alone and to free choice alone cannot happen without both the consent of the recipient and the grace of the giver. As a result, free choice is said to cooperate

1. Bernard of Clairvaux, *On Grace and Free Choice*, 1.1.

with the work of grace through its consent, *i.e.* in the process of being saved, since to consent to grace is to be saved. . . . Voluntary consent is a self-determining habit of the soul. Its action is not forced, nor is it extorted. It comes from the will rather than from necessity, denying or accepting on no issue except through the will. If consent is compelled against itself, then there is violent rather than voluntary consent. If there is no will, there is no consent, since only what is voluntary can be called consent. Therefore, where there is consent, there is also the will; and where there is will, there is freedom. This is what I understand by the term free choice.[1]

For Bernard, we see here that the focus is on free choice rather than free will, since the will is something fundamental to humanity that distinguishes us from animals, while free choice results from this. However, as already indicated, there will be other resulting freedoms that Bernard wishes to consider that clarify the nature of free choice in a manner distinct from other writers on the subject.

Having established the motivation for the work, Bernard moves on in chapter two to a series of definitions of key terms – quite a modern approach – including both consent and will, which are distinct but closely inter-related. The free nature of the will in giving consent is integral to Bernard's understanding of humanity such that, even in salvation, there cannot be absolute coercion that would determine a person's choice.

If a rational creature were made just or unjust from necessity and without the consent of its will, it should not be dejected nor could it possibly be elated because in either case it would lack the one faculty capable of happiness or unhappiness, namely the will. . . . The consent of the will – voluntary, of course, rather than necessary – shows that we are just or unjust, and also worthily makes us happy or miserable. This consent is rightly called free choice because of the enduring freedom of will and the inevitable judgement of the reason that always and everywhere accompany it. It has free disposal of itself because it retains the will and the power to judge itself because it has reason.[2]

This connection to judgement is reminiscent of many teachings by Early Church Fathers, and is developed by Bernard in the next section to allow a separation in the case of original sin as well as deal explicitly with the potential for unconscious sin:

---

1. Ibid., 1.2.
2. Ibid., 2.4.

On what basis can one impute anything to a person, whether good or bad, if they do not have free control over themselves? Necessity excuses in both cases because its presence implies freedom's absence, and where there is no freedom there can be no merit nor any judgement, apart from the case of original sin which is clearly another matter. In addition, if a person lacks a freedom of voluntary consent, he also must lack merit and judgement. Therefore, everything related to a person, excepting only the will, is free from both because it does not have free disposal of itself. . . . Concerning the will, because it is impossible for the will not to obey itself, no one does not will what they will or wills what they do not will, and so it is impossible for the will to be deprived of its freedom. An act of the will can be changed, but only into another act of the will, which means that freedom can never be lost. The will can therefore no more lose freedom than lose itself. If it were ever in a person's power to will nothing at all, or to will without the faculty of willing, then the will would be capable of lacking freedom. . . . This is why we do not impute anything that they do, whether good or bad, to the mentally deficient, to infants or to a person who is sleeping because they are not in control of their reason and so they do not retain the use of their own will or consequently a free judgement. Because the will only knows its own freedom, it is right that it should be the source of its own judgement. Slowness of mind, a weak memory, a restless nature, poor sense perception and a weakening of vitality do not in themselves constitute a person guilty, just as their opposites do not make a person innocent. This is because all these are known to occur of necessity at times, without a previous decision of the will.[1]

In chapter three, Bernard moves on to distinguishing types of freedom, which is crucial to understanding how he perceives free choice and the extent of its influence in a person's life. When introducing this, he provides one of his clearest definitions of this term:

Since the will has an innate freedom and cannot be compelled by any force or necessity to revolt against itself or consent in anything despite itself, only the will makes a creature righteous or unrighteous, capable and deserving of happiness or sorrow, inasmuch as it consents to righteousness or unrighteousness. This is why we provided a suitable definition earlier on of voluntary and

---

1. Ibid., 2.5.

free consent, on which we have seen that every act of judgement depends, as 'free choice': 'free' referring to the will; 'choice' referring to the reason.[1]

Bernard then briefly defines three forms of freedom: from sin, from sorrow and from necessity. Free choice does not relate to the first, since sin is always present in this life; it is not a freedom from sorrow, because that will only be achieved in the new creation; thus, free choice should be considered as freedom from necessity.

> There are then these three forms of freedom that we are aware of: freedom from sin, from sorrow and from necessity. The last is part of our natural condition; we are restored to the first by grace; while the second awaits us in our homeland. The first freedom can therefore be called a freedom of nature; the second a freedom of grace; and the third a freedom of life or glory. Firstly, we were created with a free will and in that we willed freedom were a noble creature in God's eyes; secondly, we are reformed in innocence as a new creature in Christ; and thirdly, we are raised up to glory as a perfect creature in the Spirit.[2]

In understanding free choice under this teaching, the effects of salvation are rather subtle. Free choice was always present in humankind since it comes from the will that is fundamental to being human. Therefore, the freedom that is won by Christ relates to the extent of the power of sin over a person and the partial conquest of this that is won for this life and that will be complete in the life to come.

> Even free choice needs a liberator, but only one who freed it not from necessity, which it did not know since this concerns the will, but rather from the sin into which it had freely and willingly fallen, and also from the penalty of sin that it carelessly incurred and willingly carried. Free choice was unable to free itself from these two evils, except through the only person who was made free from the dead; free, that is, from sin in the midst of sinners.[3]

The fact that grace does not affect the core application of human will is then asserted again in linking this faculty to will in any rational being, including God, angels and the devil.

---

1. Ibid., 3.6.
2. Ibid., 3.7.
3. Ibid.

Freedom from necessity belongs in the same way to God and to every rational creature, whether they are good or bad. It is not lost or weakened either by sin or by suffering; it is not greater in a just person than in a sinner, nor is it more complete in the angel than in a person. The consent of the human will, when it is directed by grace towards the good, makes a person freely, and in the good, free because it is voluntarily given rather than being unwillingly dragged out. In the same way, when it wills to incline towards the bad, it makes a person equally free and spontaneous in the bad. Nothing is forced to be evil by some other cause, but rather they choose to be so as a result of their own will. Just as the angels in heaven, or even God himself, remain freely good, which they do by their own will rather than from any extrinsic necessity, so the devil freely both chose evil and remains in evil not because he is coerced from without, but from his own free choice. Freedom of will therefore continues to exist even when the mind is captive, as fully in the bad as in the good, yet with greater order in the good; as complete in its own way in the creature as in the creator, but more powerfully in the creator.[1]

This clarifies that the pertinent discussion, for Bernard, is not whether free will exists in humankind, but the extent to which we have free choice and how other freedoms relate to this. Therefore, Bernard writes:

When someone complains saying, 'I wish I could have a good will, but I just can't manage it', this does not argue against the freedom that we have been speaking about, as if their will had suffered violence or were subject to necessity. Rather they are bearing witness to the fact that they lack the freedom that is called freedom from sin. Whoever wants to have a good will proves by this fact that they have a will, since their desire is directed towards the good only through their will. If they discover they are unable to have a good will then they really want one, this is because they discern the freedom that they lack, namely freedom from sin; this causes them pain that their will is oppressed, but not suppressed. Indeed, it is more than likely that the fact they desire to have a good will shows that they actually, to some extent, have it. What they want is good, and they could hardly want to do good without a good will, just as they could only want evil if they had a bad will. Therefore, when we desire good, our will is good; when we desire

---

1. Ibid., 4.9.

evil, it is evil. In either case, there is a will, and in all situations a
freedom; necessity submits to the will. But if we are unable to do
what we will, we feel that our freedom has become captive to sin
or that it is unhappy, not that it is lost.[1]

Bernard then resolves that freedom from sin and freedom from sorrow
could better be termed free counsel and free pleasure, respectively. The
first remains at the core of human experience, since it is only to the extent
that we have the wisdom of good counsel that we have the possibility of
choosing that which we ought.

> [On the prayer, 'Thy kingdom come'] This kingdom is not yet
> fully established among us, but it comes gradually closer each day,
> and daily it gradually increases and extends its boundaries. It does
> this only in those whose inner self is renewed from day to day with
> the help of God. Therefore, to the extent that grace's kingdom is
> extended, sin's power is weakened.[2]

There follows a discussion of whether free counsel or free pleasure is
possible in this life, and the incompleteness of these lead Bernard to the
ongoing role of grace in free choice:

> I think that I have clearly shown that even free choice is
> somewhat restricted when it is not accompanied, or is imperfectly
> accompanied, by the other two freedoms. It is only from this
> cause that we have this weakness that the Apostle speaks about:
> 'So that you do not do the things you would.' It is truly in
> our power to will something because we have free choice, but
> we cannot carry out what we will. I am not talking here about
> whether we will good or bad, but simply the power to will. . . .
> Creating grace gives existence to the will; saving grace gives the
> ability to achieve. However, when the will fails, it is culpable for
> this failure. Free choice therefore makes us able to will, while
> grace makes us able to will what is good. Because of our capacity
> for willing, we are able to will; but because of grace, we are able
> to will what is good.[3]

Here, there is an interesting distinction in Bernard's discussion of
grace between the grace of creation and that of salvation, which he
continues to develop:

---

1. Ibid., 4.10.
2. Ibid., 4.12.
3. Ibid., 6.16.

Simple affections are naturally present in us, as a result of our being, but additional acts affect us because of grace. This only means that grace orders what creation has given, which means that virtues are nothing more than ordered affections.[1]

This allows Bernard to give people an individual will that is yet also in some way subject either to the devil or to God.

We were created as our own to some extent with a freedom of will, but become God's as it were through a good will. In addition, the one who made the will free also makes it good and for this purpose: that we can be a kind of first fruit of His creation, because it would have been better that we would never have existed than that we would always remain our own. Those who wished to belong to themselves did indeed become like gods, knowing good and evil; but then they were not just their own, but also the devil's. Therefore, a free will makes us our own, but a bad will means we are owned by the devil and a good will means that we are owned by God. . . . Furthermore, whether we belong to God or to the devil does not stop us from also being our own. In both cases, free choice continues to work and as a result the basis for merit remains in that we are rightly punished when bad, because we have become bad from our own free choice; and we are glorified when good, because we could not have become good without a similar decision of our will. It is our own will that makes us slaves to the devil, not his power; whereas God's grace makes us subject to God, not our own will. Our will, which it must be allowed was created as good by the good God, will nevertheless only be perfect when it is perfectly subject to its creator.[2]

The summary is that free choice exists, but grace changes what that choice is capable of.

[On Romans 7:18: 'I can will what is right, but I cannot do it'] Paul realised that it was possible for him to will because he had free choice, but that to perfect this will needed grace. This is because willing what is evil is a defect in the willing faculty, and therefore it is clear that to will what is good shows a restoration of this same faculty.

Therefore, in order that the will that we have from our free choice may be perfected, we need a twofold gift of grace: this is

1. Ibid., 6.17.
2. Ibid., 6.18.

true wisdom, which involves the turning of the will to good; and full power, which means that it is confirmed in the good.[1]

The next major section of Bernard's work deals with freedom from sin and from sorrow, although the focus for our current project will be on the former, as the latter is lost at the Fall, is contingent on other freedoms to the extent that it can be experienced in this life and then is restored in the life to come. In terms of free counsel, Bernard provides a good summary of an Augustinian idea concerning the impact of the Fall:

> [On freedom of counsel and freedom of pleasure] The fact is that each of these implies two degrees of freedom, higher and lower. A higher freedom of counsel involves not being able to sin, a lower in being able not to sin. . . . Therefore, the very nature of humankind received the lower degree of each of these freedoms along with full freedom of choice; when sin occurred, humanity fell from both. In losing completing their freedom of counsel, they fell from being able not to sin to not being able not to sin. . . . There only remained, in terms of punishment, the freedom of choice through which we lost the other freedoms; this freedom we could not lose. Enslaved by the will to sin, we have deservedly forfeited the freedom of counsel. Through sin we become in debt to death, and so how could we hold on to freedom of pleasure?[2]

Following this, Bernard addresses one of the key questions concerning sin and humankind, which is why were we created with the possibility for sin by a God who is wholly good?

> Out of all living beings, only humans were given the ability to sin as part of their blessing in free choice. This was not given that we might sin, but rather that we may seems more glorious when we do not sin although we were capable of this. . . . This honour was retained for as long as they did not sin; but once sin occurred, it was lost. Adam sinned because he was free to sin, and this freedom meant that no source other than his freedom of choice was at work, which freedom contained the possibility of sinning. This was not a failure of the one granting freedom, but rather of the one who abused their freedom, who gave over to the service of sin that privilege that had been given for glory and not

---

1. Ibid., 6.18, 19.
2. Ibid., 7.21.

for sinning. Although the root cause of sin was in the ability that was received, yet Adam did not sin because he was able to, but because he willed to sin.[1]

If the power of free choice is so great that it can change the state of a person against the intention of the creator, is it then able to restore the person back to the created state?

Therefore, the sinner fell not because of the gift that allowed this, but to the evil vice of willing to sin. However, although humanity fell by the power of the will, this does not mean that they are equally free to rise again by that same power. The will was given ability to remain standing against a fall, but could not get up again once the fall occurred. It is not as easy to climb out of a pit as it is to fall into one. By the will alone, humanity fell into the pit of sin; but they cannot climb out through the will alone because now, even if we wish, we cannot avoid sinning.[2]

There is thus not sufficient strength in the human will to recover a pre-Fall state, however, this does not mean that there is no will or choice left in humanity.

Free choice therefore does still remain even after humanity sins; it is tainted by sorrow but it is intact. The fact that a person can do nothing to free themselves either from sin or from sorrow does not imply the destruction of free choice, but rather a constraint of the other two freedoms. Free choice in itself does not have within it, nor did it ever, the capacity for power or wisdom, but only for a will; it cannot make a person either wise or able, but only willing. A person cannot therefore be thought to have lost free choice if they have stopped being wise or able, but only if they cease to will. For where there is no will, neither is there freedom.[3]

Bernard now moves on to the effect of Christ and salvation on this state of humankind, which retains free choice but lacks the wisdom to know how to use it well or at times the ability to carry out that which it perceives it should do. The Christ event begins the transformation of the human condition because it brings about a change in the free counsel and free pleasure, incomplete though the changes are in this life.

---

1. Ibid., 7.22.
2. Ibid., 7.23.
3. Ibid., 8.24.

This is where Christ comes in. . . . [I]n that He is wisdom, Christ pours true wisdom back into people and so restores their free counsel; and, in that He is power, Christ renews a person's full power and so restores their free pleasure. As a result, the former makes a person perfectly good so they may now know sin no longer; while the latter makes a person completely happy, so that they may feel the sting of sin no longer. However, we must wait for this degree of perfection until the next life, when both of these freedoms that have been lost will be fully restored to our free choice. No person on earth, however perfect, is given this here, nor was it even given to the first human beings to enjoy in paradise; but the angels do possess these now in heaven. . . . [In this age] we must be content simply when we do not give in and sin from our concupiscence, which we are able to do through our freedom of counsel; and also we should not be afraid of any enemy for the sake of righteousness, which we are able to accomplish through our freedom of pleasure. However, given our sinful flesh and the evil of this day, there is no small amount of wisdom needed to avoid consenting to sin, and we cannot free ourselves from this completely; and there is no small amount of power needed to strengthen us to despise adversity for the sake of truth, and we cannot yet avoid fearing adversity at times even with all the blessings we have received.[1]

The Early Church Fathers repeatedly referred to free will as part of the image of God in humankind, and Bernard writes along similar lines, although he distinguishes between free choice, that is the image, and free counsel and pleasure, that are part of the likeness.

I believe that these three freedoms contain the image and likeness of the Creator in which we were made. The image can be found in freedom of choice, while the other two contain a certain twofold likeness. Therefore, perhaps the reason why only free choice is not reduced and does not fall away is that it contains an imprint of the substantial image of the eternal, unchanging God more than the others do.[2]

Because freedom of choice is more integral to human nature, Bernard believes that it is retained even in hell, whereas the other two are not:

---

1. Ibid., 8.26.
2. Ibid., 9.28.

As a result, nothing remains in hell of the likeness that is contained
in the freedoms of counsel and pleasure, or even can remain. But
the image in free choice does remain even there, permanent and
unchanged.[1]

In this life, while freedom of choice is always absolutely maintained,
the other two freedoms are generally changeable, although Bernard
holds that they can be either firmly held or lost again:

We lost these freedoms through our own fault, but recovered
them by grace; every day, we either progress in or lose each of
these in differing degrees. They may even be irreparably lost, but
they can also be securely possessed so that we cannot fall away
again.[2]

These considerations of other freedoms help Bernard to be nuanced
in his presentation of free choice, although they do require the reader
to work at grasping what each freedom represents and why together
they aid in our understanding of the overall topic of the human will.
Towards the end of the treatise, Bernard returns to the opening questions
concerning whether a person can take any part in his salvation based on
his construct of free choice.

Just as God was independent and the master of his own will, and
therefore not good by necessity, so the creature was also made
its own master so that they could only become evil through an
act of the will and so be justly condemned, or remain good by
an act of the will and rightly be saved. Not that a person's will
alone is capable of gaining salvation, but they would never stand
a chance of gaining this without their will. No one is unwillingly
saved.[3]

Bernard is aware of passages that might challenge this position and
responds:

[On Luke 14:23, 'Compel people to come in'] does not mean that,
because the kindly Father who wills that everyone be saved appears
as drawing people towards and compelling many to salvation,
this denies him judging as worthy of salvation only those He has
previously shown to will this. Again, in frightening and afflicting
people, the purpose of God is not to save those who are unwilling,

1. Ibid., 9.31.
2. Ibid., 9.28.
3. Ibid., 11.36.

but rather to make them willing. In this way, by changing their will from bad to good, God does not remove their freedom, but rather transfers its allegiance.[1]

The next question is the extent to which human choice is influenced negatively by temptation.

Regardless of how much a person may be attacked by temptations, either internal or external, the will always remains independent in choosing and is free to determine whether it will consent.[2]

There are additional questions raised by the negative influence of the flesh or the positive work of the Spirit:

Between these two – the divine Spirit and the desires of the flesh – what is called free choice in people, otherwise known as the human will, occupies a kind of middle position. It can go in either direction, as if it were on the sloping side of quite a steep mountain. It is greatly weakened in its desires by the flesh, so that it is only when the Spirit constantly helps with its infirmity through grace that it is capable of righteousness . . . capable of climbing from strength to strength all the way to the summit. Without the help of grace, carried along by the pull of its own weight, it would fall headlong over the precipice from one vice into another. . . . These two weaknesses that result from our mortality do not injure us, but rather test, those who do not consent; in the same way they do excuse, but rather condemn, those who do consent. Therefore, we teach that there is no salvation or condemnation without a previous consent of the will, in case freedom of choice might appear to be predetermined in any way.[3]

As the work moves towards the conclusion, Bernard seeks to show the necessity both of grace and human free choice, recognising that the first movement is always of grace but that the purpose of this is to work with the will.

God therefore works these three things in us: thinking, willing and accomplishing the good. The first he does without us; the second with us; and the third through us. In suggesting a good thought, God goes one first step before us; by bringing about a change in our evil will, God joins the will to himself through its

1. Ibid.
2. Ibid., 11.37.
3. Ibid., 12.41.

consent; and by giving to the consent the capacity and ability, God who works within us appears externally through the works that are performed. Of course, we cannot in our own strength take that first step; but the one who finds no one who is good can only save a person by himself first stepping in to lead them. Therefore, there is no doubt that the beginning of our salvation is worked by God, and this is neither through us nor with us. The consent and the accomplishment of the good, however, although they do not begin with us, are nevertheless not without us.[1]

This means that, after grace has begun a work in a person, grace and free choice work together. As Bernard explores this, there are echoes of the union of the two natures in Christ in the way Bernard describes the role of each:

We must therefore be careful when we can sense that these things are happening invisibly within us and with us not simply to ascribe them to our own will, which is weak, nor to any necessity on the part of God, since there is none. Rather it is the work of grace alone, of which God is full. It is this grace that awakens free choice when it sows the seed of good thought; which heals it when it changes its disposition; which strengthens it in order to lead it into action; and which saves it from experiencing a fall. However, grace cooperates with free choice such that only initially does it go a step ahead; at other stages, it accompanies free choice. Indeed, the whole purpose of grace taking the first step ahead is that from this point onwards it may cooperate with free choice. What was begun by grace alone is completed by grace and free choice together, in such a way that they each contribute to every new achievement not individually but together; not each in turn, but simultaneously. It is not that grace does one half of a work and free choice the other; but rather both of them do all of the work, with each making its own unique contribution. Grace performs all the work and free choice performs all the work, with just this one qualification: that just as all the work is done with free choice, so is it done of grace.[2]

Finally, Bernard summarises his position by highlighting again the beginning, process and end of grace in relation to free choice:

Therefore, whoever has true wisdom recognises three parts in a work, these not the result simply of free choice, but of the work of divine grace with or concerning free choice. The first part is creation; the

---

1. Ibid., 14.46.
2. Ibid.

second is reformation; and the third is consummation. We are first created in Christ in order to give us free will; in the second we are reformed through Christ to grant us a spirit of freedom; and thirdly we achieve fulfilment with Christ preparing us to receive eternity.[1]

Conclusion

Bernard of Clairvaux provides an interesting, indeed a novel, approach to the relationship between grace and free will (or free choice, in his terminology) that is worthy of inclusion in its own right. *On Grace and Free Choice* also offers an exemplar of a more mystical source in contrast to the approach of the Scholastic writers that surround Bernard in this volume. He clearly has Augustine's teaching in mind, and the first movement of grace is upheld. Notwithstanding, he creates a definition of free choice that allows for its full retention after the Fall and he concentrates on the experience after this in the ongoing relationship between grace and the nature of the free choice that results.

The quotations here are my own work from the Latin found in Jacques-Paul Migne's *Patrologia Latina*, working with the help of William Watkins' 1920 translation. The most recent translation is Daniel O'Donovan's in the Cistercian Fathers Series, Volume 3 (Kalamazoo, MI: Cistercian Publications, 1988).

Appendix: Peter Abelard

Useful in this context would be a chapter on Peter Abelard (1079-1142) and his doctrine of sin, which was notable in focusing more on intention than action as the locus. John Marenbon has written about this in his book, *The Philosophy of Peter Abelard* (New York: Cambridge University Press, 1997), for those who are interested. Abelard was a major thinker in early Scholasticism and possibly the greatest philosopher-theologian before Thomas Aquinas. However, the idea behind these books is to present writers' thoughts with the intention of encouraging the reader to refer to the original texts, and Abelard's significant theological works, *Theologia Summi Boni*, *Theologia Christiana* and *Theologia Scholarium*, have yet to be translated into English (two are available in German).

There are two main reasons for Abelard's continuing exclusion from mainstream theology. The first is his relationship with Heloïse, a pupil of Abelard who became pregnant during their time together, leading to

---

1. Ibid., 14.49.

Abelard's castration and her retreat into a convent. This is the dominant focus of the popular conception of Abelard, and Abelard's own account can be found in his autobiography, *The Story of my Misfortunes*, which is available in English. The second reason for his unpopularity is that he was twice convicted of heresy later in life, primarily related to his portrayal of the Trinity as power, wisdom and goodness and a supposed equivalence of the Holy Spirit with Plato's World Soul. Having previously investigated these charges through the work of Henry Mews and Abelard's own defence against the charges, I believe the convictions to be harsh at the very least. It would seem that Bernard of Clairvaux was strongly motivated in opposing Abelard's theological method, which he saw as overly rational.

Today when Abelard is taught in undergraduate theology, it is usually in the context of the Atonement and his 'subjective model' that is seen to be opposed to Anselm's more 'objective' ideas. The criticism is that Abelard focused on the Christ event more as a model to follow than as the completed work of God but, again, this seems a very unfair approach to Abelard's thought. One document that has been translated is his *Commentary on the Book of Romans*, in which his line of thought on the Atonement is briefly presented. However, when reading Abelard's wider thought, even in that Commentary but certainly when looking through the *Theologiae*, one can see that this is not the only approach that he takes. Sadly, too few teachers in this area have the ability or motivation to study Abelard's thought in the context of his wider theology and the subjective model is now tied to his name.

The most straightforward access to Abelard's theological project and style is through his *Sic et Non* (*Yes and No*), which has also been published, where he goes through many aspects of theology with the Church Fathers showing how they contrast with, if not actually contradict, each other. This should lead to a refreshing approach to theology in line with these volumes, that theological discussions should not be nailed down to a final definition but are fundamentally beyond our complete comprehension, leading to a humility before God, His word and His Church. *Sic et Non* was not widely appreciated in the early twelfth century when the early theological project rested so strongly on a perceived solid foundation of the teaching of the Church Fathers.

3.
Peter Lombard

It could easily be argued that Peter Lombard (c.1096-1160) was the prime theologian of the medieval period, and yet interest in and knowledge of his work has been sadly lacking over the last century at least.[1] Lombard was Italian by birth and studied in Paris – at that time the centre of the developing theological and philosophical climate – in the first half of the twelfth century. He became the Bishop of Paris shortly before his death. His major theological work was called the *Sentences*. This was split into four books – *The Mystery of the Trinity*, *On Creation*, *On the Incarnation of the Word* and *On the Doctrine of Signs* – each examining a number of 'Distinctions', areas of theology, broken up into relevant sections.

This work was one of the most systematic treatments of theology in the early Scholastic period and its influence was huge. The *Sentences* became the textbook for the study of theology for the next few centuries, far more foundational even than Aquinas' *Summa* after its publication in the following century. So important was Lombard's work that it became the subject of great study itself, with a number of commentaries on the *Sentences* being published, including one by Thomas Aquinas. Lombard was one of many at the time given the title 'Master', however, for Lombard this became 'The Master of the *Sentences*' and later simply 'The Master', which is how Aquinas refers to Lombard in the *Summa* – only one could be referred to as *the* Master.

Given the prominence of Lombard for so long in the history of theology, it is surprising that he has not received greater attention in recent times. There are several factors behind this, of which I would highlight three. Firstly, the senior Protestant reformer, Martin Luther, was schooled in a more Aristotelian part of the Catholic Church, where Aquinas was more dominant, thus the reaction was primarily against elements of this

---

1. The major exceptions are Marcia Colish and Philipp Rosemann, who have produced some excellent studies of Lombard's theology.

system and much future Protestant thought grew out of this context. Secondly, in the nineteenth century during a triumphal period for the Catholic Church associated with the development of Ultramontanism, Thomas Aquinas became the dominant and foundational thinker for Catholicism in a movement known as neo-Thomism with documents, such as *The 24 Thomistic Theses*, that teachers were required to approve. Thirdly, and far more obviously from the point of view of the English-speaking world, The *Sentences* were not translated until very recently and, given the decline in the teaching of Classical languages, this affected the number of people who might otherwise engage with Peter Lombard. As David Bell has wisely noted: 'It is a well known fact that the number of postgraduate dissertations dealing with any author increases in direct proportion to the degree in which that author appears in translation.'[1]

Things have begun to change in this regard, beginning with work by the Franciscan Archive, which published a translation of the first book of the *Sentences* in 2006 and seems to be continuing its work on the three remaining books. However, the great development was accomplished by Giulio Silano, who has translated all four books, published in four separate volumes by the Pontifical Institute for Mediaeval Studies between 2007 and 2010. Professor Silano and the Pontifical Institute have very generously given me permission to use the quotations from his work that appear in this chapter, and it is my hope that this work will encourage more people back to the original source. As one who had to work through the Latin of the *Sentences* for my own PhD, I am slightly envious of those who can now access Lombard so easily, but the fact that this valuable resource can be restored to its rightful position in Christian studies triumphs over this petty reaction.

On God

Lombard's thought in all areas proceeds from his understanding of God, with the entire first book of the *Sentences* devoted to a discussion of the Trinity. This is fairly remarkable in itself, but the depth of reflection this book contains, the span of themes that are addressed and the proportion of the whole that is taken up (particularly when one considers that much of the third book concerns the Son in discussing the Incarnation) demonstrate the importance of this method in the construction of Lombard's theology.

---

1. David Bell, *The Image and Likeness: the Augustinian Spirituality of William of Saint Thierry* (Kalamazoo, MI: Cistercian Publications, 1984), p.13.

It is thus unsurprising that sin receives little direct treatment as sin is not in the being of God. One important and interesting mention comes with reference to God's omnipotence, where Lombard notes that there are things that a human can do that God cannot. For actions like walking and speaking, Lombard states that: 'he can work them in creatures: he makes man walk and speak and suchlike.'[1] When it comes to sin, Lombard responds thus:

> But there are some other things which God cannot at all do, like sins: for he cannot lie and he cannot sin. But nothing is taken away or derogated from God's omnipotence in any way by this, if he is said to be unable to sin, because this would not be a matter of power, but of weakness: for if he could do this, he would not be omnipotent. Therefore, the fact that he cannot do such things is not to be ascribed to powerlessness, but to power.[2]

This indicates a view of sin that will continue through the work: that it is the negation of goodness and therefore existence (since God is these in himself and the origin of them in all creation). This is important to bear in mind in later sections.

Evil gets rather more attention as Lombard addresses this in the first book in relation to God's knowledge, since he knows all things. If there is knowledge of evil things, Lombard asks, does this mean that they are in some way in God?

> Since all things are said to be in God not by the essence of nature, but by the cognition of knowledge, and God knows good and evil things, whether it is simply to be granted that evil things are in God, or that they are in God through cognition. For God knows and has always known all things, both good and evil, even before they were done, and he had foreknowledge from eternity of those things that would be. And so, as we have said that all good things are in God through the presence of cognition, by the same reason it should be said that all evil thing are in him, since he always knew them and they were present to him through cognition.[3]

From this, Lombard concludes that evil things are not in God despite his complete knowledge of them, allowing him to differentiate between his knowledge of good and evil.

---

1. Lombard, *Sentences*, 1.42.2.
2. Ibid.
3. Ibid., 1.36.2.

Evil things are not in God because, although he knows them, yet he does not know them entirely as he knows good ones. He knows evil things as if from far away . . . And so God knows both good and evil things through knowledge; but he knows good things also through approbation and good pleasure, but not the evil ones.[1]

Lombard expands the knowledge of God to include several other core aspects of God's being in relation to creation:

And so, it is to be known that God's wisdom or knowledge, although it is one and simple, yet it is given several different names because of the varying states of things and their different effects. For it is called not only knowledge, but also foreknowledge or foresight, disposition, predestination and providence. And foreknowledge or foresight concerns only future things, but all of them, namely good and evil ones; disposition concerns things that are to be done; predestination concerns all who are to be saved, as well as the good things by which these are freed in this life and will be crowned in the future. For God, from all eternity, predestined men to good things by electing [them], and he predestined by preparing good things for them.[2]

There is a distinction drawn between the knowledge or foreknowledge of God and his predestination of things, since the latter can only be applied to good things.

For the knowledge or foreknowledge of God, by which he knows or foreknows good and evil events, is the divine nature or essence; and predestination, or his will, is the same divine essence, nor in God is it one thing to know or will, and another to be. And although God's knowledge and his will are one and the same, still not all that is said of his will is also said of his knowledge, and vice versa. Nor does God will by his own will all that he knows by his knowledge, since by his knowledge he knows both good and evil events, but by his will he only wills the good ones. Assuredly, God's knowledge and foreknowledge is of both good and evil things, but his will and predestination is only of the good ones, and yet in God knowledge and will are one and the same, as also are foreknowledge and predestination.[3]

---

1. Ibid.
2. Ibid., 1.35.2–6.
3. Ibid., 1.6.3.

While there seems to be some guarding of God's goodness in this construct, Lombard recognises that questions still remain even if God is only claimed to have knowledge of evil without predestining it. Given the completeness and infallibility of God's knowledge, does this alone not necessitate and therefore cause all that will happen? As Lombard puts it:

> Here arises a question which is not to be ignored, namely whether knowledge or foreknowledge is the cause of things, or things are the cause of God's knowledge or foreknowledge. For it seems that God's foreknowledge is the cause of things subject to it and necessitates their coming into being because there would not be any future things if God had not foreknown them, and they cannot not come to pass once God has foreknown them. But if it is impossible for them not to come to pass because they have been foreknown, then the very foreknowledge by which they have been foreknown appears to be the cause of their coming to pass. But it is impossible for them not to occur once they have been foreknown because, if they were not to happen after being foreknown, God's foreknowledge would be fallible. But God's foreknowledge is infallible, and so it is impossible for them not to happen after being foreknown.[1]

Lombard responds by clearly stating that foreknowledge cannot be the cause of events because this would mean that evil originated with God.

> But if this is so, then it is the cause of all evils, since all evil things are known and foreknown by God; which is far from the truth. For if God's knowledge or foreknowledge were the cause of evils, God would assuredly be the author of evils, which is entirely false; and so God's knowledge or foreknowledge is not the cause of all things subject to it.[2]

This in turn raises the possibility, if God foreknows all things, that what occurs is the cause of his knowledge. Again, Lombard refutes this:

> And future things too are not the cause of God's foreknowledge: for although there would not be future things unless they were foreknown by God, yet they are not foreknown because they are future. For if this were so, then the cause of that which is eternal

---

1. Ibid., 1.38.1.
2. Ibid.

would be something alien and different from it, and the Creator's foreknowledge would be dependent on creatures and something created would be the cause of something uncreated.[1]

To make clear what he means, Lombard inserts the concept of awareness into the knowledge structure of God.

That which will be is known by God before it happens, and it would not be known if it were not to be: no cause is signified there, except that without which it could not be. We also say that God's knowledge or foreknowledge is not the cause of things which happen, except in the sense that they do not happen without it; yet only if we mean by knowledge awareness alone.[2]

This then allows for a distinction between his foreknowledge of good and evil.

As for evil things, however, God knows and foreknows them before they happen, but by awareness alone, not by good pleasure. For God foreknows and foretells even those things which he will not do himself, as he knew and foretold the faithlessness of the Jews, but did not himself cause it. It is not because he foreknew it that he compelled them to the sin of faithlessness; nor would he have foreknown or foretold their evils, unless they were going to make them their own . . . But because his foreknowledge is infallible, without doubt it is not anyone else, but they themselves who sin, [and] whom God foreknew that they would sin. And so, if they had wished to do good and not evil, they would not be foreseen to be going to do evil by him who knows what each person will do.[3]

From this understanding of foreknowledge, Lombard can then move onto predestination and reprobation. Predestination provides no issues for Lombard within his concept of God, being in line with the basic concept of God's omniscience.

And so from eternity, he has predestined some to be good and blessed, that is, he elected them to be good and blessed, and he predestined, that is, prepared good things for them. Providence is concerned with governance, and it seems to be taken entirely in the same way as disposition; and yet sometimes providence is taken

1. Ibid.
2. Ibid.
3. Ibid.

for foreknowledge. Wisdom or knowledge, however, concerns all things: namely good and evil, and present, past, and future, and not only temporal things, but also eternal ones. For God does not know these temporal things so as to lose knowledge of Himself, but He alone knows Himself perfectly, by comparison with whose knowledge, the knowledge of every creature is imperfect.[1]

Within this, and in comparison with those who are not predestined, comes one of the concepts of grace found in the first book. Given that grace is a relational category, it is found in discussions of creation rather than in the intra-Trinitarian material which comprises a large amount of this book. Lombard defines the two concepts of predestination and reprobation as follows:

Predestination is the preparation of grace, that is, divine election, by which God elected whom he willed *before the foundation of the world*, as the Apostle says. Conversely, reprobation is to be understood as the foreknowledge of the iniquity of some and the preparation of their damnation. For the effect of predestination is that grace by which we are justified in the present and are assisted to live rightly and to persevere in the good, and also the grace by which we are blessed in the future. Similarly, God's reprobation, by which he has reprobated some from eternity by not electing them, is considered according to two things, of which he foreknows one, but does not prepare it, that is, iniquity; the other he foreknows and prepares, namely eternal punishment.[2]

Lombard's notion of predestination is thus tied closely to that of grace, and this strong position will affect his discussions of the nature of humanity and therefore free will. In discussing whether it is possible that those who are predestined could be damned or those destined for punishment could be saved, he states:

The reason it is said, and it is true, that the number of the elect cannot be increased or diminished is that both cannot be true at the same time: namely that anyone should be saved and not be predestined, or that anyone should be predestined and be damned. . . . For it cannot be true that he was predestined from eternity and now he is not predestined, nor can it be true simultaneously that he is predestined and he is not predestined; but yet it could be true from eternity that he was not predestined, and he could

1. Ibid., 1.35.2-6.
2. Ibid., 1.40.2.

have been not predestined from eternity. And as from eternity God was able not to predestine him, so it is granted by some that even now God is able not to have predestined him from eternity. And so God is able not to have predestined him; therefore, that person is able not to have been predestined. But if he had not been predestined, he would not be predestined; and so he is able now not to be predestined . . . But when we deal with God's foreknowledge or predestination, its possibility or impossibility is referred to the power of God, which was and is ever the same, because predestination, foreknowledge, power is one thing in God.[1]

This puts the ultimate destiny of people primarily in the good choice of God:

Therefore it is not because of faith or any merits that God has elected some from eternity or has conferred his grace of justification in time, but he has elected by his freely given goodness that they should be good.[2]

There is one final point on grace in Book One that expands the concept into God's presence, dwelling in people's spirits in a different way through grace than he is present in all things:

But in the saints, in whom he is by grace, he also dwells. For he does not dwell everywhere that he is; but where he dwells, he is. He dwells in the good alone, who are his temple and his seat.[3]

There is a distinction between this grace and that seen in the union of nature in Christ:

And moreover he exists more excellently in holy spirits and souls, namely indwelling through grace; and most excellently in the man Christ . . . For in him God dwelt not by the grace of adoption, but by the grace of union.[4]

The last aspect of the doctrine of God that should be highlighted is the extensive passage towards the end of the first book on the will of God, because all discussion that follows on angelic and human will must be understood in view of this. Unlike some other Christian writers,

---

1. Ibid., 1.40.1.
2. Ibid., 1.41.2.
3. Ibid., 1.37.2.
4. Ibid., 1.37.1.

particularly those in the Early Church, Lombard does not focus on the 'freedom' of the divine will explicitly, preferring to consider the nature of the will of the divine in relation to his transcendent being in a way that allows for a type of freedom, but one that is clearly distinct from that of humankind. Because God's will is linked into his eternal being and knowledge, it is unchangeable to some extent, and yet this does not mean that it is inevitable. For example:

> For if, in saying: 'He cannot do other than what there is reason for him to do,' you understand that he cannot do other than what is reasonable and what, if it were done, would be reasonable, then the sense is true. But if you understand that he cannot do different reasonable and good things, other than the ones which he wills and does, then the understanding is false.[1]

This quotation focuses on the will in action, but Lombard goes on to discuss the will itself and whether God's will could have been other than it is.

> And he is able to will other than what he wills, and yet his will cannot in any way be different, or new, or mutable. For although he is able to will what he never willed, yet he cannot will newly or by a new will, but only by an everlasting one; for he is able to will what he is able to have willed from eternity. For he has the power of willing both now and from eternity; and yet, what he does not will now, he did not will from eternity.[2]

There is some interesting work here with the immanent and economic Godhead, with God absolutely present both eternally and in time without allowing for any contradiction between the two. This view does create a dissimilarity between Creator and created in relation to the will that will be worked out in book two.

On Angels

Given the extent and detail of references to angelic beings in the Bible (not great in either case), it is perhaps surprising that they receive a full sub-heading in this presentation of Lombard's views on sin, grace and free will. In terms of the *Sentences*, however, this is fully deserved because, after a Distinction on creation, the next ten deal with angels and demons,

---

1. Ibid., 1.43.1.
2. Ibid.

their nature, will and fall, before Lombard moves on to considering the six days of creation and finally humankind from Distinction sixteen onwards.

The first aspect of Lombard's angelology that is relevant is their state in creation, which is a matter of debate given that some angelic beings are evil. Lombard asserts that they were created good, whatever their ultimate state.

> But it seems to others [and Lombard will support this opinion] that all angels were created good and that they were good, in the sense of without vice, at the first moment of creation; and they were just, in the sense of innocent, but not just in the sense of having practice in the virtues. For they were not yet endowed with the virtues which were added in confirmation through grace to those who remained steadfast. But the others became proud through their free choice, and so they fell. They also say that there was some small delay between their creation and fall or confirmation. And in that brief space of time, they were all good, not indeed through the use of free choice, but by the benefit of creation. And they were such as to be able to stand, that is, not to fall, through the goods of creation, and to fall through their free choice. For they were able to sin and not to sin, but they were not able to make progress toward merit of life, except through the super-addition of grace, which was added to some in confirmation.[1]

If this is the case, then they must have been created with freedom of will, a necessary condition for some to fall from their goodness.

> And four things seem certainly to have been their attributes at the beginning of their existence, namely a simple essence, that is, an indivisible and immaterial one; a distinct personal identity; and, through a naturally innate reason, intelligence, memory, and will or love; also free choice, that is, the free faculty of turning the will either to good or to evil, for through free choice, without violence and compulsion, they were able to turn toward either by their own will.[2]

There is then the question of why any would fall if they were created in a state of goodness, without a tempter to suggest evil to them. Part of the reply is that they were not blessed in their original state, but that this was only conferred on them later.

---

1. Ibid., 2.3.4.
2. Ibid., 2.3.1.

It can be said that they were created neither in [a state of] blessedness, nor in misery. For they could not be miserable before sin, because misery is from sin; indeed, if there had been no sin, there would be no misery. But those who fell were never blessed because they were unaware of what would happen to them, that is, of their future sin and punishment. For if they foreknew their fall, either they wished to avoid it but could not, and so they were miserable; or they could have but did not wish to, and so they were foolish and malign.[1]

Prior to this, Lombard states a second reason, which is that the angels were not created equal in all aspects.

Here it is to be considered whether all [the angels] were equal in spiritual substance, and rational wisdom, and freedom of will, which were present in all of them . . . And so those rational essences who were persons and spirits, simple by nature and immortal in their life, are rightly understood to have had a different fineness of essence, and a different perspicacity of wisdom, and a different aptitude for choice.

That they were spirits, and that they were indestructible and immortal, this was equal and common to all. But in refinement of essence, and understanding of wisdom, and freedom of will, they were different. As for these intelligible differences of these invisible natures, he alone was able to understand and weigh them who made all things *in weight, number, and measure*.[2]

The angels who fell therefore did so because their nature was inferior to the others, which then resulted in less grace being given to them as their lower nature resulted in rebellion.

Those spiritual natures at the beginning of their establishment received differences suitable to their purity and excellence in their essence, form, and power. As a result of these differences, some were made superior and some inferior to others by the wisdom of God, who confers greater gifts on some and lesser ones on others, so that those who at that time excelled the rest through their natural goods should afterwards also be pre-eminent over them through the gifts of grace . . . But those who were established as less fine in nature and less far-seeing in wisdom, received lesser gifts of grace and were established as less excellent by the wisdom of God, who orders all things with equitable rule.[3]

---

1. Ibid., 2.4.1.
2. Ibid., 2.3.2.
3. Ibid.

The result of this is that there was a need of conversion for angels, not from evil to good, but from a kind of intermediate or neutral position into light or darkness, the former of which is by grace.

> In those who converted, God's wisdom, by which they were given light, began to shine as in a mirror; but those who turned away were made blind. And the former converted and were enlightened by God's grace which was bestowed upon them; but the latter were blinded not by an infusion of malice, but by the desertion of grace; they were not deserted by grace in the sense that it was taken away after having been previously given to them, but in the sense that it was never given to them so that they might convert.[1]

This grace, however, is not to be viewed apart from their will which is also at work in this process.

> For all had free choice, which is a free power and aptitude of the rational will. For they were able to choose willingly what they pleased, and to make rational judgements, that is, to be discerning, and free choice consists in these things. And they were not created already willing to turn toward [God] or to turn away, but they were able to will the one or the other; and after their creation, by their spontaneous will, some chose evil and others good.[2]

Lombard moves on to discuss the nature of this grace, and makes a distinction between operating grace, which moves a person from an evil state into a just state, and cooperating grace that preserves someone in righteousness. Given the statement above, that they were created neither in blessedness nor in misery, one might expect an element of operational grace to be present, but the focus for Lombard is on cooperating grace.

> But if it is asked whether, after their creation, something was conferred on those who converted by which they might convert, that is, love God, we say that cooperating grace was conferred on them. Without such grace, the rational creature cannot make progress toward meriting life. For it can fall by itself, but it cannot make progress without the assistance of grace.[3]
>
> The angel did not need the grace by which he might be justified, because he was not evil, but the one by which he might be helped to love and obey God perfectly. That grace is called

---

1. Ibid., 2.5.1.
2. Ibid., 2.5.2.
3. Ibid., 2.5.3.

operating by which an impious person is justified, that is, from being impious he is made pious, from evil good; but cooperating grace is that by which he is assisted to will the good with efficacy, to love God before all things, to do good works, to persevere in the good, and suchlike . . . And so cooperating grace was given to the angels who remained steadfast, by which they converted so that they might love God perfectly. Thus they converted from a good which they had and had not lost to a greater good which they did not have; and this conversion was done through grace cooperating with their free choice; this grace was not given to the others who fell.[1]

The result in angels is a fixed state in goodness or evil, with their will and actions similarly determined by their initial move either to obedience or rebellion.

It was said above that the angels who remained steadfast were confirmed through grace, and those who fell were abandoned by God's grace. And certainly the good ones have been so confirmed through grace that they cannot sin; but the evil ones are so obstinate in wickedness that they cannot have a good will and are unable to will well, although what they sometimes will is good.[2]

The last phrase here seems slightly strange, but must be viewed not in terms of the goodness of the angel, but in light of the eternal will of God for his creation and creatures in which even the will and actions of the evil angels are encompassed. The relationship between will and grace remains collaborative in both good and evil:

And yet both have free choice because the good angels choose the good and reject evil without any compelling necessity, but by their own spontaneous will assisted by grace. Similarly, the evil ones, by their own free will abandoned by grace, avoid the good and pursue evil. And the evil ones have free choice, but it is so base and corrupted that they are not able to rise to the good.[3]

But for the good angels, the nature of their free will has been constrained by the grace that is present not to the detriment of their freedom but to its fulfilment, since true freedom relates only to goodness in Lombard's view.

1. Ibid., 2.5.4.
2. Ibid., 2.7.1.
3. Ibid., 2.7.2.

After their confirmation, angels were not able to sin from nature
as before: not that their free choice was weakened through grace,
but rather that it was so confirmed that the good angel is no longer
able to sin through it. And this is not at all from free choice itself,
but from God's grace.[1]

The final quotations on angels move on from their own state to their
work in creation and with humankind. Firstly, there is an interesting
passage on magic and the demonic involvement in this, which declares
that the power for evil comes from God, although its application in evil
is the result of angelic will in action.

Not even the transgressing angels and the powers of the air (who
have been cast down from their dwelling in the sublime purity of
the aether into this lowest darkness as if into a prison for their
kind), through whom the magical arts are able to do whatever they
can do, would be able to do anything, if power had not been given
to them from above. And this power is at times given to deceive
the deceitful, as when it was conferred on the Egyptians and
those very magicians, so that they should seem admirable by the
operation of the very spirits by whom they were made damnable;
at times it is given to warn the faithful against the desire to do any
such thing, as if it were a great thing to do them.[2]

Secondly, Lombard considers the way in which demons affect
humankind, whether through their influence or through their actual
presence in a person. There are historical discussions preceding and
integrated throughout this, as Lombard considers the relative worth of
different positions, before he concludes that they are not substantially
present, but effective as a result of their evil.

It also seems worthy of consideration whether demons, be they
corporeal or incorporeal, enter the bodies of men substantially and
insinuate themselves into their souls. Or are they said to enter souls
because they exercise the effect of their wickedness there, oppressing
and vexing them with God's permission, or drawing them into sin as
they please? . . . [Historical sources then quoted] By these authorities, it
is shown that demons do not enter into the hearts of men substantially,
but do so through the effect of their wickedness; and they are said to
be expelled from them when they are not allowed to do harm.[3]

1. Ibid., 2.7.4.
2. Ibid., 2.7.6.
3. Ibid., 2.8.4.

Lastly on angels (and much more could have been included here as this is only a sample of his writing – do read the original in full if this taster has proved interesting), Lombard works with the teachings of Pope Gregory the Great (c.540-604) to discuss individual human experience. Since Gregory was not covered in Volume One of this work, it is reasonable to include this idea and, in addition, it merits its place because there seem to be the roots here of an almost Disney-like idea of a devil on one shoulder and an angel on the other.

> Gregory [the Great] too says that each soul has a good angel assigned to watch over it, and an evil one to train it. For although all good angels will our good and jointly seek the salvation of all, nevertheless the one who is assigned to watch over someone especially encourages that person to the good, as we read of the angel of Tobias, and the angel of Peter in the Acts of the Apostles. Similarly, although all the evil angels desire evil for men, yet the one who is assigned to test someone incites that person more persistently to evil and encourages him more strongly to do harm.[1]

Lombard, thus, has such a strongly developed angelology at the beginning of his work on creation, and many of the concepts related to sin, grace and free will are then transferred into his presentation of humanity.

The First Human Freedom

A similar quandary to that of angels affects understanding of humans and sin; both were created by a wholly good being and thus without evil, yet in both cases evil came. For humanity, was this a result of a flaw in the design?

> It is also usual to ask, since human nature was without defect, from where did the consent to that evil come. To this it can be answered that it was from the free choice of the will. For the cause of becoming worse existed both in humankind itself and in another. In another, because it was in the devil who persuaded; in humankind itself, because it consented by the will of free choice. And since free choice is a good, that evil consent proceeded from an entirely good thing, and so evil emanated from good.[2]

---

1. Ibid., 2.11.1.
2. Ibid., 2.22.5.

Taking this further, Lombard considers whether the first sin was in the action or whether there was a movement of will that preceded this.

> But if it is asked whether the will preceded that sin, we say that that sin consisted in both the will and the act, and that the will preceded the act. But no other evil human will preceded that will itself; and that evil will issued forth from the devil's persuasion and from human choice by which humankind deserted justice and introduced iniquity; and that will itself was iniquity.[1]

The conclusion from this is that the first sin of humankind was not inevitable because of their created nature in itself, although there would be a need for cooperating grace to retain the original state. There are similarities here to the teaching on angels, that those who would become blessed would need the assistance of grace.

> And so it is to be known that, as we said of the angels, through grace help was given to man at creation and a power was granted by which he was able to stand firm, that is, not to fall from what he had received; but he could not make progress so that he could deserve salvation by the grace of creation [alone] without any other. He was certainly able, through that help of the grace of creation, to resist evil, but not to achieve good. And yet he was able in some way to live well through that help because he was able to live without sin; but without the additional help of grace, he was not able to live spiritually so as to deserve eternal life.[2]

Lombard develops a rather complex inter-relationship in aspects of humanity in order to retain a good creation with the danger of evil. He distinguishes between the will, which is at the core of humanity and that is good, and the choice in which human reason works with the will and where there is a need for grace in order that evil is avoided.

> Free choice, however, is a faculty of reason and will, by which the good is chosen with the assistance of grace, or evil without its assistance. And it is called 'free' in regard to the will, which may turn itself to either of them, but 'choice' in regard to reason, whose faculty or power it is, and to which it also belongs to discern between good and evil. And sometimes someone who has the power to discern between good and evil chooses what is evil; sometimes, that which is good. But he does not choose that which

1. Ibid.
2. Ibid., 2.24.1.

is good except with the help of grace; he chooses evil, however, by himself. For there is in the rational soul a natural will, by which it naturally wills what is good, although weakly and feebly, unless grace assists; at its coming, grace assists that will and builds it up so that it wills the good efficaciously; it is able to will evil efficaciously by itself. And so that power of the rational soul, by which it is able to will good or evil, discerning the one from the other, is called free choice.[1]

There is thus a difference between God and humankind in their free choice:

But free choice is understood otherwise in the Creator than in the creature. For God's most wise and omnipotent will, which does all things as it wills, and not by necessity, but by free goodness, is called free choice.[2]

This kind of free choice is only possible for humankind in the world to come.

The angels and saints, however, who already live happily with the Lord, and are already so confirmed in the grace of blessedness that they neither can, nor wish to bend to evil, do not lack free choice. . . . After the confirmation of blessedness, there will be in man a free choice by which he will be unable to sin, as it already now is in the angels and saints who are with the Lord; and certainly the choice will be so much the freer the more immune it is from sin and the more prone to good.[3]

Lombard helps his readers through the complexity of his thought with some categories of freedom, firstly, in outlining four states of free choice and, secondly, by defining three kinds of freedom. The four states relate to the various phases of human experience from their created state to their redeemed state.

And four states of free choice can be noted in man. For before sin, nothing impeded man from the good, nothing impelled him to evil; he did not have a weakness toward evil, and had a help toward the good. Then, reason was able to judge without error, and the will was able to desire the good without difficulty. But after sin, before the restoration of grace, he is pressed down and overcome

1. Ibid., 2.24.3.
2. Ibid., 2.25.2.
3. Ibid., 2.25.3-4.

by concupiscence; he has weakness toward evil, but does not have grace toward good; and so he can sin and cannot not sin, even damnably. After the restoration and before confirmation, however, he is pressed down by concupiscence, but not overcome; and he also has weakness toward evil, but grace toward good, so that he is able to sin because of his freedom and weakness, and he is able not to sin unto death because of his freedom and the help of grace. Nevertheless, he does not yet have the power not to sin entirely or the inability to sin, because his weakness has not yet been entirely removed and grace has not yet been entirely perfected. But the confirmation, when the weakness will have been entirely destroyed and grace achieved, he will have the power to be neither overcome nor pressed down, and then he shall have the inability to sin.[1]

The three kinds of freedom are freedom from necessity, freedom from sin and freedom from misery. The first of these, freedom from necessity, is part of human nature and is present through all the phases presented above.

Choice is equally free from necessity both before and after sin. For just as it could not be compelled then, so it cannot be now. And so it is rightly concluded that there is a will in God which is always free from necessity and can never be compelled. Where there is necessity, there is no freedom; where there is no freedom, there is no will; and so there is no merit. This freedom is in all, both good and evil.[2]

This is an important principle in Lombard's theology, that there can be no absolute compulsion towards good or evil, which means that the human will is involved despite the great power and importance that Lombard grants to grace.

The second kind of freedom is freedom from sin, a state that humankind had before the fall but that was then lost and can only be regained as a result of the work of grace.

This freedom frees us from the servitude of sin and renders us servants of justice, just as conversely the servitude of sin frees us from justice . . . Man lost this freedom by sinning . . . Those alone whom the Son frees and restores through grace now have this freedom, which is from sin: not in such a way that they are entirely without sin in this mortal flesh, but that sin will neither dominate, nor rule in them. And this is the true and good freedom, which

---

1. Ibid., 2.25.6.
2. Ibid., 2.25.8.

gives birth to the good servitude, namely of justice . . . There is
another freedom that is not true, attached to the evil servitude,
which is that of doing evil: where reason dissents from the will,
judging that what the will desires is not to be done. But in doing
good, reason agrees with the will, and so there is a true and pious
freedom.[1]

Peter Lombard does not hold to a pure Augustinian line that freedom
is only when the will has the choice to do good, although he does
recognise the position.

It seems to some that this is freedom of choice, which is always
good; but because of the servitude of sin, it becomes freer and
more prone to sin, and so it is said not to be true freedom, because
it is for evil. But it seems to others that this freedom to do evil,
which Augustine has recalled above, is not freedom of choice
itself, but is some proneness and bent towards sinning, which is
from sin and is evil.[2]

In Lombard's understanding of will and choice, freedom does relate
both to evil and to good, but the role of grace is protected.

But it pleases us more that freedom of choice itself be both that by
which one is free to do evil, and that by which one is free to do the
good. For it is called different things because of different causes. It
is called freedom to do evil before it is restored through grace; but
once it has been restored through grace, it is called freedom to do
good, because before grace, the will is free toward evil, but through
grace it is made free toward the good.[3]

Finally, there is the third kind of freedom, freedom from misery, which
was the human experience before the Fall and will be again in the life to
come, but is not present now.

Man had this freedom before sin, because he lacked all misery and
was touched by no trouble; and he shall have it more fully in his
future blessedness, where he will not be able to be miserable. But in
this life, which is between the first sin and the final confirmation,
no one is free from misery, because no one lacks the punishment
of sin.[4]

1. Ibid.
2. Ibid.
3. Ibid.
4. Ibid.

This last section has moved slightly away from the first freedom of humans, but has done so in line with Lombard's writing which seeks to explain that freedom both in itself and in comparison with the changes that resulted from sin. His conclusion on the three kinds of freedom is that: 'Freedom from sin and from misery is through grace, but freedom from necessity is through nature.'[1]

Sin and its Effects

Peter Lombard leaves the definition of sin until rather late in the discussion, which seems slightly strange and here it will be moved up to the beginning. He works with two definitions of sin from Augustine: 'Sin is every word or deed or desire which happens against the law of God' (from *To Faustus*); 'Sin is the will to obtain or retain what justice forbids' (from *On the Two Souls*). Considering these, Lombard writes:

> In either description, what is discussed is actual and mortal sin, not venial sin. By the first description, it is shown that sin is an evil will, or depraved speech and deed, that is, an evil action, whether interior or exterior. By the second, it is shown to be only an interior action, for the will, as was said above, is a movement of the spirit; and so the action is interior.[2]

He develops his ideas in the next part of this Distinction:

> It can well be said and it must be freely taught that sin is an evil action, interior and exterior, namely an evil thought, speech, and deed. Yet, sin exists primarily in the will, from which, like evil fruits from an evil tree, proceed evil deeds.[3]

As in the above section on angels, the question arises how this sin could result from a good creation, and in the discussion of humankind the former teaching is revived.

> The cause and first origin of sin was a good thing, because before the first sin there was nothing evil from which it might arise. For since it had an origin and cause, either it had it from good, or from evil. But there was no evil before; and so it arose from good. For sin first arose in the angel, and afterwards in man; and what was

---

1. Ibid., 2.25.9.
2. Ibid., 2.35.1.
3. Ibid., 2.35.2.

the angel other than a good nature of God? It was not from God that the evil which was in the angel arose; it was not from anyone other than the angel, and so it arose from good.[1]

The distinction that was drawn between God and creation is also important, since God's will as part of his nature is unchangeable, unlike that of humans or angels.

See, you have here that the first will of a changeable good, that is, of the angel or of man, falling away from the unchangeable good, that is, from God, is the cause of the evil things which pertain to us, because it is the cause of both the sins and the punishments by which human nature is oppressed. And so the first origin and cause of sin was a good; and the second, an evil which had arisen from the good.[2]

For humans, there is the additional factor of the temptation that came through the devil, which is influential but not a controlling or necessitating element in the fall into sin.

An exterior temptation occurs when an evil extrinsic to us is visibly suggested to us by some word or sign, so that the one to whom the suggestion is made may bend to consent to sin. And such a temptation is done only by the adversary. But an interior temptation occurs when an evil intrinsic to us is suggested invisibly. And this temptation is sometimes done by the enemy, sometimes by the flesh. Indeed, both the devil invisibly suggests evil, and an unlawful motion and depraved titillation arises from the corruption of the flesh. And for that reason, the temptation which is from the flesh does not occur without sin; however, the one which is from the enemy does not cause sin, unless consent is extended to it, but is matter for the practice of virtue.[3]

One of the most important results of the first sin for Lombard is the transmission and nature of original sin that is received by each generation and affects humanity at its core and in its relationship with God.

Now it remains to see what is original sin itself. And since it is not actual sin, it is not an act or movement of the soul or of the body. For if it is an act of the soul or of the body, it is certainly an actual sin. But it is not actual; and so it is not an act or movement. What then is it? Original sin is called the incentive to sin, namely

1. Ibid., 2.34.2.
2. Ibid., 2.34.3.
3. Ibid., 2.21.6.

concupiscence or the attraction to pleasure, which is called the law of the members, or the weakness of nature, or the tyrant who is in our members, or the law of the flesh.[1]

Lombard seems to lessen slightly the concept of concupiscence in comparison with Augustine, although he is clearly building on the great theologian. He clarifies the concept by stating that for infants it is a potential rather than an actual part of their being.

But by the term concupiscence, [Augustine] signified not the act of desiring, but the first vice, when he called it 'the law of the flesh.' . . . What is the concupiscence with which we are born? Surely, it is the vice which makes the child able to become concupiscent, and which renders the adult [actually] concupiscent.[2]

This is not Pelagianism of any form, since there is no indication that concupiscence can be avoided and, therefore, Lombard does make a clarification in the case of Christ so that he is not held to have received this flaw in his nature.

It has already been shown what original sin is, and how it passes from parents to children and into the soul through the flesh. From these comments, it also becomes clear why it is called original sin: namely, because it is transmitted by the vicious law of our origin in which we are conceived, namely by the lustful concupiscence of the flesh, as was said above. For it is not because we are conceived from the flesh drawn from Adam that we derive this sin. The body of Christ was also formed from the same flesh which descends from Adam, but his conception did not occur by the law of sin, that is, by the concupiscence of the flesh, but by the operation of the Holy Spirit, and so his flesh was not sinful. But our own conception does not occur without lust, and so it is not without sin.[3]

For people, Lombard retains the importance of baptism in this area that he received from Augustine.

And so original sin is said to be remitted in baptism by a double reason: because through the grace of baptism, the vice of concupiscence is weakened and attenuated, so that it will no longer reign, unless its vigour is restored by our consent; and because the guilt for it is absolved.[4]

1. Ibid., 2.30.8.
2. Ibid., 2.30.9.
3. Ibid., 2.31.7.
4. Ibid., 2.32.1.

Lombard offers extensive teaching on the nature and effects of sin that cannot be presented here due to the constraints of space, but are well worth exploring. Here just two will be noted specifically, the first of which concerns the nature of free choice that resulted from sin.

> And so it is manifest that, in addition to other penalties, because of that sin man incurred a punishment in the corruption and suppression of free choice. For by that sin, natural goods became corrupt in man and the goods of grace were taken away . . . And so freedom of choice was corrupted through sin and was in part lost . . . [On Augustine] See, he says that man lost free choice: not because he did not have free choice after sin, but because he lost the freedom of choice, not indeed all of it, but only the freedom from misery and sin.[1]

Lombard also shows the effects of sin not only on the individual and the extension of sin through generations, but also its effects on the world and society. Sin is seen to pollute the world, with resulting confusion about what is sin and what is the punishment of sin.

> And yet it is not held to cause any prejudice to truth if one were to say that the very things which are sins are essentially, so to speak, punishments, that is, chastisements for preceding sins, which are just and are from God. Nevertheless, they are not from God insofar as they are sins; nor are they punishments for sin insofar as they are sins. And yet, insofar as they are sins, they are privations of the good; but, as we said above, they are called privations causally and actively.[2]

The Experience of Grace

We have already seen something of Lombard's understanding of grace in relation to the angels and the created state of humankind, in which there was a need for grace in order to obtain or maintain the blessed condition. Following sin, the experience of grace explained by Lombard falls into two major categories: his work with Augustine's phases of grace in understanding the transformation of the human person in book two; and an extensive treatment of the sacraments in book four.

In line with the heritage of Christian thought, Lombard stresses the fact that grace must come first, prevenient grace, in the process of salvation: 'And if you contemplate it with diligence, it will likewise be

1. Ibid., 2.25.7.
2. Ibid., 2.36.4.

shown to you what the grace that goes before and prepares the will is, namely faith with love.'[1] This first grace is not in the choice of the individual, but affects the resulting nature of choice.

> And that prevenient grace, which is also a virtue, is not the use of free choice, but rather the good use of free choice comes from it. It is ours from God, not from ourselves. But the good use of choice is from both God and ourselves; and so it is a good merit. In the one case, God alone works; in the other, God and man [work together].[2]

While this first movement is not from the person, the works that result from this prevenient grace are not seen as purely God's work but rather from grace and the awakened human choice.

> And so, when good merits are said to be and begin from grace, either the grace that freely gives, that is, God, is meant; or better, the grace that is freely given, which precedes the will of man; for it would not be a great thing if these things were to be said to be from God, from whom are all things. It is rather his freely given grace, from which good merits have their beginning, that is meant. But when they are said to be from grace alone, free choice is not excluded, because there is no merit in man which is not through free choice. But in deserving goods, principality of cause is attributed to grace because the principal cause of good merits is grace itself, by which free choice is roused, and the will of man is healed and aided so that it may be good.[3]

Lombard depicts this process creatively through an agricultural analogy:

> The earth is bathed by the rain in order to germinate and produce fruit, but the rain is neither the earth, nor the seed, nor the fruit; the earth is neither the seed, nor the fruit; the seed is not the fruit. In the same way, the rain of divine blessing is freely poured into the earth of our mind, that is, the choice of our will, that is, it is inspired by grace – which God alone does, and not man with him. By this grace, the will of man is bathed so as to germinate and produce fruit, that is, it is healed and prepared to will the good, according to which the grace is called operating; and it is assisted to do the good, according to which the grace is called cooperating.[4]

---

1. Ibid., 2.26.3.
2. Ibid., 2.27.7.
3. Ibid., 2.27.3.
4. Ibid., 2.27.2.

Here we have two more Augustinian terms for grace that were highlighted earlier in the chapter, operating and cooperating grace. For Lombard, operating grace is closely associated with prevenient grace, while cooperating grace is that which follows once the transformation has begun.

> This is operating and cooperating grace. For operating grace prepares the will of man to will the good; cooperating grace helps it not to will in vain . . . The operating one is that which goes ahead of the good will, for it is by it that man's will is freed and prepared in order to be good and to will the good efficaciously; and cooperating grace accompanies the will which is already good in order to aid it . . . the will of man is first visited and prepared by the grace of God so that it may be made good, not so that it may be made a will, because it was a will even before grace, but it was not a good and righteous will.[1]

My presentation here of Lombard's thoughts on sin, grace and free will has sought to treat each separately to aid comprehension. In the *Sentences*, the quotations cited thus far are integrated, with Lombard moving fluidly through discussions of human nature and experience. The last major section on grace is separated into a book of its own, book four, which is a masterful treatise on the sacraments. The first forty-two Distinctions are devoted to this discussion, with the last eight then discussing eschatology.

Presenting Lombard's work on the sacraments here poses several issues. Firstly, it must be noted that the entire sacramental theology is related to grace, based on his classic definition: 'A sacrament is a visible form of invisible grace.'[2] He develops this shortly afterwards:

> For a sacrament is properly so called because it is a sign of God's grace and a form of invisible grace in such a manner that it bears its image and is its cause. And so the sacraments were not instituted only for the sake of signifying, but also to sanctify.[3]

The struggle results from three factors: the sheer amount of material in book four; the great number of quotations from the Church Fathers that Lombard uses (this volume tries to analyse the writers' own theology rather than their presentation of previous works); and his lack of explicit language about grace. The result of processing all this follows, with my encouragement for those interested in the sacraments to dive into the seeming ocean of thought in book four of the *Sentences*.

---

1. Ibid., 2.26.1.
2. Ibid., 4.1.2.
3. Ibid., 4.1.4.

I shall focus on two of the sacraments here, baptism and penance, because they have the clearest explicit application of grace, which is more implicit in the remaining five sacraments. On baptism, Lombard stresses that adult baptism is not a magical rite that confers grace regardless of the attitude of the supplicant.

> By these and other testimonies, it is plainly shown that the grace of remission is not conferred upon adults at baptism in the absence of faith and repentance, because remission is not even given in baptism to children without someone else's faith, since they are unable to have their own. And so, if one approaches under false pretences, not having true contrition in his heart, he receives the sacrament without the thing.[1]

Similarly, for children who have been baptised, the grace that is received is not controlling to the extent that they can then live any life they choose under its protection.

> It is also usual to ask whether a grace is given to children in baptism by which, when the time comes for the use of their free will, they may will and run. For it is not doubted that adults who receive the sacrament worthily obtain operating and cooperating grace. This grace is given to them *in vain*, if they afterwards sin mortally by their free will, and by reason of sin lose deservedly the grace that was given to them. They are then even said to offer an affront to the Holy Spirit, and to chase Him away from them.[2]

Lombard argues that the grace received is latent in children and will need their choice to retain, when they will have the cooperation of grace to will and act as they should.

> But as for children who do not yet have the use of reason, the question is whether they receive grace in baptism by which, when they come to a later age, they can will and work the good. . . . Some hold that operating and cooperating grace is given to all children in baptism, but in gift, not in use, so that, when they come to a later age, they may draw the use from the gift, unless, of their free will, they extinguish the use of the gift by sinning. And so it is from their fault, and not from a defect of grace, that they become evil, if being able to have a good use from God's gift, they have refused it by their free will, and chosen an evil use.[3]

---

1. Ibid., 4.4.2.
2. Ibid., 4.4.7.
3. Ibid.

The second sacrament that is closely tied to the themes of this book is penance, which Lombard links to both sin and grace. Working with Pope Gregory the Great's writing about 'The Lord makes it rain', Lombard writes:

> And what is called *rain* is that self-restraint by which one is recalled from the work of sin, because from the font of God's grace it is instilled in the heart either that he come gradually to penance in this way, or that he be punished by God less who might have accumulated a greater torment for himself by the longer delight in an act of sin.[1]

Lombard states that one is cleansed from sin at the moment a person proposes to confess, rather than tying the grace into the formal elements of the sacrament.

> Sins are blotted out by contrition and humility of heart, even without confession by the mouth and payment of outward punishment. For from the moment when one proposes, with compunction of mind, that one will confess, God remits; because there is present confession of the heart, although not of the mouth, by which the soul is cleansed inwardly from the spot and contagion of the sin committed, and the debt of eternal death is released.[2]

As a result, he is content that forgiveness can be received without confession to the priest, if there is a fear of what people might think, after consideration of certain historical texts.

> By these authorities, they support themselves who contend that it suffices to confess sins to God, without a priest. For they say that, if one fears to reveal his fault before men lest he have to suffer shame because of it, or lead others to sin by his example, and so he is silent before men and reveals it to God, he receives forgiveness.[3]

This would seem to bring into question the role of the priest in the sacrament of penance, if there is no absolute need for a person to confess to a priest. To some extent, Lombard accepts that God alone is responsible for granting forgiveness.

> But others say that God alone, and not the priest, remits the debt of eternal death, just as he be himself also vivifies the soul interiorly. They do not deny, however, that to priests was given the power

1. Ibid., 4.15.3.
2. Ibid., 4.17.2.
3. Ibid.

of remitting and retaining sins, to whom it was aid: Whose sins
you shall remit, *etc*. For as Christ retained to himself the power of
baptism, so also he retained that of penance; therefore, as his grace
enlightens the soul inwardly, so also it simultaneously relaxes the
debt of eternal death. For he covers over the penitents' sins by
himself; and he covers them over, when he does not reserve them
for punishment; and so he covers them over, when he dissolves the
debt of punishment.[1]

Yet there is a role given to the Church, and therefore to priests,
indicated in Scripture that Lombard does uphold.

We may truly say and feel this: that God alone remits and retains
sins, and yet he confers upon the Church the power of binding
and loosing. But he binds and looses in one way, and the Church
in another. For he remits sins by himself alone in such a way that
he both cleanses the soul from inward stain and absolves it from
the debt of eternal death.[2]

The work of the Church is to recognise the work of God and to
confirm this to people.

[Based on Jerome and scriptural references] It is plainly shown
here that God does not follow the Church's judgement, for
sometimes the latter judges through deception and ignorance;
but God always judges according to truth. And in remitting and
retaining faults, the priests of the Gospel have the same right and
office which formerly the priests of the Law had in curing lepers.
And so they remit or retain sins when they judge and show that
God has remitted or retained them.[3]

Lombard writes of two elements of Church practice in relation to
penance that are used to communicate to people the Church's belief
about their state before God. The first of these is the satisfaction of
penance, which confirms that a person is seen to be penitent.

The priests also bind when they impose the satisfaction of penance
upon those who confess; they loose when they remit some of the
same, or when they admit to the communion of the sacraments
those who have been purged through it. . . . And it is to be noted
that, when they bind people by the satisfaction of penance, by

1. Ibid., 4.18.4.
2. Ibid., 4.18.5.
3. Ibid., 4.18.6.

that very deed they show them to be absolved from sins, because penitential satisfaction is not imposed on anyone, except by him whom the priest adjudges to be truly penitent; if he does not impose it on someone, he thereby indicates that the sin has been retained by God.[1]

The second is excommunication, which punishment is intended to move a person to humility and repentance in order that they may be received back into the communion of the Church.

> There is another manner of binding and loosing, which is done by excommunication. This happens when someone, in accordance with canonical discipline, has been called three times to the amendment of a manifest crime; if he refuses to make satisfaction, he is cut off by the Church's sentence from the place of prayer, the communion of the sacraments, and the fellowship of the faithful, so that he may blush and, converted by the shame of his crime, he may repent so that his *spirit may be saved*. If he should come to his senses and make profession of penance, he is admitted to the communion denied to him and he is reconciled to the Church. And this anathematization of the Church inflicts this penalty on those who are struck down for a good reason: because God's grace and protection is further taken away from them, and they are left to their own devices, so that they are free to fall into the ruin of sin. And greater power to savage them is also given to the devil. And the prayers of the Church and the aids of blessings and merits are not thought to help them in any way.[2]

Conclusion

Peter Lombard has been one of the most influential theologians in the history of the Church, and yet wider appreciation of his contribution has fallen away significantly in recent decades. It is to be hoped that the translation of his great work will help to re-establish Lombard as an interlocutor in modern theological studies. His method in relation to sin, grace and free will is certainly interesting in the extensive discussion on the nature of God and the distinction between this and all of creation, followed by a large amount of material on the angels and their fall, before dealing with humankind. The highlight of this

---

1. Ibid.
2. Ibid.

is perhaps his work on the sacraments in book four, entitled *On the Doctrine of Signs*, which is far more thorough in this area than any previous work.

For those wanting to read Lombard for themselves, the four books of the *Sentences* have been translated by Professor Giulio Silano and published by the Pontifical Institute of Mediaeval Studies (Toronto: University of Toronto, 2007-2010). Recent studies about Lombard are still rather thin on the ground, with the prime work undoubtedly being Marcia Colish's two-volume work *Peter Lombard* (Leiden: E.J. Brill, 1994), which is very thorough but not intended for beginners. Silano's introductions to each volume of his translation are the easiest route into an overall understanding of Lombard's work.

4.

Thomas Aquinas on Sin

Thomas Aquinas (1225-1274) was a member of the Dominican monastic order, known as the Friars Preaching. He came from a noble family in the south of Italy, his father being the Count of Aquino, and he seems to have been a rather large, meditative child, highly interested in discussing God from a young age. He decided to join the Dominican Order against the wishes of his family; they actually abducted him and held him captive for two years, at one point his brothers even brought a prostitute to him to tempt him from his chosen life of dedication to God – he chased her out of the room.

Following this, he was released and allowed to join the order, spending the last thirty years of his life studying, writing, teaching and preaching around Europe. His education was conducted in Cologne and Paris, while later in life he was in great demand and spent a lot of time travelling, particularly visiting the Italian states. Although he was only around fifty when he died, he wrote over sixty works, some short and some massive. His approach to theology was quite philosophical, with Aristotle proving a major influence at times in Aquinas' understanding of God and humanity.

About four years ago my mentor and colleague at the London School of Theology, Professor Tony Lane, suggested that we read through Aquinas' *Summa Theologiae* together in weekly sessions. Most weeks we get through 50-60 pages, Latin and English alongside each other, and as I write this we are about to finish Book Four of the *Summa* after 160 sessions.[1] There now only remains the Supplement, concerning topics that Thomas didn't cover before his death, collected from other writings – we reckon it will take about another six months to finish this.

---

1. For more on perseverance, see chapter six, below, 'Thomas Aquinas on Free Will'.

From this, it can be deduced that the *Summa* is a massive work, over 6,000 pages in most translations, and the presentation of Aquinas' thought here will be limited to this one book. Another work that could have been considered was the *Summa Contra Gentiles*, an explanation of Christian doctrine, but there was a need to provide some limit to the amount of material from Aquinas in this volume. He also wrote an extensive number of commentaries on Scripture and tracts on various theological themes, most of which are readily available to those who want a bit of extra bedtime reading.

One of the great strengths of the *Summa Theologiae* as a source for Christian theology is its arrangement; areas for presentation and discussion are clearly separated to aid the reader to find a direct approach to the specific aspect of thought that they are looking for. The *Summa* is divided up into four major parts, which are divided up by treatises on certain subjects: God, man, grace, sacraments. These are then further sub-divided into specific Questions that are explained through a series of Articles that approach the Question from every angle of which Thomas is aware. These Articles start with a series of Objections to the main Christian position that Aquinas will defend, followed by a '*Sed contra*' (On the contrary) that is generally from an authoritative source. Thomas then provides his own answer to the question, with the Article finishing with responses to the Objections that had been raised. The whole process creates nuggets of theology that, with the exception of some of the language and philosophical concepts used, are easily accessible answers to a vast array of theological questions.

At times this does create sections that seem very strange to the modern reader, either because of the theological climate, or because of the influence of a particular philosophical strain (generally Aristotle) that informs the theology. A good example of this would be Book One, Question 79, which discusses the 'Intellectual Powers' in a series of thirteen Articles comprising:

(1)   Is the intellect a power of the soul or its essence?
(2)   If it is a power, is it a passive power?
(3)   If it is a passive power, is there an active intellect?
(4)   Is it something that is in the soul?
(5)   Is the active intellect one in all?
(6)   Is the memory in the intellect?
(7)   Is the memory distinct from the intellect?
(8)   Is the reason a power that is distinct from the intellect?
(9)   Are the superior reason and the inferior reason distinct powers?

(10)   Is the intelligence distinct from the intellect?
(11)   Are the speculative intellect and practical intellect distinct powers?
(12)   Is 'synderesis' a power of the intellectual faculty?
(13)   Is the conscience a power of the intellectual faculty?

Quite frankly, at times like this it seems that you can sense your brain begin to melt before you get into the content, and it can get worse when you find out that 'synderesis' is distinguished from the 'irascible, concupiscible and the rational'.

However, despite these difficult sections, the *Summa* is an incredibly helpful voice in considering a wide range of theological topics, both in the clarity (generally) of the ideas communicated and in the use of Scripture and historic Christian voices to support the case. Where Aquinas is influenced by other sources, notably Aristotle, these are referenced (Aristotle is referred to as 'the Philosopher') and one can discern their influence. At times, there seems to be extensive use of Aristotle and one might wonder why a Greek philosopher could be cited as an authority on Christian theology. However, all theology uses philosophical tools in processing revelation, explicitly or implicitly, knowingly or unknowingly, and Aquinas does at least make it clear where such influence is to be found in his work. Of additional importance is the role of Aquinas in Catholic theology, to a certain extent in the medieval period (since his ideas were important in the Protestant reformers' teaching against the Church) but, more particularly, after the second half of the nineteenth century when neo-Thomism (the 'New Thomas') made Aquinas central to Catholic theological method.

This presentation of Aquinas' thought will be broken into three separate chapters on sin, grace and free will because of the sheer extent of material. Even with this approach, there is a need for a massive edit and at times indications will be made of a wider method that Aquinas has employed across a range of similar topics, with passages quoted that exemplify Aquinas' teaching. For the most part the quotations will be from Aquinas' answers, with context given where useful from the introductory Objections. Occasionally there will also be sections from his replies to the Objections where these demonstrate the theology he is teaching in illustrative application.

In this chapter on sin, we shall start by looking at how Aquinas deals with sin and God, which is largely found in Book One of the *Summa*, followed by his teaching on how the good creation of a good God is marred by the sin of angels and then the first humans. After this, we shall follow Aquinas' method in looking at the results for humankind in our relationship to sin and evil, with a separate section on habits and vices, which take up a large amount of the second half of Book Two. Finally, Aquinas examines what all this means for the Christ who comes into a sinful world to overcome the power and effects of sin.

Sin and God

The first major treatise of the *Summa* is on the one God, beginning with questions about God's unity, simplicity and perfection. The first indication of existence that departs from this picture that strongly equates being and goodness is in a consideration of the knowledge of God in Question 14. Here we find some important principles that underpin Aquinas' understanding of sin and evil that result from a consideration of the relationship between God's knowledge and causation. In Article 8, Aquinas agrees with the notion that God's knowledge is the cause of things under a model of his will as encompassing all things. Therefore, to the extent to which anything happens, it is at least allowed to happen by God and must in some way come under the sovereign will of God.

As the discussion moves towards evil, Aquinas considers whether God knows things 'that are not'. This is a root understanding of evil as 'the privation [absence] of good' and, therefore, the absence of being/existence, since this comes from a God who is wholly Good. In Article 10, Aquinas then answers whether God knows evil things.

> Whoever knows a thing perfectly, must know everything that is accidental [that results from its existence] to it. Now there are some good things that have the corruption of evil as accidents. Therefore, God would not have perfect knowledge of good things unless he also knew evil things. Now something can be known to the degree in which it exists. Therefore since it is the essence of evil that it is the privation of the good, from the fact that God knows good things he must also know evil things, as darkness is known by light.[1]

This secondary relationship of God to evil, through the good that he creates, is developed in the discussion of the will of God and whether this can be for evil.

---

1. Aquinas, *Summa Theologiae*, 1.14.10. The notation system used in these footnotes refers to Book.Question.Article in the *Summa*.

God wills his own goodness above any other good, yet he also wills one good more than another. In no way does he will the evil of sin, which is the loss of right order tending towards the divine good. He does will the evil of natural defects or punishment by willing the good that such evils are attached to. So in that God wills justice, he wills punishment; and in that God wills the preservation of the natural order [in goodness], he wills that some things are naturally corrupted [by evil].[1]

It is noticeable that, with these brief exceptions, there is almost nothing on evil and sin in the first four treatises of the *Summa* on God, Trinity, creation (as created, rather than in its fallen state) and the distinction of things.[2] All told, this takes up about eight per cent of the whole *Summa* and shows the importance for Aquinas of understanding reality in light of a fundamental concept of God and creation, rather than trying to delve too quickly into issues that we face as fallen humanity entangled in our understanding by the effects of sin and grace. Even then, Aquinas moves on from a brief look at the nature and cause of evil to angelic beings and thirteen Questions on their good nature, before addressing evil and the angels.

In Question 48, Aquinas addresses the nature of evil, defining it in the first Article as 'the absence of good'.[3] He again helps the reader to understand what he means by using the darkness/light analogy.

One opposite is known from the other as we know about darkness from light. Therefore, we must know what evil is from the nature of goodness. Now we have said that good is everything desirable, and therefore since every nature desires its own being and perfection, we must also say that the being and perfection of any nature is good. Therefore, evil cannot signify being, form or nature.[4]

Because evil is this negation of being, the question arises whether it can extinguish being completely, which Aquinas does not admit – although aspects of good can be destroyed.

Evil cannot completely destroy good. In order to prove this, we must consider three aspects of good. One kind of good is completely destroyed by evil, which is the good opposed to evil; in

---

1. *Summa*, 1.19.9.
2. Chapter five, below, 'Thomas Aquinas on Grace', will deal with the teachings on providence and predestination that do contain a little more teaching in that context on sin and evil.
3. *Summa*, 1.48.1.
4. Ibid.

the same way light can be completely destroyed by darkness and sight by blindness. A second kind of good is neither completely destroyed nor diminished by evil, which is the good that is the subject of evil; so, darkness does not harm the substance of the air. Finally, there is a kind of good which is diminished by evil, but not completely removed, which good is the capacity of a subject to achieve something.[1]

In this Article, Aquinas starts to write about sin specifically in the context of evil: 'Likewise, sins can add to the infinite, whereby the capacity of the soul to receive grace is increasingly lessened; and these sins are like obstacles placed between us and God.'[2]

Aquinas moves on in Question 49 to the cause of evil and to explaining how good can cause evil (there being no other option, given that only goodness has real existence). The important aspect for Aquinas is that there must be some defect in some aspect of the good being that causes evil, rather than that it comes out of the core substance.

In an action evil is caused through the defect of some principle of action, either of the main or the instrumental agent. So, a defect in the movement of an animal may happen because of the weakness of the moving power, as in the case of children, or only due to the ineptitude of the instrument, as in the lame. On the other hand, evil is caused in something – but not in the proper effect of the agent – sometimes by the power used by the agent and sometimes because of a defect either in the agent or in its substance. However, the fact that it is caused by a deficient being is accidental to good, which is the ultimate cause of the action. It is therefore true that evil only has an accidental cause, and in this way good is the cause of evil.[3]

Good therefore does cause evil, not from itself but from a corruption of that created by the good. What does this mean for God? Does God cause evil?

It is clear that the form that God mainly intends for the things he has created is the good order of the universe. Now, as has been said, the order of the universe requires that there should be some things that can, and sometimes do, fail [this is addressed more fully in Question 22 on providence]. Therefore God, who causing things to aim towards the good order of the universe, consequently

1. *Summa*, 1.48.4.
2. Ibid.
3. *Summa*, 1.49.1.

and, as it were, by accident causes the corruption of things. . . .
Nevertheless, the order that is justice is part of the order of the
universe, and this requires that a punishment should be given to
sinners. So, God is the author of the evil that is the punishment,
but not of the evil that is the fault.[1]

The last major comment for this section comes considerably later in
Book One in a consideration of the government of the universe, which is
part of the work of God, where there is a discussion of whether anything
can occur outside this government.

It is possible that something can happen outside the order of a
particular cause, but not outside the order of the universal cause.
The reason for this is that something only occurs outside the order
of a particular cause through some impeding cause. This other
cause must ultimately result from the first universal cause. As an
example, indigestion can occur outside the order of the nutrition
by an impediment such as the coarseness of the food; this can be
ascribed to another cause, and so on until we come to the first
universal cause. Therefore, because God is the first universal cause,
not only of one genus but of all being, it is impossible for anything
to occur outside the order of divine government. However, the
fact that, from one point of view, something seems to escape the
order of divine providence, when this is considered in regard to
one particular cause, this necessarily comes back to divine order as
it regards some other [root] cause.[2]

This is clarified when Aquinas responds to a potential objection that
God orders all things (taken from the writing of Boethius) and, therefore,
even secondary causes must be within the order of divine government.

There is nothing completely evil in the world because evil is always
based on good, as I have shown above. Therefore, something is said
to be evil because it escapes from the order of a particular good. If
it completely escaped from the order of the divine government, it
would wholly cease to exist.[3]

In terms of the doctrine of God, it is clear that Aquinas denies that
evil or sin have any root in God's being or action and thus it is important
to move onto angels and created humanity to find the active cause of sin.

1. *Summa*, 1.49.4.
2. *Summa*, 1.103.7.
3. *Summa*, 1.103.7. Reply to 1.

Sin and Angels

Aquinas takes some time to build up an understanding of angels, one aspect of which is the nature of their will that he defends as being free because he holds that there is reason in the angels. This will is instinctively towards the good (as is the will in all things), and Aquinas argues that one moment of 'charity' (*charitas* has the idea of active love) is sufficient for an angel to receive their blessed state from which they cannot then fall into sin.[1]

In dealing with the sin of the angels, the first step for Aquinas is to explain on what basis they are able to sin, which he puts down to their creaturely nature – only God cannot sin in his nature.

> An angel or any other rational creature considered in its own nature can sin. Whatever creature that can not sin has this ability as a gift of grace, not from its nature. The reason for this is that sinning is only a deviation from the righteousness that an act ought to have, whether we speak of sin in nature, act or morals. . . . But every created will has a righteousness in its actions only insofar as it is regulated according to the divine will, to which the ultimate purpose is referred. So, every desire of a subordinate ought to be regulated by the will of their superior; for instance, a soldier's will should be ruled according to the will of his commanding officer. Therefore, there can be no sin only in the divine will, whereas there can be sin in the will of any creature when we consider the condition of its nature.[2]

One of the clearest statements on the nature of angelic sin comes in a Reply in this Article considering whether there could be sinful desires in angels:

> This kind of sin does not presuppose ignorance, but simply the absence of consideration of things that ought to be considered. The angel sinned in this way in seeking his own good from his own free will, not in obedience to the rule of the divine will.[3]

Aquinas explores the sin of the devil as pride and envy before stating that, 'the angel sinned by seeking to be like God'.[4] He clarifies that this is not seeking to be the equal of God, but to be like God in respect to having a power over himself apart from God's influence. Were the angels

1. The discussion of this is found in Book One, Question 62.
2. *Summa*, 1.63.1.
3. *Summa*, 1.63.1, Reply to 4.
4. *Summa*, 1.63.3.

then corrupt in their creation? Aquinas naturally argues not, since they were created by God. He deals with this firstly in relation to those that would become demons:

> Now it is clear that every intellectual nature inclines towards good in general, which it is able to apprehend since this is the chief object of the will. Therefore, because the demons are intellectual substances they cannot have a natural inclination towards any evil, and so they cannot naturally be evil.[1]

After this, he writes of the devil. Aquinas notes two positions he regards as false, the first being that the devil's will was faulty in its created state (which would imply no fall from perfection) and the second that the angels sinned in the first instant of their creation, but this would seem to again imply that the sin was linked to their creation, and therefore to God. Aquinas replies as follows:

> We must state that it was impossible for the angel to sin in the first instant of its existence by a wrongly ordained act of free will. Although a thing can begin to act in the first instant of its existence, the operation which begins with existence comes from the agent that created its nature . . . Therefore, if there is anything that derives its nature from a defective cause, which is then the cause of a defective action, it can in its first instant of existence have a defective operation . . . But the agent that brought the angels into existence, namely God, cannot be the cause of sin. Therefore, it cannot be said that the devil was wicked in the first instant of his creation.[2]

There must therefore be a separation between the creation of the angel and the movement of the will that is not in obedience to the will of God so that the fall of the devil is in no way a result of the being or action of God. This separation is in order rather than time, however, so Thomas' teaching

> is that the devil sinned immediately after the first instant of his creation. This must be maintained if we believe that he received the capacity for free will in the first instant of his creation and that he was created in grace.[3]

Aquinas continues to hold that there is no connection between God and sin.

---

1. *Summa*, 1.63.4.
2. *Summa*, 1.63.5.
3. *Summa*, 1.63.6.

Sin and Adam

This principle is carried on to the discussion of the first sin of
humankind, which Aquinas holds is purely the result of human
disobedience and cannot be placed even at the hands of the devil, let
alone God, in order that full responsibility for sin lies with us. Aquinas
considers whether the first humans could have been deceived and
denies this in case we could lay the blame for sin on the serpent: 'it
is clear that the righteousness of the first state was not compatible
with a deception of the intellect.'[1] Regarding that first sin, building
on the work of Augustine, Aquinas writes: 'Although the woman was
deceived before she sinned in her action, yet this was not before she
had sinned through interior pride.'[2]

In the following Question, Aquinas considers what this means for the
first humans' will.

> The passions of the soul are in the sensual appetite, and their
> objects are good and evil. Therefore, some of the passions of the
> soul are aimed at what is good, such as love and joy; while others
> tend to what is evil, such as fear and sorrow. In the primitive state,
> evil was not present nor was it imminent and there was no lack
> of good that a right will could desire, therefore, as Augustine says,
> Adam had no passion tending to evil, such as fear, sorrow and so
> on; neither did he have passions regarding goods that he did not
> yet possess creating a burning concupiscence.[3]

The question raised by this is how the first humans did fall into sin,
but the answer does not appear for some time. Book One of the *Summa*
has them still in the garden, but even Book Two, Part One, which looks
through many aspects of sin (as we shall see below) including original
sin, does not deal with this, nor does most of Book Two, Part Two that
explores seemingly every aspect of sin that Thomas can think of. In fact,
it is not until Question 163 of Book Two, Part Two that we finally come
to the first sin and its subsequent discussion.

---

1. *Summa*, 1.94.4.
2. *Summa*, 1.94.4, Reply to 1.
3. *Summa*, 1.95.2. Concupiscence is a word loaded with meaning from the time
   of Augustine, who had used it to refer to the bound will of fallen humanity
   desiring evil with every aspect of its being. The root Latin word (*concupiscentia*)
   is more neutral, indicating any desire. The indication here is a negative desire
   from the adjective 'burning' but Aquinas had not defined his understanding of
   concupiscence at this point in the *Summa*.

The context is a treatise on steadfastness and moderation that begins at Question 123, which has reached as far as pride as a sin against humility. After a general consideration of pride, Aquinas then states that this is the nature of the first man's sin.

> Many movements can come together resulting in one sin, and the character of the sin is found in the first one where there is disorder. It is clear that this is in the inner movement of the soul before it is in the external act of the body . . . therefore the first sin occurred when his desire was directed to an inordinate end. Now humans were created in the state of innocence, and therefore there was no rebellion of the flesh against the spirit. From this we can say that it was not possible for the first wrong human desire to result from coveting a physical good that the concupiscence of the flesh tends to against the reason. Therefore, it must be that the first disordered human desire resulted from a wrong desire for some spiritual good. This could not have been a disordered desire if he wished for it according to his measure as established by the divine rule. Therefore, it follows that the first human sin consisted in Adam desiring some spiritual good above his measure, and this pertains to pride. Therefore, it is clear that the first human sin was pride.[1]

In terms of the sin itself, there is little exploration except for an Article discussing whose sin was the more grievous – Adam or Eve – that concludes that Eve's was more serious for three reasons: a greater pride; the fact of leading Adam into sin; and because Aquinas believes Adam's sin is mitigated by a desire to please Eve.[2]

There are two further Questions that concern the first sin: one dealing with punishment in death and the other results mentioned in Genesis chapter three; and the other looking at the temptation. The first Article here is a common approach: to ask whether it was suitable for humans to be tempted by the devil, where one knows that the answer is yes, because that is what happened in Scripture, and one only wonders on what basis it will be defended. Of importance are the concepts present in both Articles that affirm human responsibility for sin despite the presence of the tempter.

> God's wisdom 'orders all things sweetly' (Book of Wisdom 8:1) in that his providence appoints to every creature that which is fitting according to its nature . . . Now it is a part of human nature that one

---

1. *Summa*, 2:2.163.1 (the second book of the *Summa* is split into two parts, the second of these indicated here in the notation 2:2).
2. *Summa*, 2:2.163.4.

individual can be helped or impeded by another. Therefore it was
right that God should both allow humans in their state of innocence
to be tempted by evil angels and that they should be helped by good
angels. By a special work of grace, it was granted that no creature
outside the person could harm them against their own will, and
therefore they were even able to resist the temptation of the demon.[1]

These three Questions far into the second half of the second book
of the *Summa* constitute the main study of the sin of Adam in itself,
and Aquinas then moves on to discuss 'Studiousness' and other virtues
and vices. It seems rather strange that such an important theological
discussion is so buried in other material.

Sin and Humankind

This section will be split into two basic sections mirroring Aquinas'
approach, looking first at the nature of sin, which Aquinas does in the
context of a study of the human will, and then at sins in particular. This
second part will necessarily be heavily selective since a large proportion
of the Questions from 10 to 170 in Book Two, Part Two of the *Summa*
discuss a range of sins in different categories.

The more general discussion of sin is in Book Two, Part One,
beginning with a study of the acts of humankind that explores the
nature of the will and how this leads to action (more on this in the
chapter below on free will). It is at the end of this first treatise that
Aquinas approaches evil in human action. The main principle at this
stage comes from Aristotle's idea of being linked to form and purpose
and the relation of the will to these as evidence for good or evil. Thus,
Aquinas writes in terms of the object of an action that 'the primary evil
is when something does not realise its specific form'.[2] Will and action
are intrinsically linked throughout this section, with the ultimate end
desired (in line with Aristotle) the most important factor.

> The will is the actively-forming agent in regard to that which results
> in the external action because the will uses the limbs as instruments.
> External actions do not have any measure of morality except
> insofar as they are voluntary. Therefore, the nature of a human act
> is considered in its moral form as regards the final purpose, but in
> itself as regards the immediate goal of the external action.[3]

---

1. *Summa*, 2:2.165.1.
2. *Summa*, 2:1.18.2.
3. *Summa*, 2:1.18.6.

Aquinas gives an example from Aristotle to support this, that if a person steals in order to commit adultery, the major crime is the adultery intended since the theft is a means to this end. Thomas questions whether actions are all good or bad or could be indifferent, answering that if there is reason involved, then there is a purpose that is either towards or away from completeness that characterises the action (he gives the example of someone picking up a bit of straw from the ground as something indifferent).

In the next Question on the interior movement of the will, there is a complex but important discussion of the root intention of the will, regardless of the action itself, where Aquinas states that good or evil is found in the response to reason, rather than the nature of the action itself.

> In matters of indifference, a will that works against an incorrect reason or conscience is evil in some way because of the event purposed, on which the goodness or evil of the will depends. This is not due to the event as it is in its own nature, but as it is at that point understood by the reason as something evil to do or to avoid. Since the object of the will is proposed by the reason, when a thing is proposed by the reason as something that is evil, the will that desires this becomes evil. This is not only the case in indifferent matters, but also in those that are good or evil in themselves. Not only indifferent matters can be considered good or evil in certain circumstances, but even that which is good can receive the character of evil, or that which is evil can receive the character of goodness, because the reason understands it in this way. For instance, to refrain from fornication is good. However, the will does not desire this good except insofar as it understands this through the reason. If a person's reason wrongly proposes this good as an evil thing, the will understands it as something evil. In this situation the will is evil because it wills evil; not something that is evil in itself, but that which is evil in this case because it is understood as such by the reason. . . . We must therefore conclude that, absolutely speaking, every will that disagrees with the reason, whether right or wrong in its understanding, is always evil.[1]

What does this mean for sins committed in ignorance? Are they still sins? Aquinas answers this based on prior teaching that ignorance excuses a person to the extent that they could justly claim ignorance, but if this is something that they should know from their nature or within their understanding, there is no excuse.

---

1. *Summa*, 2:1.19.5.

I call ignorance a pure part of the will when it is a core part of
the act of the will; and ignorance an impure part that results
from negligence, because a person does not wish to know what
they ought to know. If reason or conscience is mistaken impurely,
either in its designs or through negligence, so that a person does
not know what they ought to know, then such an error by the
reason or conscience does not excuse the will that follows a wrong
reason or conscience from being evil. But if an error results from
ignorance of circumstance, without any negligence, so that the act
is truly involuntary, then the error of reason or conscience does
excuse the will that follows the wrong reason from being evil. For
instance, if a wrong reason tells a man to go to another man's wife,
the will that follows that wrong reason is evil because the error
results from ignorance of the divine law, which one is bound to
know. But if a man's reason mistakes another for his wife, and if
he wishes to give the lady her right when she asks for it, his will is
excused from being evil because the error results from ignorance
of circumstance, which ignorance excuses and causes the act to be
purely involuntary.[1]

One wonders at the end how the man has purely and completely
mistaken another for his wife, but Thomas does convey his overall point
effectively.[2]

For Aquinas, as we see, the internal disposition is crucial and only
once this is thoroughly examined does he turn to external actions where
he is consistent in affirming that, while something may be good itself,
it is only good for a person insofar as it is desired for the right reasons.

External actions can be seen as good or bad in two ways. Firstly,
in regard to their nature and the circumstances connected with
them; in this the giving of alms, if the required conditions are
observed, is said to be good. Secondly, a thing is seen as good or
evil from its relation to the purpose; and, therefore, the giving of
alms for self-promotion is said to be evil. Since the final purpose
is the will's proper object, it is clear that this aspect of good or evil,
which the external action receives from its relation to the final
purpose, is to be found firstly in the act of the will, from which the
external action results.[3]

---

1. *Summa*, 2:1.19.6.
2. If you are thinking drunkenness as the reason for misidentification, then this is
   probably though not absolutely a pure excuse as we shall see below.
3. *Summa*, 2:1.20.1.

The final interesting aspect of this first presentation of sin and evil is the relationship between the two terms and the extent to which the concept of sin is dependent on that of evil.

> Evil is more comprehensive than sin, as good is greater than right. Every limitation of good, in whatever subject, is an evil, whereas sin truly consists in an action that is done for a certain purpose and lacks goodness in that purpose. . . . When an action strays from this goodness, it comes under the notion of sin. In those things that are done by the will, the immediate rule is the human reason and the supreme rule is the Eternal Law. When a human action tends to the right end, according to the order of reason and of the Eternal Law, then that action is right. When it turns aside from that goodness, then it is said to be a sin. It is clear that every voluntary action that turns away from the order of reason and of the Eternal Law is evil, while every good action is in accord with reason and the Eternal Law. Therefore, it follows that a human action is right or sinful by reason of its being good or evil.

After this foundational material, we move into three realms of human experience that were fundamental to Aquinas' understanding of humanity but that take some work for us to access today: passions, habits and virtues. The first treatise is on the passions, and what Aquinas means by passion is best explained through what he ultimately discusses – love, joy, hope, sorrow, fear – all of which are responses of the whole self, reason and senses working together, to external stimuli. Thomas divides these up under the terms 'concupiscible' and 'irascible', the first of which covers those passions that 'regard good or evil absolutely', such as love and hate, joy and sorrow; the second regards those that involve an innate struggle to gain or to lose them, such as hope and fear.[1]

Passions

When discussing the passions, there is little language of sin used by Aquinas, although related concepts of evil and incompleteness are used. Early in this section there is an Article about moral good and evil in the passions where the answer echoes the teaching above on the importance of the orientation of the will.

> If the passions are considered to be subject to the command of the reason and will, then moral good and evil are found in them because the sensitive appetite [the desire related to the emotions] is nearer

---

1. *Summa*, 2:1.23.1.

than the body to the reason and will. However, the movements and actions of the body are morally good or evil only inasmuch as they are voluntary. Insofar as they are voluntary, the passions can therefore more reasonably be considered morally good or evil, and they are deemed voluntary either because they are commanded by the will or because they are not checked by the will.[1]

This point is not built on as the 'Treatise on the Passions' progresses and, even in discussing hatred, Aquinas states that love is the cause of hatred because the object of hatred has departed from something that should be loveable.[2] There are three Questions on sorrow before the idea of evil is brought up as a possible element, and then it is allowed that the fact of sorrow must result from evil but that the fact that one is sorrowful is good in recognising evil as evil.[3]

In these concupiscible (absolute) passions, the focus is on the created nature as good and other aspects as reflections on some loss of the good, rather than on evil or sin in themselves. This largely continues in the irascible (contentious) passions, although the three discussed – fear, daring and anger – more naturally engage with brokenness at their centre. This is recognised in the first Article on fear that clarifies this as avoidance, and therefore firstly related to evil, rather than the pursuit of good.[4] Because there is an innate struggle in any irascible passions, Aquinas does not seek absolute judgements on them but recognises that context is vital to understand where there is good and evil. Therefore, there is right fear (of God, of evil) and right anger (against evil) and all these passions result from evil not in a person but in the fact that the object has suffered from evil, while the one who is fearful or angry must reflect on how their nature affects the fear or anger that they experience.

Habits

The next category that receives a Treatise is habits, defined by Aquinas through a quote from Aristotle as, 'the disposition whereby that which is disposed is disposed well or ill, and this, either in regard to itself or in regard to another'.[5] The concept of habits incorporates a wide range of subjects, including bodily habits (health and sickness) and scientific habits (knowledge and ignorance), that deal with the experience of life in different realms. The second Treatise related to habits concentrates on

1. *Summa*, 2:1.24.1.
2. *Summa*, 2:1.29.2.
3. *Summa*, 2:1.39.1.
4. *Summa*, 2:1.42.1.
5. *Summa*, 2:1.49.1.

virtues and vices on a macro level (the individual elements are explored in the next section both for Aquinas and in this book) and, in the work on vices, Aquinas digs into the idea of sin. Aquinas initially clarifies a difference between sin, malice and vice: sin works against 'that to which virtue is ordained', which is goodness and completeness; malice works against the good implied in the virtue; while vice works against the essence of a virtue.[1]

In the first Article dealing with this topic, we are confronted with venial and mortal sins for the first time, venial sins staining the soul to a greater or lesser extent, while mortal sins sever the soul from the state of grace. Aquinas writes of these in the context of 'infused virtues' and 'acquired virtues', the latter being the transformed human self that is affected or corrupted by venial sins, the former being the ongoing work of the Spirit in a person's life that is rejected by a mortal sin.[2]

Aquinas moves on to consider whether all sin is active and defends this even in sins of omission.

> When we consider the causes in the sin or occasions of omission, then this must necessarily include some act because there is no sin of omission unless we do not do what we could, and turn aside so that we do not do what we could do . . . If the reason for this is not in a person's power, the omission will not be sinful, as is the case when anyone does not go to church because they are sick . . . insofar as it is voluntary, omission must always include some act, at least an inner act of the will, which bears directly on the omission, as when a person wills 'not to go to church' because it is too much trouble . . . Sometimes, however, the act of the will bears directly on something else that stops the person from doing what they ought, whether this something else is linked to the omission, as when a person wants to play at the time they ought to go to church, or precedes the omission, as when a person chooses to stay up late at night, with the result that they do not go to church in the morning. . . . Therefore it is clear that the sin of omission has an act linked to or preceding the omission, but that this act is accidental to the sin of omission.[3]

Question 72 concerns the distinction of sin, and begins by recognising that all sins share the fact that they are against the ordination of God but not the specific object in each case.

---

1. *Summa*, 2:1.71.1.
2. *Summa*, 2:1.71.4.
3. *Summa*, 2:1.71.5.

> Sins differ specifically in terms of the voluntary acts, but not in
> their corrupt nature that is inherent to sin. Voluntary acts differ
> in type according to their objects, as was proved above. Therefore,
> it follows that sins are rightly distinguished from each other by
> their objects.[1]

This distinction leads to an assessment of the relative punishment of
sins, focusing on the difference between venial and mortal sins.

> It is evident that punishment is outside the intention of the sinner,
> and thus it is a result of sin on the part of the sinner. Nevertheless,
> it is also related to sin by an external power, the justice of the
> judge, who imposes various punishments according to the manner
> of sin. . . . The difference between venial and mortal sin results
> from the diversity of the corruption that constitutes the notion
> of sin. For the corruption is twofold, one destroying the principle
> of order, and another that creates corruption in what follows the
> first act without destroying the principle of order. As an example,
> the frame of an animal's body may be so broken that the vital
> principle is destroyed, which is the corruption of death; on the
> other hand, maintaining life, there may be an imbalance in the
> bodily humours, and then there is sickness. . . . When the soul is
> so corrupted by sin that it turns away from its ultimate purpose,
> God, to whom it is united by love, there is mortal sin; but when it
> is corrupted without turning away from God, there is venial sin.
> . . . In practical matters, one who through sinning turns away from
> God, when we consider the nature of this sin, falls irreparably and
> therefore is said to sin mortally and to deserve eternal punishment;
> whereas when a person sins without turning away from God, their
> disorder can be repaired due to the nature of the sin because the
> principle of order is not destroyed. Such a person is said to sin
> venially, because they do not sin so as to deserve to be punished
> eternally.[2]

Later in the Question Aquinas considers the different types of
sin – thought, word and deed – and what this means for the nature of sin.

> Sins are divided into these three, thought, word and deed, but not
> into separate complete types. The consummation of sin is in the
> deed, and therefore sins of deed are complete; but the beginning
> of sin is its foundation, as it were, in the sin of thought; the

1. *Summa*, 2:1.72.1.
2. *Summa*, 2:1.72.5.

second stage is the sin of word, when a person is ready to make a declaration of their thought; while the third stage consists in the consummation of the deed. Therefore, these three differ in respect of the various degrees of sin, but it is clear that the three belong to the one complete species of sin because they proceed from the same motive. The angry man, through desire for vengeance, is first disturbed in thought, then he breaks out in words of abuse and, lastly, he goes on to commit wrongful deeds. The same applies to lust and to any other sin.[1]

This idea of degrees of sin, that some are worse than others, is picked up in its own Question, which begins by stating that the extent to which someone turns from righteousness (linked to reason) affects the severity of the sin.[2] This Question goes on to compare bodily and spiritual sins.

Spiritual sins carry greater guilt than bodily sins, but this does not mean that each spiritual sin carries greater guilt than each bodily sin. Rather, considering the sole difference between spiritual and bodily sins, spiritual sins are more grievous than bodily sins, all other elements being equal. Three reasons may be given for this. The first concerns the subject: because spiritual sins belong to the spirit, whose proper action is to turn to God yet one turns away from him; whereas bodily sins are carried out in the carnal pleasure of the desire, whose proper action is to look to the good of the body. Bodily sin therefore indicates more a 'turning to' something, and for that reason, implies a closer connection; whereas spiritual sin indicates more a 'turning from' something, from which the notion of guilt arises and for this reason it involves a greater guilt. A second reason concerns the person against whom sin is committed: because bodily sin is against the sinner's own body, which they ought to love less in the order of love than God and neighbour, against whom they commit spiritual sins. Therefore, spiritual sins carry greater guilt. A third reason comes from the motive, since the stronger the impulse to sin, the less grievous the sin is, as we shall state later. Now bodily sins have a stronger impulse due to the innate desires of the flesh. Therefore, spiritual sins carry greater guilt.[3]

---

1. *Summa*, 2:1.72.7.
2. *Summa*, 2:1.73.2.
3. *Summa*, 2:1.73.5.

Question 74 concerns the subject of sin, where Aquinas affirms that sin exists in the will, in the sensitive desires and in the reason, before Question 75 looks at the causes of sin, which is found in the will of a person.

> The will, lacking the direction of the rule of reason and the divine law and intent on some changeable good, causes the act of sin directly, and directly makes the act and the intention disordered. For the lack of order in the act results from a lack of direction in the will.[1]

If there is this fault in the will and the reason, is it possible to absolve a person of responsibility if there is external pressure involved in this process? Aquinas does not believe so.

> As stated above, the internal cause of sin is both the will, which completes the sinful act, and the reason, which is lacking right understanding, and the desire, which inclines to sin. Therefore, something external may be a cause of sin in three ways, by moving the will itself immediately, or by moving the reason or by moving the desire. Now, as stated above, nothing can move the will inwardly except God alone, who cannot be a cause of sin, as we shall prove later. It must follow that nothing external can be a cause of sin except by moving the reason, as a person or devil by enticing to sin, or by moving the desire, as certain external attractions move it. However, no external enticement moves the reason of necessity in matters of action, nor do things proposed externally of necessity move the desire, unless it is disposed to move in a certain way. Even the desire does not necessarily move the reason and the will. Therefore, something external can be a cause moving a person to sin, but not the sufficient cause of the sin; and the will alone is the sufficient active cause of sin being carried out.[2]

Aquinas takes some time to look at the relationship between ignorance and sin, distinguishing between not knowing and ignorance – the former implying something that can or should be known, the latter something beyond one's knowledge.

> All are bound to know the articles of faith and the universal principles of right, while each person is bound to have knowledge about their duty or state. There are other things that a person may

1. *Summa*, 2:1.75.1.
2. *Summa*, 2:1.75.3.

have a natural aptitude to know but they are not bound to know them, such as geometrical theories and contingent particulars, except in some individual case. It is clear that whoever neglects to have or to do what they ought commits a sin of omission. Therefore, through negligence, ignorance of what one is supposed to know is a sin. However, it is not imputed as a sin if a person fails to know what they are unable to know. Consequently, ignorance of such things is called 'unconquerable' because it cannot be overcome by study. For this reason, such ignorance, not being voluntary because it is not in our power to be rid of it, is not a sin. Therefore, it is clear that no unconquerable ignorance is a sin. On the other hand, conquerable ignorance is a sin if it is about matters one is supposed to know; but not if it is about things one is not supposed to know.[1]

Thomas concludes his teaching on this point a couple of Articles later.

Because every sin is voluntary, ignorance can diminish sin insofar as it diminishes how voluntary it is. If it does not make it less voluntary, it in no way alleviates the sin. Now it is clear that ignorance which excuses from sin altogether (through making it altogether involuntary) does not diminish a sin but does away with it altogether. However, ignorance which is not the cause of the sin committed, but is current alongside the sin, neither diminishes nor increases the sin.[2]

Aquinas returns to the relationship between God and sin in this discussion in questioning the extent to which God could be deemed an agent in human sin, which is dealt with in three sections. Firstly, God is not the direct or indirect cause of sin.

God cannot be the direct cause of sin either in himself or in another, since every sin departs from the order that works to God as the end, whereas God inclines and turns everything to himself as their last end . . . In the same way he cannot cause sin indirectly. It does happen that God does not give to some the help through which they may avoid sin, whereas if he did give them such help then they would not sin. However, he does this according to the order of his wisdom and justice, because he himself is Wisdom and Justice. Therefore if someone sins, it cannot be imputed to God as though he were the cause of that sin. In the same way,

1. *Summa*, 2:1.76.2.
2. *Summa*, 2:1.76.4.

a pilot is not said to cause the wrecking of his ship because he is not steering the ship unless he stops steering while he is able and bound to steer. It is therefore evident that God is in no way a cause of sin.[1]

The second stage is to accept that God is the cause of all being, and is in this sense indirectly a cause of action, but is not responsible for the free use made of the will that he created.

The act of sin is both a being and an act, and in both respects it is from God. This is because every being, whatever the mode of its existence, must be derived from the first being . . . Therefore, God is the cause of every action in that it is an action. However, sin indicates a being and an action with a defect, and this is from the created cause, the free will, which falls away from the order of the first agent, God. Therefore, this defect does not have God as its cause, but the free will, just as the defect of limping has a crooked leg as its cause, but not the moving power that does cause whatever movement there is in the limping. In this way, God is the cause of the act of sin but he is not the cause of sin, because he does not cause defect to be present in the act.[2]

Finally, Aquinas recognises that God does withhold his grace (indicated in the first of these quotes) and this plays a role in the existence of sin.

Spiritual blindness and hardness of heart imply two things. One is the movement of the human mind in holding to evil and turning away from the divine light. Regarding this, God is not the cause of spiritual blindness and hardness of heart just as he is not the cause of sin. The other is the withdrawal of grace, which results in a mind that is not enlightened by God to see correctly and a heart that is not softened to live correctly. Regarding this, God is the cause of spiritual blindness and hardness of heart. . . . God, of his own accord, withholds his grace from those in whom he finds an obstacle. The reason for grace being withheld is therefore not only the person who raises an obstacle to grace, but God who, of his own accord, withholds his grace. In this way, God is the cause of spiritual blindness, deafness of ear and hardness of heart.[3]

---

1. *Summa*, 2:1.79.1.
2. *Summa*, 2:1.79.2.
3. *Summa*, 2:1.79.3.

Having clarified the role of God in relation to human sin, Aquinas then discusses the role of the devil in more detail, beginning by making it clear that this is limited to persuading or propositioning.

> The will can be moved by two things: firstly, by its object, so the object desired is said to move the desire; and, secondly, by an agent which moves the will inwardly, and this is only the will itself or God, and God cannot be the cause of sin. Therefore, it follows that in this respect, a person's will alone is directly the cause of their sin. As regards the object, a thing may be understood to move the will in three ways. Firstly, the object itself that is offered to the will and so we can say that food arouses a person's desire to eat. Secondly, one who proposes or offers the object. Thirdly, one that persuades the will that the object is good because they also, in a way, offer the will its proper object, which the reason deems a real or apparent good. In the first way, the external object moves a person's will to sin. In the second and third ways, either the devil or a person may incite to sin, either by offering a desired object to the senses, or by persuading the reason. But none of these three ways are the direct cause of sin, because the will is not forcibly moved by any object except its end [God]. Therefore, neither the thing offered nor any that proposes it or persuades is the sufficient cause of sin. It must follow that the devil is neither a direct nor sufficient cause of sin, but only one who persuades or proposes the object of desire.[1]

This role is clarified in the next Article as darkening a person's reason by encouraging desire through presenting forms to the imagination. While there is power here, it is a power that is allowed by God and is resistible by people.

> Unless he is restrained by God, the devil in his own power can compel a person to do an act which is a sin in its nature, but he cannot bring about the necessity of sinning. This is clear from the fact that a person does not resist something that moves them to sin except by their reason, the use of which the devil is able to impede completely by moving the imagination and the desire, as is the case with a person who is possessed. In this case, the reason being so constrained, whatever a person may do is not imputed to them as a sin. If, however, the reason is not completely constrained, then, it can resist sin to the extent that it is free. It is therefore evident that the devil can in no way compel a person to sin.[2]

---

1. *Summa*, 2:1.80.1.
2. *Summa*, 2:1.80.3.

The next stage is to look at original sin and the corruption that is received as a result of the Adamic sin.

> All who are born of Adam may be considered as one, in that they have one common nature that they receive from their first parents. . . . Therefore, the multitude of people born of Adam are so many members of one body. Now the action of any part of the body, of the hand for instance, is not through the will of that hand but by the will of the soul, the first mover of all the parts. Therefore, a murder that the hand commits is not seen as a sin of the hand considered by itself, apart from the body, but is carried out by the hand as something belonging to the person and moved by the soul. In this way, the corruption which is in a person born of Adam is voluntary, not by their will, but by the will of the first parent who, through generation, moves all who originate from him, even as the soul's will moves all the parts of the body to their actions. In this way, the sin that is transmitted by the first parent to his descendants is called 'original', just as the sin that flows from the soul into the parts of the body is called 'actual'. Just as actual sin committed by a part of the body is not the sin of that part, except as that is a part of the whole person (for which reason it is called a 'human sin'), so original sin is not the sin of this person, except as this person receives their nature from the first parent, for which reason it is called the 'sin of nature'.[1]

The ultimate result is that, 'Christ alone excepted, all who are descended from Adam contract original sin from him, or else all would not need redemption, which is through Christ.'[2]

Finally, in this section on the habits, which is the context for all of this, there is the question of the stain that sin inflicts on a person after a sin is committed.

> The stain of sin remains in the soul even when the act of sin is past. The reason for this is that the stain indicates a blemish in the brightness of the soul because it has withdrawn from the light of reason or of the divine law. Therefore, so long as a person remains out of this light, the stain of sin remains in them; but as soon as, moved by grace, they return to the divine light and to the light of reason, the stain is removed.[3]

---

1. *Summa*, 2:1.81.1.
2. *Summa*, 2:1.81.3.
3. *Summa*, 2:1.86.2.

Virtues

Book Two, Part Two opens with three lengthy treatises on the theological virtues (Questions 1-46), the cardinal virtues (Questions 47-122) and on steadfastness and modesty (Questions 123-170). It may seem unlikely given these titles that there should be much material on sin, however, much of these sections take the method that something can be known from its opposite and so there is an extensive list of sins that are presented and discussed. More than any other topic in these books so far, there is far too much material for the space available here and so certain sins will be looked at for significance or interest, while there is an appendix to this chapter that contains the full list of sins by their Question number for those who wish to research something specific.

A good example of the approach to these sins is in the first mentioned, unbelief, which follows on from a section on faith. The assessment may be interesting:

> Unbelief may be taken in two ways: firstly, as a pure negation, so that a person may be called an unbeliever simply because they do not have faith; secondly, unbelief may be taken to mean opposition to the faith, when a person refuses to hear the faith or despises it . . . It is this that completes the idea of unbelief and it is in this sense that unbelief is a sin. If we take it to mean pure negation, as it exists in those who have heard nothing about the faith, it bears the character of punishment, not sin, because this ignorance of divine things results from the sin of our first parent. If such unbelievers are damned, it is due to other sins, which cannot be taken away without faith, but not due to a sin of unbelief.[1]

One sin that was mentioned at times in volume one of this series is blasphemy against the Holy Spirit, a worrying sin in that it is held up as the one unforgiveable sin, either in this age or in the age to come, and yet the Bible doesn't actually tell us what this sin is. Aquinas deals with it in Question 14 in four separate Articles, outlining three major historical positions in his answer without nailing his colours to any one specific mast. This is one of the very few occasions when Aquinas does not indicate what his own view is, and the issue is made more complex in Article 2 when he outlines six kinds of sin against the Holy Spirit.

When discussing most of the sins in this section, Aquinas seeks to help the reader to understand the exact nature of the sin by explaining why it is considered a sin, by stating the virtue that it is opposed to and by assessing whether it is a mortal sin or not. Some sins have many

---

1. *Summa*, 2:2.10.1.

further elements due to their own complexity, or how they are dealt with in particular Biblical passages or theological discussions, but generally there is a familiar rhythm to the discussions.

An early example of some interest is presumption, which receives four Articles looking at the nature of presumption, whether it is a sin, what it is opposed to and from what vice it arises. Aquinas highlights two roots of presumption, one in a reliance on human power and one in a false reliance on divine power.

> As to the hope whereby a person relies on the power of God, there may be presumption through immoderate hope in the fact that a person wishes for a good by the power and mercy of God when it is not possible, for instance by hoping to receive pardon without repenting or glory without merits. This presumption is, properly understood, the sin against the Holy Spirit because by presuming in this way a person removes or despises the assistance of the Holy Spirit, who is able to save a person from sin.[1]

In looking at the concupiscible passions above, we noted a fairly neutral approach to the concept of hatred in that the evil there was present in the object primarily. In this section on the virtues, Aquinas takes a different line in focusing on the one hating.

> Hatred is opposed to love, as stated above, so that hatred of a thing is evil insofar as the love of that thing is good. Now, love is due to our neighbour because of what they receive from God in respect of nature and grace, but not in what they have of themselves and from the devil, in respect of sin and a lack of justice. Consequently, it is lawful to hate the sin in one's neighbour and whatever pertains to a lack of divine justice, but we cannot hate our neighbour's nature and grace without sin. Now, it is a part of our love for them that we hate the fault and the lack of good in others, since a desire for another's good is equivalent to hatred of his evil. Therefore, the hatred of one's neighbour, if we consider it simply, is always sinful.[2]

Folly is held to be a sin as contrary to wisdom, which is always directed for Aquinas to humankind's ultimate end and purpose, *i.e.* God, and sections like the following challenge a modern perspective in the Church that seems to give great emphasis to wisdom directed to earthly matters.

---

1. *Summa*, 2:2.21.1.
2. *Summa*, 2:2.34.1.

Folly denotes a dullness of sense in judging, chiefly regarding the highest cause that is the last end and the sovereign good. A person may in this respect contract dullness in judgement in two ways. Firstly, from a natural indisposition, as in the case of the simple, and such folly is no sin. Secondly, by plunging their sense into earthly things whereby a person becomes incapable of perceiving divine things . . . even as sweet things have no savour for a man whose taste is infected with an evil humour. Such folly is a sin.[1]

Aquinas strikes an interesting tone when discussing distributive justice, asking whether undue respect for persons is a sin.

Respect for persons is opposed to distributive justice. For the equality in distributive justice consists in allotting things to various persons in proportion to their personal dignity. . . . For instance, if you promote someone to a professorship on account of their having sufficient knowledge, you consider the due cause, not the person; but if, in conferring something on someone, you consider not the fact that what you give them is proportionate or their due but the fact that they are this particular person, then there is respect of the person because you give them something not for some worthy cause, but simply because it is this person. Any circumstance that does not involve a reason why a person may be worthy of a gift is referred to the person. For instance, if someone is promoted to a prelacy or a professorship because they are rich or a relative, it is respect of persons. It may be that a person's circumstance makes them worthy of one thing but not another. Family ties make a person worthy to be appointed heir to an estate, but not to be chosen for a position of ecclesiastical authority. Therefore, consideration of the same circumstance will amount to respect of persons in one matter but not in another. It follows that respect of persons is opposed to distributive justice in that it fails to observe due proportion. Nothing but sin is opposed to virtue, and therefore respect of persons is a sin.[2]

Aquinas addresses sins that he sees present in the Church such as simony:

Accordingly, we must answer that receiving money for the spiritual grace of the sacraments is the sin of simony, which cannot be excused by any custom whatever since 'custom does not prevail over natural or divine law'. By money we understand anything

---

1. *Summa*, 2:2.46.2.
2. *Summa*, 2:2.63.1.

that has a pecuniary value, as the Philosopher states. On the other hand, to receive anything for the support of those who administer the sacraments, in accordance with the statutes of the Church and approved customs, is not simony nor is it a sin because it is received not as a price for the goods but as a payment for their need.[1]

There is a series of areas that Aquinas addresses that result from his idea that something is right when it is complete in doing that which it was created to do. This creates a series of statements that may seem extreme to us today. On lying, Aquinas asks whether every lie is a sin.

> Any action that is naturally evil in what it is cannot be good and lawful because, in order for an action to be good, it must be right in every respect. This is because good results from a complete cause, while evil is the result of any single defect, as Dionysius asserts. A lie is evil in what it is as an action related to what is not right. Because words in their nature are signs of intellectual acts, it is unnatural and unworthy for a person to indicate by words something that is not in their mind. Therefore, the Philosopher says that 'lying is evil in itself and should be rejected, while truthfulness is good and worthy of praise.' Therefore, every lie is a sin, as Augustine also states.[2]

Aquinas writes about irony, which in his understanding of the Greek term indicates a false humiliation in denying one's own strengths. He considers this to be a sin.

> One may speak to belittle oneself in two ways. Firstly, in order to protect the truth, such as when a person hides greater abilities but discovers and asserts lesser abilities that they perceive in themselves. When one belittles oneself in this way it is not irony, nor is it a sin in what it is, except through a corruption of one part. Secondly, a person belittles themselves by rejecting the truth, for instance by claiming to own something that they do not believe that they possess, or by denying something great that they recognise that they do possess. This relates to irony and it is always a sin.[3]

As this is a sin in a false assessment of oneself, so flattery is always a sin in an incorrect recognition of another.[4] On similar lines, Aquinas

---

1. *Summa*, 2:2.100.2.
2. *Summa*, 2:2.110.3.
3. *Summa*, 2:2.113.1.
4. *Summa*, 2:2.115.

believes that ambition is a sin as a false view both of one's own dignity and the work of God in a person's life.

> Honour indicates a reverence that is shown to a person as a witness of their excellence. In this, two things must be considered in regard to a person's honour. The first is that a person is not the source of that gift in which they excel because this is something divine in them; as a result, honour is due principally not to the person but to God. The second point to bear in mind is that the gift in which a person excels is given by God so that others may profit from this. Therefore, a person should be pleased that others are witnesses to their excellence because this helps them to benefit others. The desire for honour may be excessive in three ways: firstly, when a person wants to be recognised for an excellence they do not have, which is to desire more than the right share of honour; secondly, when a person desires honour for themselves without recognising the source as in God; thirdly, when a person's desire is for honour itself, without recognising that this should be for the profit of others. Since ambition indicates a wrong desire for honour, it is clear that it is always a sin.[1]

There are some sections in the lists of sins where a great balance is shown: Aquinas states that fear can be a sin when it is not ordered correctly (there are some things that we should fear and then it is the right response); in the next Question Aquinas shows that fearlessness is a sin when there is an undue confidence resulting from 'a lack of love, a pride in the soul or a limited understanding'.[2] One is aware through all this of Thomas' care with words, recognising precisely what is involved in the language that he uses. An example of this would be magnificence, which is held as a virtue because the Latin best translates as 'great deed' and this is in line with the purpose of creation rather than seeking a false greatness.[3]

Some of the 'seven deadly sins' are presented fairly late in the long list of sins, including gluttony, lust and pride. Drunkenness comes under the area of gluttony and leads to the question whether drunkenness absolves a person from committing a sin.

> Two aspects should be noted when discussing drunkenness, namely the preceding action and the resulting wrong. In relation to the resulting wrong, in which the use of reason is limited,

---

1. *Summa*, 2:2.131.1.
2. *Summa*, 2:2.125-126.
3. *Summa*, 2:2.134.

drunkenness may be seen as an excuse for sin in that it causes an act to be involuntary because of ignorance. However, on the part of the preceding action, there must be a distinction made because, if there is no sin that leads to drunkenness, the resulting sin is entirely excused from blame, as may be seen in the case of Lot. If, however, the preceding action was sinful, then the person is not completely excused from the resulting sin because then this sin is voluntary due to the freedom of the preceding action, in that it was by doing something unlawful that the person committed the resulting sin. Nevertheless, the resulting sin is diminished just as the voluntary character of the action is diminished.[1]

Aquinas goes into some detail when discussing lust, breaking down the parts of lust into twelve Articles dealing with a range of related issues from kissing to incest. Aquinas can be fairly blunt in his language and the topics that he deals with, and one of the most instructive answers he gives in terms of his method, relates to 'Whether Nocturnal Pollution is a Mortal Sin?' This receives a lengthy consideration, beginning with the event itself that is not considered a sin because the reason is not directly involved: 'What a person does while they sleep and do not have the judgement of reason is not considered a sin, in the same way as the actions of a mad or mindless person are not sins.'[2] However, Aquinas recognises that the thoughts of a sleeping person can result from what they have done in their waking state among other reasons. While the result in sleep is still not a sin, it is necessary to recognise when it may have stemmed from a sinful cause.

Before this section finishes, it must be noted again that the precise sections that have been presented here are selective. There is a full list of all the sins considered by Aquinas at the end of this chapter for the reader looking for further detail. One Article that does stand out in light of the modern leisure culture concerns whether a lack of play or mirth is a sin. It may be unsurprising that Aquinas considers an excess of play or mirth to be a sin, but he likewise judges that it is sinful to be lacking in these areas (although his choice of authorities, Seneca and Aristotle, seems rather strange).

In human affairs, a sin is something that is against reason. Now it is unreasonable for someone to be a burden to others by offering no pleasure to them or by hindering their enjoyment. Therefore, Seneca says: 'Let your conduct be guided by wisdom so that no

1. *Summa*, 2:2.150.4.
2. *Summa*, 2:2.154.5.

one will think you rude or despise you as a scoundrel.' Any person who is without mirth is not only lacking in playful speech but is a burden to others because they are deaf to their reasonable mirth. Therefore, they are vicious and are said to be coarse or rude, as the Philosopher states. Therefore, since mirth is useful for the rest and the pleasures it affords, and because pleasure and rest for humans are not sought for their own sake but to help them to work, as stated by the Philosopher, it follows that 'a lack of mirth is less sinful than an excess'.[1]

Given the extent of material on sins of all kinds, it is unsurprising that, when he considers the states of life, Aquinas denies the possibility of perfection in this life.

The perfection of the Christian life is found in love. Perfection implies a certain universality because, according to the Philosopher, 'the perfect is that which lacks nothing'. Therefore, we may consider three types of perfection. One is absolute and involves a totality not only on the part of the lover but also by the object loved, so that God is loved as much as he is loveable. This kind of perfection is impossible for any creature, but is found in God alone who is completely and essentially good. A second perfection involves a totality on the part of the lover, so that the love of a person always tends to God as much as it can. This kind of perfection is impossible while we are on the way, but we shall have it in heaven. The third perfection involves no totality either by the object or by the lover in terms of always tending to God, but the lover does remove any obstacles to the movement of love towards God, of which Augustine says that 'bodily desire is a barrier to love; to have no bodily desires is the perfection of love'. This kind of perfection can be had in this life in two ways. Firstly, by the removal from a person's affections of all that is a barrier to love, such as mortal sin. There can be no love apart from this perfection, and therefore it is necessary for salvation. Secondly, by the additional removal from a person's affections of whatever barriers there are to the mind's affections focusing completely on God. Love is possible without this perfection, for example, in those who are beginners in the faith and in those who are proficient.[2]

---

1. *Summa*, 2:2.168.4.
2. *Summa*, 2:2.184.2.

Sin and Christ

The final section of this chapter looks at Aquinas' writing on the relationship of Christ to sin, given that He took on human nature in order to overcome sin. The first half of the third book of the *Summa* looks at the Incarnation. In the first Question, Aquinas considers whether sin was the cause of the Incarnation, recognising that there have been different views on this point.

> There are different opinions about this question. Some say that, even if people had not sinned, the Son of Man would have become incarnate. Others assert the opposite and it seems right that we should agree with this opinion. For such things that come from God's will and are beyond what we deserve can only be made known to us by being revealed in the Sacred Scripture, where we learn about the divine will. Therefore, since everywhere in the Bible the sin of the first man is given as the reason for the Incarnation, we should agree with this and say that the work of the Incarnation was ordained by God as a remedy for sin. Had sin not existed, we say that there would have been no Incarnation. However, the power of God is not limited by this since, even if sin did not exist, God could have become incarnate.[1]

Having discussed elements of the Incarnation, Aquinas considers whether Christ took on sin in assuming human nature.

> Christ assumed our defects in order that he provide satisfaction for us, that he might prove the truth of his human nature and that he might become an example of virtue to us. It is clear through these three things that he did not assume the defect of sin. Firstly, this is because sin in no way works for our satisfaction, but rather it impedes the power of satisfying . . . Secondly, the truth of his human nature is not proved by sin because sin does not belong to human nature, which is the result of the work of God; rather sin has been sown in human nature for its corruption by the devil. Thirdly, by sinning Christ could not be an example of virtue because sin is opposed to virtue. Therefore Christ in no way assumed the defect of sin, either original or actual, according to what is written [1 Pet. 2:22]: 'He committed no sin, and no deceit was found in his mouth.'[2]

---

1. *Summa*, 3.1.3.
2. *Summa*, 3.15.1.

Later Aquinas addresses Mary because Christ receives his human nature from her and there is a discussion of her relationship to sin. Aquinas does not teach the position that would become the Catholic Doctrine of the Immaculate Conception of Mary, but rather states that she was sanctified before birth in the womb.

> Nothing is stated in the canonical Scriptures about the sanctification of the Blessed Mary as happening in the womb, indeed they do not even mention her birth. However, as Augustine (in his treatise on the assumption of the Virgin) reasonably argues, since her body was assumed into heaven and yet Scripture does not mention this, so it may be reasonably argued that she was sanctified in the womb.[1]

The important aspect in this discussion, as always in considering the nature of Mary, is the issue of original sin and how Christ does not receive this in his human nature. Aquinas holds that Mary does receive original sin at her conception, but is then sanctified and set apart in preparation for the Incarnation.

> Original sin is transmitted from the origin, in that through human nature is transmitted from its source, and original sin affects the resulting nature, correctly speaking. This takes place when the offspring that has been conceived is animated. Therefore, nothing stops the conceived offspring from being sanctified after animation. After this, it does not remain in the mother's womb in order to receive human nature, but for the perfecting of that which it has already received.[2]

The desire is for Christ to receive all the aspects of human nature that must be redeemed for the resurrection, and thus none of the nature or effects of sin can be a part of his humanity or these would also be in the resurrected human nature.

Conclusion

As with most areas of theology, Aquinas provides an incredibly thorough window into the study of sin that, due to the structure of the *Summa*, is accessible, although the concepts that underpin his language and affect his method are at times rather too driven by an Aristotelian method.

---

1. *Summa*, 3.27.1.
2. *Summa*, 3.27.1, Reply to 4.

This makes his distinctions on the lines of passions, habits and virtues quite foreign to those studying theology today and creates a layer of work in approaching Aquinas' thought, a work that does reap benefits when one understands the resulting discussions.

The quotations in this chapter are my own work from the *Summa*, which can easily be accessed online in translation, and I would suggest using the version at www.newadvent.org/summa as that website contains a Catholic encyclopaedia that can be helpful for understanding the particular terminology that Aquinas uses, through simple links to informative articles. Paul Glen has written *A Tour of the Summa* (Rockford, IL: Tan Books, 1978), which takes the reader briefly through each of the Articles in summary form and is useful for anyone seeking to take on the mammoth task of reading the *Summa*. A great assessment of Aquinas' thought is Eleonore Stump's *Aquinas* (London: Routledge, 2003), a massive and comprehensive work that is particularly useful because of her awareness of the philosophical dimension underpinning Aquinas' theological project.

Appendix: A List of Virtues and Sins by Question Number

The following list of Questions comes from Book Two, Part Two of the *Summa* in the treatises on the theological virtues, cardinal virtues and fortitude and temperance. I have left in the names of the Questions on virtues so that the reader can see the context in which the sin is discussed, however, those concerning sin are highlighted in italics. The aim here is to direct the reader to the relevant Question without having to trawl through each of these and the Articles that comprise them.

Question 1   Of Faith
Question 2   Of the Act of Faith
Question 3   Of the Outward Act of Faith
Question 4   Of the Virtue Itself of Faith
Question 5   Of Those Who Have Faith
Question 6   Of the Cause of Faith
Question 7   Of the Effects of Faith
Question 8   Of the Gift of Understanding
Question 9   Of the Gift of Knowledge

5.
Thomas Aquinas on Grace

As with the concept of sin, Aquinas grounds his doctrine of grace in his doctrine of God at the beginning of the *Summa*, before getting into the application of grace to creation and the effects of sin in later sections. There is a noticeable difference in his method of treating the two subjects as grace is a distinct theological term and therefore there is far less Aristotelian material that is directly applicable, with the strong guiding hand held by Scripture and the tradition of the Church.

Aquinas' teaching on grace is generally contained in clear sections relating to phases of his theological project, except for the early material on grace and God where references are more sporadic. The first major treatise comes at the end of Book Two, Part One, following the work on the nature of sin, bridged by a section on law that ends with indications of grace. Grace is discussed in terms of its nature and role in light of the work in this part of the *Summa*. Book Two, Part Two deals with the habits and virtues related to humanity and after this there is a section on the gratuitous graces, the charismata, that are the detailed work of God above and beyond the natural, fallen human condition. The third book of the *Summa* deals with salvation in the Incarnation and the Church, with grace discussed in relation to the Christ event and, then, as central to the sacramental work in the second half of the third book. Grace is also discussed briefly in the Supplement, where sacraments are presented from Aquinas' writings that were not finished at the time of Aquinas' death.

Given Aquinas' reputation as a great philosopher-theologian, it may seem surprising that grace plays such a heavy role in his understanding of humanity and salvation. However, there should really be no surprise when one considers the project that he is engaging in. Aquinas is not seeking to subject theology to philosophy but to use philosophy as a tool for understanding theology, as far as this allows, always retaining the authority of the faith of the Church that has been passed down through the centuries. The result, for the most part, is a very Augustinian position since Augustine is an easier tool to work with, when dealing with grace, than Aristotle or any other philosopher.

Grace and God

The first work on grace is to define it as part of the being and action of God in Book One of the *Summa*. In the first Question of the *Summa*, a stand-alone treatise on the nature of sacred doctrine, there are a couple of important references to grace that indicate its nature and role in Aquinas' thought. The first concerns the work of God.

> Although we cannot know what the essence of God consists of, in this science we make use of his effects, either of nature or grace, in place of a definition, in whatever element we are dealing with in this science concerning God, just as philosophical sciences understand a cause from its effect by using the effect as part of the definition of the cause.[1]

The focus on the grace highlighted here is the specific work of God, in addition to that seen in creation, what is often termed 'common grace', both giving us a knowledge of God. Grace is further referenced in relation to rational enquiry into the faith, which would seem to make theology a purely human endeavour.

> Sacred doctrine even makes use of human reason, not to prove faith (since in this case faith would have no worth) but to clarify other aspects that are considered in this doctrine. Therefore, since grace does not destroy nature but rather perfects it, natural reason should provide aids to faith as the natural attitude of the will provides an aid to love.[2]

The nature/grace relationship is picked up in the Question on the existence of God, in an Article considering whether and how God is in all things.

> God is said to be in something in two ways: in one way he is present as the efficient cause, and in this way he is in all things that are created by him; in another way he is in a thing as a worker knows the subject of his work; and this is seen in the operations of

---

1. *Summa*, 1.1.7, Reply to 1.
2. *Summa*, 1.1.8, Reply to 2.

the soul, since the thing known is in the one who knows and the thing desired is in the one who desires. In this second way God is especially in the rational creature that knows and loves him actually or habitually because the rational creature possesses this ability by grace, as will be shown later. He is therefore said to be in the saints through grace.[1]

This is developed later in Book One when the mission of the divine persons is discussed.

> The divine person is rightly sent in that he exists afresh in a person, in that he dwells with a person, and these can only be by sanctifying grace. . . . No other effect is the reason why the divine person is in the rational creature in a new way except by sanctifying grace. Therefore the divine person is sent and proceeds temporally only through sanctifying grace. Again, we possess only what we can freely use or enjoy, and the power of enjoying the divine person can only be from sanctifying grace. The Holy Spirit is possessed by a person and dwells within them in the very gift of sanctifying grace.[2]

This Article illustrates the point that this grace is not simply the presence of the Holy Spirit but the work of the Spirit.

> Working miracles manifests sanctifying grace as does the gift of prophecy and other gratuitous graces. This is why gratuitous grace is called the 'manifestation of the Spirit' (1 Cor. 12:7). The Holy Spirit is said to be given to the apostles for the working of miracles because sanctifying grace was given to them along with the external work of the Spirit. If only the sign of sanctifying grace was given without the work of grace, the Holy Spirit would only seem to be given in light of some qualifying term. In this way, we read of certain people receiving the gift of the spirit of prophecy or of miracles, so that they receive from the Holy Spirit the power of prophesying or working miracles.[3]

This does not only refer to the presence of God by grace, but even to the apprehension of God as he is, which the reason alone cannot do but which requires a movement of grace.

> It is impossible for any created intellect to see the essence of God through its own natural power because knowledge is dependent on the extent to which this is in the one knowing. . . . The

---

1. *Summa*, 1.8.4.
2. *Summa*, 1.43.3.
3. Ibid.

knowledge of a being is dependent on its nature. Therefore, if a being exceeds in nature the being of the one knowing, it must result that knowledge of that being is above their nature. . . . The knowledge of a self-existent being is only natural to the divine intellect and thus beyond the natural power of a created intellect, since no creature is its own existence but derives this from another. Therefore, the created intellect cannot see the essence of God unless God, through his grace, unites himself to the created intellect as something that it can understand.[1]

Aquinas develops this point later in the same Question.

We have a more perfect knowledge of God by grace than through our natural reason, as can be shown by the following. The knowledge from our natural reason contains two things: images received from our senses' perception of things; and the natural light of intelligence that enables us to deduce coherent concepts from these. In both of these aspects, human knowledge is assisted through the revelation of grace. For the natural light of intelligence is strengthened by the infusion of the light of grace, and sometimes images are formed in the human imagination by God in order to help us understand divine things better than we would from our senses' perception, as happens in prophetic visions. In addition, physical things or even voices can be formed by God to express divine meaning, as occurred in the baptism [of Jesus] when the Holy Spirit came in the form of a dove and the voice of the Father was heard.[2]

There is some material on grace in the work on the predestination of God and the 'Book of Life', consecutive Questions that are part of the treatise on the being of God. Much of the material here relates more to free will and will be dealt with in the next chapter, but grace is closely linked to the nature of predestination without being a defining feature.

Grace is not part of the definition of predestination as something that belongs to its essence, but predestination does imply a relationship to grace, similar to cause and effect or an action and its object.[3]

This is clarified in the following Article that looks at reprobation – the assigning of some to punishment.

---

1. *Summa*, 1.12.4.
2. *Summa*, 1.12.13.
3. *Summa*, 1.23.2.

Just as predestination includes the will to confer grace and glory,
so reprobation includes the will to allow a person to fall into
sin and then to impose a punishment of damnation because of
that sin. God loves all people and all creatures in that he wishes
them all some good; but he does not wish every kind of good to
all of them. Therefore, to the extent that he does not wish this
particular good, eternal life, he is said to hate or reprobate them.
However, reprobation differs in its causation from predestination.
In the latter case, this is the cause of both what is expected in the
future by the predestined, which is glory, and what is received in
this life, which is grace. However, reprobation is not the cause of
the present sin, but it is the cause of the abandonment by God
that results from the sin. It is the cause of what will come in the
future, which is eternal punishment. Guilt comes from the free
will of the person who is reprobate and deserted by grace.[1]

Returning to the positive of predestination, Aquinas argues that,
despite a role of the will in salvation, because even this is the result
of grace (the work of God), there is no purely human role that can be
identified.

There can be no distinction between what results from free will
and what from predestination, since there can be no distinction
between what results from a secondary cause and what from a first
cause. The providence of God produces effects through secondary
causes, as was shown above, and so that which results from free
will is also from predestination. We must therefore say that the
effect of predestination may be considered in two ways. Firstly,
in the particular, in which there is no reason why one effect of
predestination should not be the reason or cause of another. So, a
later result can be the reason for a previous action as its final cause;
or the previous action could be the reason for the later result as
its meriting cause, which depends on how the event is viewed. We
could say that God preordained that he would give glory on account
of some merit, or that he preordained to give grace in order to merit
glory. Secondly, the result of predestination may be considered
in general. It is then impossible that the whole of the results of
predestination in general should have any cause coming from us
because whatever is in a person preparing them for salvation is all
part of the results of predestination, even the preparation for grace.[2]

1. *Summa*, 1.23.3.
2. *Summa*, 1.23.5.

When Aquinas moves on in the next Question to look at the Book of Life, often linked to the concept of predestination, he distinguishes between those whose names are found there either by predestination or by grace, which seems a strange distinction to make given the above quotes that inter-relate the two themes, and the explanation does not seem to resolve the difficulties.

> The Book of Life is inscribed with the names of those ordained to eternal life, to which a person is directed from two sources: from predestination, whose direction never fails; and from grace, since whoever has grace by this fact is prepared for eternal life. This latter direction fails sometimes because some obtain possessing grace that allows them to receive eternal life, but they fail to receive this because of mortal sin. Therefore, those who are ordained to receive eternal life through divine predestination have their names written down in the Book of Life simply because they are written there that they might have eternal life in reality; these are never blotted out from the Book of Life. However, those who are ordained to eternal life through grace, but not through divine predestination, are said to have their names written in the Book of Life relatively, not simply, because they are written there not to receive eternal life itself, but only its cause. Although these latter names can be blotted out of the Book of Life, this must not be referred to God, as if God foreknew a thing and then later did not know it. Rather it must relate to the one known because God knows a person who is first ordained to receive eternal life and then not ordained when they fall from grace.[1]

This twofold access to the Book of Life, by predestination and grace, the former being certain and the latter contingent on the life lived following the receipt of grace, will seem increasingly strange as we go through Aquinas' teaching which would seem to describe grace in ways more similar to the presentation of predestination here than to the uncertain language of grace.

Grace in the Creation State

It is here necessary to recognise the role of grace in the nature of angels and humankind before there is sin, since the understanding of the corruption of sin and subsequent grace (in the case of humans; there is

---

1. *Summa*, 1.24.3.

no restoring grace for fallen angels) is set in the context of the created state. The first quotation relates to angels and their need for grace to turn to God.

> The angels needed grace in order to turn to God as the object of a blessed state. As was observed above, the natural movement of the will is the basis of anything that we will, but the natural inclination of the will is towards whatever is in keeping with its nature. Therefore, the will cannot naturally incline towards anything above its nature unless it is helped by some supernatural principle. . . . Consequently, no rational creature's will can move towards the blessed divine nature unless it is moved by a supernatural agent. This is what we call the help of grace. Therefore, an angel could not turn their own will to the divine except by the help of grace.[1]

The angels are thus seen to attain their blessed state through a work of grace, which was therefore lacking to the angels who fell. This grace, accompanied by the varying nature of the angels, then led to the various ranks and duties ascribed to angels.

> It is reasonable to state that gifts of grace and the perfection of a blessed state were given to the angels in accordance with their natural gifts. There are two sources behind this teaching. Firstly, God in his ultimate wisdom established various degrees in the nature of angels. This nature was created by God so that they might attain to grace and blessedness, and the degrees of the angelic nature were intended for various degrees of grace and glory . . . It seems that God destined the angels he created with a higher nature for greater gifts of grace and more complete blessedness. Secondly, the same teaching comes from our understanding of angels. The angel is not comprised of different natures, with the inclination of one in any way inhibiting the will of the other, as happens in humans when the will of the intellect can be inhibited by the will of the senses. When there is nothing that inhibits a nature, it is moved by its whole energy. Therefore, we can say that the angels that received a higher nature were turned to God with greater power and effect. The same thing can be seen in people, since greater grace and glory are given to those who turn to God with greater dedication. Therefore, it seems that the angels who received greater natural powers had greater grace and glory.[2]

1. *Summa*, 1.62.2.
2. *Summa*, 1.62.6.

There are certain echoes of this teaching when Aquinas deals with the created nature of humankind, where he states that this must have been in grace, although he recognises that not all would agree with this view.

> Some say that humankind was not created in grace, but that this was given later and yet before sin; many saintly authorities declare that people possessed grace in the state of innocence. But the very righteousness of the first state given to people by God requires that, as others teach, humans were created in grace, in line with Ecclesiastes 7:30, 'God made humankind upright.' . . . It is clear that the first subjection of reason to God through virtue was not simply a natural gift, but was rather a supernatural gift of grace because it is not possible that the effect should have greater importance than the cause. . . . Therefore, if the loss of grace removed the obedience of the flesh to the soul, we may gather that the inferior powers were subject to the soul through the grace that this possessed.[1]

There is thus an initial state of grace from which humankind is removed through sin, a state granted by God. The salvation after sin then is similarly seen to be through the work of grace under this understanding that humankind in its created, pure nature could not worship that which is superior in nature to it; even more so, therefore, the sinful, fallen human nature could not turn of itself to God.

Law, Grace and Salvation

Following a discussion of the passions and habits of humans, those internal aspects that affect the nature and will of a person in leading to their actions, at the end of Book Two, Part One, Aquinas deals with external forces that are at work. In this he recognises that the devil is involved in temptation and then considers two aspects of the work of God:

> the external principle that moves us to good is God, who both teaches us through his law and assists us by his grace. Therefore, we will speak first of the law, and secondly of grace.[2]

The presentation of the law understandably focuses on the Old Testament for the most part, before at the end moving on to the new law/covenant where grace and the work of the Spirit is emphasised.

---

1. *Summa*, 1.95.1.
2. *Summa*, 2:1.90, Prologue.

The dominant aspect of the law of the New Testament, that on which its entire power is based, is the grace of the Holy Spirit that is given through faith in Christ. Therefore, the new law is primarily the grace itself of the Holy Spirit, which is given to all who believe in Christ. . . . The new law contains certain things that make us ready to receive the grace of the Holy Spirit and that pertain to the use of that grace. Such things are to be seen as of secondary importance in the new law, but the faithful do need to be instructed about them in both word and writing, concerning what they should believe and what they should do. Consequently, we believe that the new law is first one that is written on our hearts, but secondarily is also a written law.[1]

In this section bridging the old and new covenants, moving from law to grace, there is a consideration of the role of external actions in the new covenant and how these relate to the means of grace in Christ and the resulting life in the new covenant.

The new law mainly consists of the grace of the Holy Spirit, the evidence of which is a faith that works through love. People receive this grace through God's Son made man, whose humanity was first filled with grace and from that source flowed out to us. . . . Therefore, it is right that we should receive the grace flowing from the Incarnate Word through certain external objects; and that this inner grace, in which the flesh is subject to the Spirit, certainly results in external works. External actions therefore have two connections with grace. Firstly, as in some way leading to grace, such as in the sacraments instituted in the new law, such as Baptism and Eucharist. Secondly, there are external acts that result from the movement of grace, in which we may note a distinction. Some are necessarily either in line with or in opposition to inner grace, which consists of faith working through love. These are either prescribed or forbidden in the New Law: confession of faith is prescribed, while denial of faith is forbidden . . . On the other hand, there are works that are not necessarily in line with or opposition to a faith working through love, and these are neither prescribed or forbidden in the new law in its initial institution, but Christ the lawgiver leaves these to the discretion of the individual. Each person is thus free to decide what they should do or avoid; and each leader should direct his followers in these things regarding what they should do or avoid.

1. *Summa*, 2:1.106.1.

This is why in this area the Gospel is called the 'law of freedom', since the old law decided many points and left little to the choice of people.[1]

The treatise that examines sin follows this Question and starts by stating and exploring the necessity of grace in every positive aspect of humanity from knowledge to action, salvation and perseverance. Aquinas believes that fallen human nature is capable only of utilitarian goods – building houses, planting vineyards – but for knowledge and will for the intended nature and life there is a need for grace. Aquinas states clearly that grace is necessary for salvation, which cannot be secured by works of merit.

> The natural endowments of humankind cannot produce meritorious works that can secure everlasting life, but a higher force is needed for this, which is grace. Therefore, without grace a person cannot merit everlasting life, but they can perform works that lead to a natural good for humankind [growing crops, eating, making friends].[2]

In the next Article, Aquinas goes back a further stage to show not only that grace is necessary for salvation, but that it is necessary to awaken a person to the need for this grace.

> There are two elements in the preparation of the human will for good. Firstly, it is prepared to work correctly and to enjoy God, and this preparation of the will cannot take place without a constantly accompanying [as a habit] gift of grace, which is the basis of any good work, as stated above. Secondly, the human will must be prepared for the gift of constantly accompanying grace. In order that a person is prepared to receive this gift, we do not presuppose a further constant work of grace in the soul, otherwise this chain would go on to infinity. Rather we presuppose a gratuitous gift of God that moves the soul inwardly and inspires the desire for good. . . . That people 'turn' to God can only result from God having 'turned' them. Therefore, it is clear that to prepare oneself for grace is to be turned to God, just as a person whose eyes are turned away from the sun's light prepares to receive this by turning their eyes towards the sun. Therefore it is clear that a person cannot be prepared to receive the light of grace unless they receive the gratuitous help of God moving them inwardly.[3]

---

1. *Summa*, 2:1.108.1.
2. *Summa*, 2:1.109.5.
3. *Summa*, 2:1.109.6.

When discussing the work of grace in salvation, given the effects of sin on humankind, Aquinas describes three elements of corruption and shows how in each case grace is necessary to overcome sin.

> A person cannot rise from sin on their own in any way without the help of grace. Because the act of sin ends and yet the guilt of sin remains, as stated above, to rise from sin is not the same as ceasing the act of sin. Rising from sin means that a person has restored what they lost by sinning. Sinning involves a threefold loss as we have seen: the stain of sin, the corruption of the natural good and a debt of punishment. The stain of sin tarnishes the brightness of grace through the deformity of sin. Natural good is corrupted because human nature is disordered in the will no longer being subject to God. Without this right orientation, the result is that the whole human nature is disordered. Finally, there is the debt of punishment because sinful people deserve everlasting damnation. Now it is clear that none of these can be restored except by God. The brightness of grace comes from the rays of divine light, and thus it cannot be restored unless God sheds his light anew. This means that a constantly accompanying gift is necessary, which is the light of grace. In the same way, human nature can only be put back in order, so that the will is subject to God, when God draws the will to himself, as we have seen. Finally, the guilt leading to eternal punishment can only be remitted by God, against whom the offence was committed and who is the judge of all. Therefore, for a person to rise from sin there must be a work of grace, both as a continually accompanying gift and as the internal movement of God.[1]

Having stated so strongly the essential role of grace in every aspect of a person's faith – he continues in a later Article to talk of the role of persevering grace in a person's life.[2] Aquinas writes about the essence of grace and then the division of grace. This starts by contrasting 'gratuitous' grace, which is given to help another towards God, with sanctifying grace that unites a person with God. The next Article speaks of the difference between operating and cooperating grace, common terms coming from Augustine.

> When our mind is moved and does not move itself, when God is the only mover, the work is attributed to God and it is in this regard that we talk of 'operating grace'. But when our mind both

1. *Summa*, 2:1.109.7.
2. *Summa*, 2:1.109.10.

moves itself and is moved, the work is not only attributed to
God but also to the soul and it is in this regard that we talk of
'cooperating grace'. There is a twofold action in us. Firstly, there is
the inner act of the will, and in this the will is something moved
and God is the mover. This is particularly the case when the will,
which up to this point had only willed evil, begins to will the
good. Therefore, because God moves the human mind for this act,
it is termed operating grace. There is another, exterior act that is
commanded by the will, and as we have seen the work of this act
is attributed to the human will. Because God assists us in this act,
both strengthening our inner will in order that we might perform
the act and granting outwardly the capability of performing the
work, this is termed cooperating grace.[1]

Aquinas goes on to write about five effects of grace, with each former
stage being considered 'prevenient' grace (that which comes before)
allowing for the next 'subsequent' grace.

There are five effects of grace in us: the first is to heal the soul;
the second that we might desire good; the third to perform the
good proposed; the fourth to persevere in goodness; the fifth to
reach glory. As grace causes the first of these in us, it is called
prevenient in relation to the second; as it causes the second, it is
called subsequent in relation to the first. As an effect comes after
one and before another, so that each effect of grace can be called
prevenient and subsequent in relation to various others.[2]

When considering the cause of grace, Aquinas begins by stating that
God alone can be the cause of grace:

the gift of grace exceeds every capability of a created nature because
it is nothing short of partaking in the divine nature, which exceeds
every other nature. Therefore, it is impossible that any creature
should cause grace.[3]

Is there any role then for the human will? There is a need for a right
disposition of the will, although even this is a result of grace.

If we are talking about grace as a help from God to move us to the
good, no preparation is required on the human part to anticipate
divine help; rather, every preparation of a person must come from

1. *Summa*, 2:1.111.2.
2. *Summa*, 2:1.111.3.
3. *Summa*, 2:1.112.1.

the help of God moving the soul to the good. Therefore, even the good movement of the free will that prepares a person to receive the gift of grace is an act of the free will that has been moved by God.[1]

After establishing the cause of grace as God, Aquinas moves onto the effects of grace, focusing on the justification of the ungodly. Grace is established as necessary and attention then turns to the relationship between this and human free will and faith – do these have a role to play? There is a need for free will but, building on the previous Question, this is the result of the work of God.

> The justification of the ungodly is accomplished by God moving people to justice. . . . God moves people to justice in line with human nature, which nature has free will as its proper condition. Therefore, for those who have the use of reason, God's movement to justice does not occur without a movement of the free will. However, God infuses the gift of justifying grace and simultaneously moves the free will to accept the gift of grace in those who are capable of being moved in this way.[2]

Indicated here is an answer to the question concerning those who are unable to use their free will, and Aquinas explicitly deals with those who would fit into this category.

> Infants are not capable of using free will, and so God moves them to justice by the simple infusion of grace into their souls. This cannot be brought about without a sacrament because original sin, from which they are justified, does not come from their own will but through their birth. In the same way, Christ gives them grace through spiritual rebirth. The same reason holds good for the mad or simple that have never had the use of their free will.[3]

In considering faith in the next Article, Aquinas states that this is the first aspect of the will's God-inspired move towards God: 'The mind must move towards God in order for the ungodly to be justified. The first turning to God is by faith.'[4] Aquinas builds on this at the beginning of the second part of Book Two when considering faith in affirming the role of grace against a Pelagian emphasis on free will in faith: 'Therefore

---

1. *Summa*, 2:1.112.2.
2. *Summa*, 2:1.113.3.
3. *Summa*, 2:1.113.3, Reply to 1.
4. *Summa*, 2:1.113.4.

faith as the assent that is the main act of faith is from God moving a person inwardly by grace.'[1] There is an indication in the first section of a continual turning of a person to God beyond justification, raising the issue of whether justification is finished or ongoing. The answer of Aquinas is ultimately both, but the first response focuses on the complete work at the initial infusion of grace.

> The complete justification of the ungodly originates in the infusion of grace, since it is by grace that the free will is moved and sin is remitted. This infusion of grace takes place in an instant and without succession because, if a form is not immediately impressed on its subject, it is either because that subject does not will it or because the agent needs time to prepare the subject. . . . We noted that God does not need preparation to infuse grace into the soul, except his own preparatory grace. Sometimes God prepares a person for the reception of grace suddenly, sometimes gradually and successively. . . . Since the divine power is infinite, it can suddenly prepare anything for its intended form; this is particularly the case with human free will, whose movement is instant in its nature. Therefore, God's justification of the ungodly takes place in an instant.[2]

The final element in this treatment on grace concerns its relation to the merit of human works and their place in the matrix of the Christian experience. Given that this is the last Question in a treatise on grace, it is unsurprising that merit is firmly placed under the role of grace for people who have a sinful nature.

> Because sin is an offence against God that excludes us from eternal life, as we have seen before, no one who lives in the state of mortal sin can merit eternal life unless they are first reconciled to God through their sins being forgiven, which is achieved by grace.[3]

It is hard to conceive of a higher view of grace than that found in these questions that set the foundation for the rest of the discussion of God, sin and grace in relation to the human life. Following this section of the *Summa*, Aquinas discusses the list of sins (found in the appendix to the previous chapter) before returning to grace in looking at the charismata.

---

1. *Summa*, 2:2.6.1.
2. *Summa*, 2:1.113.7.
3. *Summa*, 2:1.114.2.

Gifts of Grace

This section follows work on the habits and virtues that are inherent
to people affected by sin and grace. The charismata are distinct because
they are not habits but are particular gifts given by God for a specific
time and purpose. There are five gifts discussed in this treatise, beginning
with a series of questions on prophecy and followed by rapture (as in
a heightened spiritual experience, rather than an end-times rapture),
speaking in tongues, particular words and finally miracles.

The precise language of grace does not appear frequently in this
treatise on the gratuitous graces, rather the concept is implied in the
fact that the gifts are above human nature and are thus the work of
God.

> The prophetic light is not in the mind of the prophet as an
> abiding form or the prophet would always be able to prophesy,
> which is clearly wrong. . . . A person's intellectual light exists in
> them as an abiding and complete form, aiding the intellect mainly
> by helping it to know the principle of things seen by that light.
> Therefore the light of the active intellect helps a person to know
> the principles of things that are known naturally. God himself
> is the principle of things related to supernatural knowledge, and
> these are manifested by prophecy. The prophets do not see God in
> his essence, although he is seen by the saints in heaven who have
> the light of supernatural knowledge as an abiding and complete
> form.[1]

The section on speaking in tongues is particularly interesting given
the modern Pentecostal and charismatic interest in this area.

> Christ's first disciples were chosen to make disciples throughout
> the whole world and to preach the faith everywhere . . . it was not
> right that those who were sent to teach others should need others
> to teach them, either how to speak to other people or how to
> understand people who spoke to them . . . In addition, those sent
> were poor and powerless and nor could initially have easily found
> someone who could interpret their words faithfully to others or
> explain what others said to them, particularly as they were being
> sent to unbelievers. Therefore, it was necessary for their task that
> God provide them with the gift of speaking in tongues so that,
> as the languages of the nations were separated when they fell

---

1. *Summa*, 2:2.171.2.

into idolatry, as we learn in Genesis 11, so when the nations were called back to the worship of the one God the gift of tongues provides a remedy to this separation.[1]

The gift of words builds on this idea of grace enabling communication beyond that which would be possible naturally.

Because the Holy Spirit does not fail in anything that would be of profit to the Church, the Spirit provides members of the Church with speech so that a person does not only speak to be understood by different people, which is the gift of tongues, but also with particular effect, which relates to the grace of the 'word'. This happens in three ways. Firstly, to teach the intellect, which is the case when a person speaks 'to teach'. Secondly, to move the affections so that people willingly listen to the word of God. This is the case when someone speaks 'to please' his listeners, not in order to gain favour but to encourage them to listen to God's word. Thirdly so that people love that which is taught by the word and want to obey it, and this is the case when someone speaks in order 'to sway' people.[2]

These two elements of language, the gift of tongues and the grace of the word, allow the Church to communicate the Gospel to people clearly in order that they might understand the message. Then, however, the gift of miracles is given in addition in order that the power of the Gospel is shown in support of the teaching.

The knowledge that the Church receives from God needs to be given to others for their benefit, which is done through the gift of tongues and the grace of the word. In addition, the spoken word needs to be confirmed in order for it to be credible. This is done by the working of miracles . . . and reasonably so. It is natural for people to accept intelligible truth because of its effects in life. So as people are led by natural reason to attain a knowledge of God through the natural effects from his creation, in the same way people gain supernatural knowledge of the faith through supernatural works that are called miracles. Therefore, the working of miracles is a gratuitous grace.[3]

It may seem slightly strange to some readers that a Scholastic philosopher-theologian like Aquinas would spend this time working with the charismata, but it emphasises again that his greatest source

---

1. *Summa*, 2:2.176.1.
2. *Summa*, 2:2.177.1.
3. *Summa*, 2:2.178.1.

remains Scripture and the tradition of the Church and that philosophy is intended to act as a tool to aid understanding rather than a rule by which the theology is judged.

Grace and Christ

As an example of how broadly the concept of grace is used in the *Summa*, we need to include this short section not on grace as a result of Christ's work but as a factor in Christ's own identity as the Incarnation is explored at the beginning of Book Three. In the second Article that discusses the mode of the union, Aquinas states that this is by grace.

> Grace can be understood in two ways: firstly, as the will of God gratuitously granting something; and, secondly, as the free gift of God. Human nature needs the gratuitous will of God in order that it might be lifted up to God because this is above its natural capability. In addition, human nature is lifted up to God in two ways: firstly, through activity as the saints know and love God; and, secondly, by personal being, and this way belongs exclusively to Christ who has assumed human nature so that he might be in his person the Son of God. . . . We must say that if grace is understood as the will of God gratuitously doing something or reckoning something as pleasing or acceptable to him, the union in the Incarnation was by grace, just as the union of the saints with God is through knowledge and love. But, if grace is understood as the free gift of God, then the uniting of human nature to the divine person may be called a grace because it occurred without any preceding merits, but not as the result of a habitual grace that was the cause of the union.[1]

While this habitual grace or grace in nature was not the cause of the union, Aquinas does show that it was a result of the union.

> It is right to state that there was habitual grace in Christ for three reasons. Firstly, because of the union of his soul with the Word of God. The nearer any recipient is to the cause working on it, the more it receives from that influence. It is God who pours out grace . . . and therefore it was right that Christ's soul should receive the inpouring of divine grace. Secondly, because of the dignity of this soul, which was to draw close to God by knowledge and love, a place to which human nature must be raised by grace. Thirdly,

---

1. *Summa*, 3.2.10.

because of the relation of Christ to the human race since Christ, as a human, is the 'mediator between God and humankind', as is written in 1 Timothy 2:5, and therefore it was right for Christ to have grace which would then overflow onto others.[1]

This grace that is a part of Christ's incarnate nature is then developed in the following Question that looks at the grace of Christ as the head of the Church.

The soul of Christ received grace in the highest form; therefore, from this pre-eminent grace that He received, this grace is then bestowed on others, which belongs to the nature of the head. In this way, the personal grace by which the soul of Christ is justified is essentially the same as the grace by which He is the head of the Church and justifies others.[2]

Later in the treatise on the Incarnation, Aquinas considers the relationship of Christ to original sin, a stage of which discussion we have already looked at in the sanctification of Mary immediately following her conception. For Christ there is no need for this because the grace of sanctification is part of the union of human and divine.

The abundance of grace that sanctifies Christ's soul flows from the very union with the Word . . . in the first instant of conception, Christ's body was both animated and assumed by the Word of God. Therefore, in that first instant of his conception, Christ had fullness of grace sanctifying both body and soul.[3]

This grace of the union is later applied to the two natures of Christ after his death, and presumably (though not stated here) after the ascension of Christ.

What God's grace gives is never withdrawn unless there is some fault. . . . The grace of union in which the Godhead was united to human nature in Christ's person is greater than the grace of adoption, by which people are sanctified. In addition, it is more naturally enduring because this grace effects a personal union, whereas the grace of adoption refers to a certain affective [*i.e.* relational rather than ontological] union. Yet we know that the grace of adoption is never lost unless there is some fault. Therefore, because there was no sin in Christ, it was impossible

1. *Summa*, 3.7.1.
2. *Summa*, 3.8.5.
3. *Summa*, 3.34.1.

that the union of the Godhead with human nature could be dissolved. Consequently, just as Christ's human nature was united personally and hypostatically with the Word of God before his death, it remained united after his death so that the hypostasis of the Word of God was not different from that of Christ's human nature even after death.[1]

Finally, and leading into the last section of this chapter that looks at the sacraments, the treatise on the Incarnation includes material on Christ's baptism by John and the nature of that baptism, which is seen as part of John's whole preparatory ministry.

> The whole teaching and work of John was a preparation for Christ, just as work of the servant and the under-craftsman prepare something for the form that is given by the master-craftsman. Grace would be conferred on humankind through Christ, according to John 1:17: 'Grace and truth came through Jesus Christ.' Therefore, John's baptism did not confer grace, but only prepared the way for grace and it did this in three ways: firstly, through John's teaching, which led people to faith in Christ; secondly, by prefiguring for people the rite of Christ's baptism; and, thirdly, through Penance, preparing people to receive the effect of Christ's baptism.[2]

These passages reinforce Aquinas' whole method, which is to ground human experience in the nature of God, creation and redemption so that the effects that we perceive in ourselves as we experience sin and grace are understood under this greater framework.

Grace and Sacraments

The *Summa* finishes with Aquinas' treatment of the sacraments still incomplete, with the sacrament of Penance begun but not finished while Extreme Unction, Holy Orders and Matrimony are not considered. After Aquinas' death, therefore, his writings in these areas were collected into the first part of a substantial Supplement, which finishes with his teaching on matters relating to eschatology. The sacraments were the prime means of receiving grace for Christians in the Medieval Church and a study is thus vital for this chapter, although the primacy of grace is not always apparent to the reader because Aquinas spends large amounts

---

1. *Summa*, 3.50.2.
2. *Summa*, 3.38.3.

of time considering aspects of the rituals and often far less time on the effects of the sacraments. Initially, Aquinas highlights three elements of a sacrament.

> A sacrament is something ordained by God that signifies our sanctification, in which three aspects may be considered: the cause of our sanctification, which is Christ's death; the form of our sanctification, which is by grace and the virtues; and the final end of our sanctification, which is eternal life. All these are signified by the sacraments, which are signs that are a reminder of the past, of the death of Christ; indications of the effects of Christ's death in us, which is grace; and look forward as they foretell of future glory.[1]

Aquinas goes on to show a belief that sacraments are not merely signs of grace, but instruments of God that cause grace in the believer.

> We have to say that in some way the sacraments of the new law cause grace, since it is clear that people are incorporated into Christ through the sacraments of the new law . . . and people are made members of the body of Christ through grace alone. However, some say that they do not cause grace by their own work, but only insofar as God causes grace in the soul when people partake of the sacraments. . . . But if we examine the question properly, we will see that this view would see the sacraments as merely signs. . . . Therefore, according to this opinion the sacraments of the new law would only be signs of grace, whereas the authority of many saints shows that the sacraments of the new law not only signify but also cause grace.
>
> We would therefore say that the efficient cause is twofold, principal and instrumental. The principal cause works from the power of its form, and the effect is a likeness of this form . . . In this way, only God can cause grace because grace is only a participating likeness of the divine nature . . . But the instrumental cause does not work by the power of the form, but only by the motion caused by the principal agent. In this, the effect is not simply the result of the instrument, but is attributed to the principal agent . . . it is in this way that the sacraments of the new law cause grace because they were instituted by God to be used in order to confer grace.[2]

Aquinas returns to this theme of principal agent (God) and instrumental agent (sacrament) a couple of times to help his readers understand that the sacraments do not have any inherent power except

1. *Summa*, 3.60.3.
2. *Summa*, 3.62.1.

that which God chooses to give them: 'If we believe that a sacrament is an instrumental cause of grace, we must allow that the sacraments have certain instrumental power bringing about the effects of the sacrament.'[1] However, this instrumental power only exists when it is 'moved by the principal agent, which works on its own'.[2] An additional instrument is brought into the sacramental system in the form of the minister, who again plays a part in the receipt of grace that remains primarily the gift of God to the believer.

> The inner sacramental effect can be the work of a person insofar as they work as a minister. A minister has the nature of an instrument because the action of both [minister and sacrament] concerns something external, while the inner effect is the result of the power of God, the principal agent.[3]

This distinction is vitally important in seeking to prevent the sacraments from taking on a magical quality as if they had a power in and of themselves. The results of Aquinas' teaching are seen a few questions further on in his consideration of the case of someone who wishes to receive Baptism but is prevented by circumstances from doing this – is the grace withheld because they do not come into contact with the instruments of grace? Not according to Aquinas.

> A person may not receive the sacrament of Baptism but yet desire it. For example, a person may wish to be baptised, but through some misfortune they are prevented from receiving Baptism by death. Such a person can obtain salvation without actually being baptised through their desire for Baptism, which is the result of 'faith working through love', in which God, whose power is not limited to the visible sacraments, sanctifies a person inwardly.[4]

The concept of intention is picked up later in this question, again warning against considering the sacraments as means of grace apart from a right relationship between the believer and God. In discussing Baptism, Aquinas states that 'it is necessary for the recipient to have the will or the intention of receiving the sacrament' in order for the grace to be received.[5] In fact, if a person receives Baptism without a right intention, according to Aquinas, they should then be rebaptised:

1. *Summa*, 3.62.4.
2. Ibid.
3. *Summa*, 3.64.1.
4. *Summa*, 3.68.2.
5. *Summa*, 3.68.7.

If an adult lacks an intention to receive the sacrament, they must be rebaptised. However, if there is any doubt, then the words used should be: 'If you are not baptised, I baptise you.'[1]

The following Article moves from the role of intention to that of faith in Baptism, with Aquinas interestingly showing why right faith both is and is not necessary to receiving grace in his view. The first, on why faith is necessary, is fairly simple to understand.

Firstly, right faith is necessary for Baptism as something without which grace, which is the ultimate effect of the sacrament, cannot be received because, as is shown in Romans 3:22, justification by God is by faith in Jesus Christ.[2]

However, given that the grace of salvation that effects a change in a person's nature and character is the free gift of God rather than something earned, Aquinas argues that in this sense faith is not necessary.

Secondly, something is necessary for Baptism because without it a person cannot receive the character resulting from Baptism. In this way, right faith is not necessary in the person who is baptised any more than it is in the person who baptises, so long as the other essential conditions of the sacrament are met. This is because the sacrament is not made effective by the righteousness of the minister or the person being baptised, but by the power of God.[3]

In the Question dealing with the effects of Baptism, Aquinas mentions the work of grace in a number of the Articles:

It is clear that in Baptism a person dies to the old life of sin and begins to live in the new life of grace. . . . The fullness of grace and the virtues flows from Christ the head to all members of his body. . . . Therefore, it is clear that a person receives grace and virtues in Baptism. . . . Those who are baptised are enlightened by Christ with the knowledge of truth, and are made fruitful by him with the fruitfulness of good works that come from the infusion of grace.[4]

---

1. *Summa*, 3.68.7, Reply to 2. This is important, given the Reformation discussion about rebaptism and the group known as the Anabaptists (which literally means, 'rebaptism'), which the Catholic and major Protestant reformers all taught against.
2. *Summa*, 3.68.8.
3. Ibid.
4. *Summa*, 3.69.1, 4, 5.

Grace is more explicitly and extensively related to the sacrament of
Baptism than to the other sacraments. Here it should be recognised that,
when Aquinas writes about the action of God in and through the other
sacraments, he is writing about the work of the Holy Spirit and therefore
about grace, often without directly mentioning either. Before looking
at the remaining six sacraments of the Catholic Church, Aquinas does
compare the grace received in Baptism to that received in circumcision
before the advent of Christ, acknowledging parallels but deeming the
earlier sacrament more limited in its effects.

> We have to say that grace was given in circumcision in all of its effects,
> but not in the same way as in Baptism because the grace of Baptism
> is given by the power of Baptism itself, which power is given to
> Baptism as the instrument of Christ's death that has already occurred.
> However, circumcision gave grace as a sign of faith in Christ's future
> death. Therefore, a person who was circumcised professed that
> they had that faith whether as an adult they made a profession for
> themselves or, being a child, someone else made that profession for
> them.... Since Baptism receives its instrumental power from Christ's
> death, whereas circumcision did not, Baptism therefore imprints a
> character that binds a person into Christ and grants a greater gift
> of grace than circumcision because the effect of something already
> present is greater than the hope of something yet to come.[1]

The next sacrament that Aquinas deals with is the second of the
'sacraments of initiation', which is Confirmation. We see in the brief
reference to grace here the move from saving grace to sanctifying grace,
which is the grace that is at work in the remaining sacraments (Penance
and Extreme Unction have elements of saving grace when dealing with
the effects on mortal sins). Confirmation is linked to the experience of
the Apostles at Pentecost, and thus the grace could be seen as charismatic
rather than sanctifying, but Aquinas does not make this distinction.

> In this sacrament, the Holy Spirit is given to those who have been
> baptised to strengthen them, just as the Spirit was given to the
> apostles on the day of Pentecost, as we read in Acts 2, and as the
> Spirit was given to those who had been baptised by the laying on of
> the apostles' hands, as we read in Acts 8:17. Now we have seen above
> that the Holy Spirit is only sent or given with sanctifying grace, and
> therefore it is clear that sanctifying grace is given in this sacrament.[2]

1. *Summa*, 3.70.4.
2. *Summa*, 3.72.7.

The third of the Sacraments of Initiation is the Eucharist, in which one can detect many aspects of grace behind the ideas of transubstantiation in the work of God on the elements without explicit references. It is in the consideration of the effects of the sacrament, again, where the relevant grace is most clearly discussed.

> The effect of this sacrament should first be considered from what is contained in this sacrament, which is Christ. Through Christ's coming into the world, he visibly bestowed the life of grace on the world . . . in the same way as he comes sacramentally into a person and is the cause of a life of grace . . . since Christ and his death are the cause of grace, and because spiritual refreshment and love are the result of grace, it is clear that that this sacrament grants grace.[1]

Penance takes up a good amount of space both at the end of Book Three of the *Summa* and at the beginning of the Supplement, given that it is dealt with in relation to both venial and mortal sins and is then discussed in related issues of contrition, confession, satisfaction, the power of the keys, excommunication and indulgences.[2] One of the most useful quotes in relation to Aquinas' understanding of Penance comes in a Reply in the Supplement.

> The infusion of grace is sufficient for the remission of sin, but a sinner still owes a debt of temporal punishment after the sins have been forgiven. In addition, the sacraments of grace are ordained so that people can receive an infusion of grace; before a person receives them, either actually or intending to do so, they do not receive grace. This is clear in Baptism and the same applies to Penance. A penitent person expiates their temporal punishment as they experience the shame of confession, as they submit to the power of the keys and as the priest oversees the accompanying satisfaction based on the kinds of sins he knows through the confession.[3]

Aquinas states that Penance is an important part of forgiveness in the change of a person's will back to God since one cannot remain opposed to God when there is forgiveness.

---

1. *Summa*, 3.79.1.
2. The power of the keys is the concept that the Church, in being granted through the apostles the capacity to retain or loose sins (John 20:23), holds metaphorical keys that can open the gates to heaven and hell through the granting (or not) of grace.
3. *Summa*, Supplement.6.1, Reply to 1.

It is impossible for an actual mortal sin to be pardoned without Penance, when Penance is spoken of as a virtue. Because sin is an offence against God, it is pardoned in the same way that an offence committed against God is pardoned. Since an offence is directly opposed to grace, when a person is said to be offended by another they are excluded from their rival's grace. As stated above, the difference between the grace of God and the grace of humans is that the latter does not cause goodness, but rather presumes real or apparent goodness in the one graced; whereas the grace of God actually causes goodness in the one graced because the good will of God (which is contained in the word 'grace') is the cause of all goodness in creation. . . . Therefore, for God to pardon an offence against himself, it is necessary for a person's will to be changed so that it turns to God and for that person to reject whatever else they have sought.[1]

However, Aquinas is quick to point out that God's grace is not limited by the decision of a person to undergo Penance, highlighting the example of the adulterous woman:

The sacrament of Penance is made perfect by the priestly office of binding and loosing; yet God can forgive sins without this, just as Christ pardoned the adulterous woman as we read in John 8.[2]

Aquinas moves on to look at whether one can be penitent for one sin and not for another, an idea that he does not agree with.

Penance cannot remove one sin without another. Firstly, this is because sin is overcome by grace removing the offense against God. . . . Since every mortal sin is opposed to and excludes grace, it must be impossible for one sin to be pardoned without another. Secondly, a mortal sin cannot be forgiven without real Penance, which involves renouncing sin because it is against God (this is common to all mortal sins). . . . A person cannot be truly penitent if they repent of one sin but not another. If one particular sin were displeasing because it was against the love of God above everything else (which is the necessary cause of true repentance), it follows that they would repent of all their sins. . . . Thirdly, this idea would go against the perfection of God's mercy. However, because God's works are perfect, whoever is pardoned by God is completely pardoned.[3]

---

1. *Summa*, 3.86.2.
2. Ibid.
3. *Summa*, 3.86.3.

It is difficult to choose sections to highlight from the extensive material on Penance as a sacrament, but given its importance at the root of the Reformation, it seems worthwhile to deal with indulgences as they were understood by Aquinas. It is clear that, even by Aquinas' time, there was some dispute about the nature, purpose and effect of indulgences and Aquinas seeks to clarify the teaching of the Church in light of all the preceding work on sin and grace. Be warned, it is quite a lengthy summary of the different positions and of Aquinas' own conclusions.

> There are many opinions on this point. Some people hold that indulgences do not have the power that is imputed to them, but that they only help each individual in proportion to their faith and devotion. Those who would say this therefore state that the Church publishes indulgences as a kind of holy deception to encourage people to do what they ought, in the same way that a mother encourages her child to walk by holding out an apple. However, this seems to be a very dangerous claim. . . . If any error were found in the preaching of the Church, her doctrines would have no authority for deciding on questions of faith.
>
> Therefore, others believe that indulgences do aid as the Church claims, to the extent of a just estimate; this is not decided by the one granting the indulgence (who may grant it too high a value) nor by the recipient (who may consider too highly the gift received), but a just estimate according to good people who bear in mind both the condition of the person who is affected and the use and needs of the Church, because the Church's needs are greater at one time than at another. However, it does not seem possible that this opinion is right. Firstly because, in this case, indulgences are not a remission of sins but merely put off the penalty. Secondly, the Church's preaching is not excused from untruths because sometimes indulgences are granted far above the requirements of such a just estimate that considers all the conditions mentioned. An example of this would be when the Pope granted an indulgence of seven years to anyone who visited a certain church; this was granted by Blessed Gregory for the Roman Stations.
>
> Others then say that the amount of remission given by an indulgence cannot be measured by the devotion of the recipient, as the first opinion taught, nor by the quantity of what is given, as the second opinion indicated. Rather, it is according to the cause for which the indulgence is granted, and from this a person is deemed

to be worthy of receiving this indulgence. In this, the extent to which a person was close to that cause would determine whether they obtain a partial or complete remission of sins. Yet this also does not explain the custom of the Church, since at times a greater or lesser indulgence is granted for the same cause. So, in the same circumstances, those who visit a church are sometimes granted a year's indulgence and sometimes only forty days, according to the graciousness of the Pope granting the indulgence.

Therefore, we must say that the amount of remission granted by an indulgence is not measured by the cause that makes the person worthy, but that the amount of effect is in proportion to the magnitude of the cause. The cause of the remission of punishment that results from indulgences is only the abundance of the Church's merits, which is sufficient for the remission of all punishment. The effective cause of remission is not the devotion, work or gift of the recipient; nor is it the cause that the indulgence was granted for. We cannot work out the quantity of remission by any of these, but only by the merits of the Church, which are always superabundant. Therefore, a person receives remission as these merits are applied to them. In order for them to be applied, there needs first to be authority to bestow this treasure; secondly, a union between the recipient of the remission and Christ who merited it, which is brought about by love; and thirdly, a reason for giving out of this treasury so that the intention of those who undertook these deserving works is safeguarded, because they were done for the honour of God and the good of the Church in general. Therefore, when the given cause is for the good of the Church and the honour of God, there is sufficient reason to grant an indulgence. For this reason, others believe that indulgences do have precisely the power claimed for them, so long as the person who grants them has the authority, the recipient has love, and that there is piety in the cause that includes the honour of God and the profit of our neighbours.[1]

We will bring this section to a close with a brief quotation on each of the remaining three sacraments, beginning with Extreme Unction (or Anointing the Sick), which for Aquinas was far more about healing spiritual sickness than physical sickness.

> Each of the sacraments was instituted for one main effect, although it may have other effects that result.... This sacrament is conferred as a kind of medicine (just as Baptism is conferred as a kind of

---

1. *Summa*, Supplement.25.2.

washing), and the purpose of a medicine is to remove sickness. Therefore, the main purpose of the institution of this sacrament is to cure the sickness of sin. In the same way that Baptism involves a spiritual regeneration and Penance a spiritual resurrection, so Extreme Unction is a spiritual healing or cure. In the same way that a bodily cure presupposes bodily life in the patient, so a spiritual cure presupposes spiritual life. Therefore, this sacrament is not an antidote to any defects that might deprive a person of spiritual life, in other words original or mortal sin, but is a remedy for any defects that weaken a person spiritually and deprive them of perfect strength to carry out the deeds associated with a life of grace or glory. These defects only consist of a weakness and unfitness in us that is the result of actual or original sin. This sacrament strengthens a person against these weaknesses. Since this strength is given by grace, which is incompatible with sin, it follows that one result is that any sin, either mortal or venial, is removed in terms of the guilt, so long as there is no obstacle in the recipient.[1]

Holy Orders, as with Confirmation, could have come under charismatic grace if Aquinas had created any such distinction, but Orders is included as a part of sanctifying grace.

The works of God are perfect, and therefore whoever receives power from above also receives that which enables them to exercise that power well. This is the case in nature, where animals are provided with bodies through which their souls are able to achieve their due actions unless there is a defect in their bodies. Now, in the same way that sanctifying grace is necessary for a person to receive the sacraments in a worthy manner, so is it necessary for a person to dispense the sacraments in a worthy manner. Therefore, as in Baptism through which a person is prepared by sanctifying grace to receive the other sacraments, so in the sacrament of Order a person is ordained that they might dispense the other sacraments.[2]

Finally, there is the sacrament of Matrimony, the last of the sacraments to be added and still the cause of some disagreement concerning its nature and relationship to grace.

There have been three opinions on this point. For some said that Matrimony is in no way a cause of grace, but only a sign of grace. However, this cannot be supported because in that case it would

1. *Summa*, Supplement.30.1.
2. *Summa*, Supplement.35.1.

not surpass the sacraments of the Old Law in any way, and then there would be no reason to include it among the sacraments of the New Law . . . Therefore, others held that grace is conferred in Matrimony in a removal of evil, because the act [of sex] is excused from sin, which it would have been outside Matrimony. However, this would be too little effect because this was also the case under the Old Law. As a result, such people argue that it makes a person withdraw from evil by restraining evil desires that lead to something outside the blessings of marriage, but that this grace does not help a person to do good works. However, this cannot be the case because the same grace that removes sin also inclines the will to good, just as the same heat that removes cold also gives heat. Therefore, others believe that Matrimony, because it is contracted in the faith of Christ, does confer the grace that enables us to perform those good works that are required in Matrimony. This is a more probable understanding, because whenever God gives a person the ability to do something, he also gives the assistance that enables them to make a right use of that ability. As a result it is clear that each of the soul's powers have corresponding bodily parts that allow those powers to act. Therefore, because a man in Matrimony receives by divine institution the ability to join with his wife to beget children, he also receives the grace that allows him to do this in a right way.[1]

This may seem a lengthy presentation on sacramental grace, but the scale of editing is shown by the fact that the original presentation of the sacraments takes up over 1,000 pages of the *Summa*, showing the importance of this area for Aquinas' understanding of the nature and reception of grace. Each area has a mass of sub-topics that could be explored, but these generally have little mention of grace and are either matters of form and ritual or areas that result from considerations of the major topic.

Conclusion

What comes through strongly in this presentation of Aquinas' thoughts on grace is his method that starts with the nature of God and creation and delves deep into that understanding since it is there that we find indications of things as they ought to be, including a pure experience of grace. Only once the task of exploring this is complete does Thomas

---

1. *Summa*, Supplement.42.3.

move on to aspects of grace that become necessary because of sin and its effects, which grace saves and restores to some degree through sanctification. One is always aware, however, that this restoration is not complete in this world and that pure grace untainted by sin will only be experienced after the resurrection.

For pointers to the original source and accompanying secondary literature, please see the conclusion to the previous chapter on Aquinas' views of sin.

6.

Thomas Aquinas on Free Will

The previous two chapters have highlighted Aquinas' method in, first, establishing divine/pre-Fall concepts thoroughly before, then, seeking to move on to the effects of sin and grace on the nature and experience of humankind in itself and its relationship with God, angels and each other. This method is in greater evidence in his approach to free will than the other two concepts because it is foundational to the nature of a being – divine, angelic or human – and is worked out in the sins that are committed or helped to resist by the grace that is experienced. The will is therefore not something that is fundamentally in flux but is rather more fixed; this is consistent with the Latin tradition that distinguishes between the will as the core orientation of a person and the realisation of that will in the choice that is made.

In terms of the structure of the *Summa*, almost all of the significant material on free will therefore appears in Book One, which deals with the original nature of God, angels and humankind, and then in the early sections of the first part of Book Two, in which the effects of sin on human nature are discussed. These effects are then worked out in the lengthy treatises on the passions, habits, virtues and vices that cover the manifestation of the will in sins and the restorative effects of the graces of salvation and sanctification, the latter of course being primarily embodied in the sanctifying grace of the sacraments. There is some additional work on the freedom of the will in sections on sin and grace at the end of the first part of Book Two, and then in relationship to Christ and the final condition of humanity after judgement day.

This presentation will largely follow Aquinas' order, certainly in beginning with the nature of God that is the basis for understanding all that is created by God. This includes sections on the providence, predestination and foreknowledge of God that are crucially important for the nature of the will of something created that should always understand its existence as derived from a higher, supreme being, who is sovereign and orders all things according to his will, and whose nature and will are beyond our comprehension. Following this there will be a short look at angelic will before a more lengthy exploration of human will in its original state. In looking at the will after the Fall, as indicated above, the first presentation of the fundamental effects on human nature will take up the bulk of this section before highlighting a few other passages, ending with short sections on the will of Christ and of the redeemed and the damned. Some of this later material has already been engaged with to some extent in the chapters on sin and grace.

Free Will and God

Given the comment above that the Latin understanding of the will is that it is the 'core orientation' of a person, rather than the choices they make, there is an immediate need to establish the nature of will in the divine before one can explore the extent to which such a will might be 'free'. Given that the early Questions of the *Summa* concerning the nature of God include discussions of the simplicity, perfection and immutability of God, it would seem to be difficult to attach a modern notion of free will to such a being.

In this respect, it is significant that Aquinas looks first at the knowledge of God before looking at the will of God, since the universality of the former will necessarily affect the nature and impact of the latter. In discussing the knowledge of God, Aquinas asks whether this knowledge is the cause of things and states that they can be considered the cause by consequence, but not by essence.[1]

> The knowledge of God is the cause of things because this knowledge relates to all creatures in the same way that a craftsman's knowledge relates to the things he makes. The craftsman's knowledge causes the things that he makes because he works using his intellect. . . . When he [Origen] says that the reason God foreknows things is because they are in the future, this must be understood as a cause of consequence, not a cause of essence.[2]

Crucially for what follows, Aquinas then relates the knowledge of God to the being of God in its infinite immensity, meaning that there

---

1. This point was mentioned in chapter four, above, on sin, and Aquinas' position allows God's complete knowledge without making God the cause of sin.

2. *Summa*, 1.14.8, 8, Reply to 1.

is no past, present and future for God as there is for us, and this will be important when Aquinas moves on to questions relating to providence and predestination.

> As was shown above, God knows all things, not only actual things but also whatever is possible for him and for his creatures. Since some of these for us are dependent on the future, it follows that God knows things that are contingent on the future. As evidence of this, we can see that something that is contingent can be considered in two ways. Firstly, it can be considered in itself, insofar as it currently exists, and in this sense it is not considered to be future, but present . . . Secondly, it can be considered in terms of its cause, and in this sense it is considered to be future and as something not yet absolutely determined. This is because a contingent cause relates to opposite things, and thus cannot be the subject of certain knowledge. In this understanding, a person's knowledge only of the cause of something that has not yet come about only conjectures concerning their knowledge of it. God knows all contingent things not only in terms of their causes, but also as they each actually exist. Despite the fact that contingent things become actual in succession, God still knows them as they exist simultaneously, rather than successively as we know them. The reason for this is that his knowledge is measured by eternity, as his being is. Eternity comprises the whole of time being simultaneously complete, as we said above, and therefore everything that exists in time is present to God in this eternity. This is not simply because he has types of things present with him, as some say, but because his gaze from eternity covers all things as they exist in any present form. Therefore it is clear that God infallibly knows future contingent things because they are in the divine sight in a present form; however, they are future contingencies in terms of their own causes.[1]

A few Questions later, Aquinas moves on to the subject of the will of God with this understanding of God's knowledge at its base. Before moving on to the freedom or even movement of the will of God, Aquinas asserts that there is a will in God and seeks to present its nature.

> There is will in God, just as there is intellect, because will results from the intellect. In the same way that the form of natural things gives them their actual existence, so we can understand the

---

1. *Summa*, 1.14.13.

intellect through the form of its communication. . . . Intellectual natures have a natural inclination to their natural good that can be understood from their form of communication. This encourages them to rest in that good when it is achieved, and to seek it when the nature does not have it, both of which pertain to the will. Therefore, there is will in every intellectual being, just as there is an animal appetite in every sensible being. There must be will in God, therefore, because there is intellect in him, and just as his intellect is his existence, so is his will.[1]

This equation of will with intellect and being in God means that the will is immutable, as God is.

The will of God is completely unchangeable. In this regard, we must acknowledge that changing the will is one thing, but it is another thing to will that certain things should be changed. It is possible to will that something be done now and later the opposite thing, and yet the will can forever remain the same. However, there would be a change in the will if one began to will what had not before been willed, or stop willing what had previously been willed. This in the will cannot occur unless there is a change in either the knowledge or the disposition of the willing being's substance.[2]

We saw above that Aquinas held that God's absolute knowledge did not necessarily cause things to occur, in his view, and the same question comes up concerning God's will. If this is unchangeable, then surely everything that God wills must happen or alternatively God's will can be ineffective. Again, Aquinas does not want to allow either position – the first would seem to have God willing evil, the second a weak God – and thus he argues that it can be God's will that some things be contingent on other factors.

God's will imposes a necessity on some things that are willed, but not on all things. Some believe that the reason for this is the creation of intermediate causes, that God creates what is necessary through necessary causes and contingency through contingent causes. This seems to be an insufficient explanation for two reasons. Firstly, because the effect of a necessary cause would become contingent due to the secondary cause, since its effect would be limited by the deficiency in the contingent cause, just as the power of the sun can

---

1. *Summa*, 1.19.1.
2. *Summa*, 1.19.7.

be ineffective because of a defect in a plant. However, no defect
in a secondary cause could prevent God's will from producing
the desired effect. Secondly, because, if the distinction between
necessary and contingent only relates to secondary causes, the
separation must occur independently of the divine intention and
will, which cannot be accepted. Therefore, it is better to say that
this happens from the power of the divine will. . . . Since the divine
will is perfect in power, it not only follows that things are done
that God wills, but also that things are done in the way that God
wills. God wills that some things are done necessarily and some
contingently, all to create a right order and to build up the universe.
Therefore, for some things God has created necessary causes that
cannot fail, but to other things he gives defective and contingent
causes that lead to contingent effects. Therefore, it is not because
the immediate causes are contingent that the results that God
willed happen contingently, but because God prepared contingent
causes for them since it was his will that they happen contingently.[1]

In this way, Aquinas seeks to argue that God's unchanging will
includes provision for the exercise of free will in his creation, but what
freedom is left for God's will?

We have free will in those areas where we do not will from
necessity or from natural instinct. The will to be blessed does not
concern free will, but natural instinct. So other animals whose
natural instinct stimulates action are not said to be moved by free
will. God necessarily wills his own goodness, but does not will
other things necessarily, as shown above, and he therefore has free
will in those things that he does not necessarily will.[2]

Having analysed the will of God, Aquinas does not move on
immediately to topics that flow naturally from this discussion –
providence, predestination, the Book of Life – but first deals with
Questions on the love of God and on the justice and mercy of God
because these are more fundamental to our understanding of God.
Following this, Aquinas takes up the issue of providence and the fact
that everything must come under the order of God.

We must say that everything is subject to divine providence,
not only in general but also in each individual case. This is clear
because every agent works for a purpose, and the ordering of

1. *Summa*, 1.19.8.
2. *Summa*, 1.19.10.

actions towards that purpose is effective to the extent that the
causality of the first agent reaches. . . . The causality of God, the
first agent, extends to everything that exists, not only in terms of the
basic principles that comprise species, but also to those principles
that form individuals; not only for incorruptible things, but also
corruptible things. . . . Therefore, because the providence of God
is nothing less than the archetypal ordering of things towards an
end, as said above, it follows that everything, to the extent that it
participates in existence, must to that degree be subject to divine
providence. We have also shown that God knows everything,
both the universal and the particular. Since his knowledge can be
compared to things in themselves . . . everything must necessarily
be ordered by him.[1]

In the next Article, Aquinas notes that, while the order of every single
thing in creation is directed by God, the working out of that order – what
he terms 'government' – is carried out through intermediaries including
humans.

Providence comprises two things: the type of order of things that
is directed in advance towards an end; and the working out of
this order, which is called government. In the first of these, God
has immediate providence over everything because the type of
everything, even the smallest thing, is in his intellect and he gives
everything the power to carry out whatever particular effects
he assigns to each thing. Therefore he must have the type of all
those effects always present in his mind. For the second aspect of
providence, God works through certain intermediaries, governing
inferior things by things that are superior, not because of any
defect in his power but because of the abundance of his goodness,
which means that even creatures are given the dignity of causality.[2]

The result of this employment of intermediaries in God's providence
is that the order of everything is not necessarily achieved since there is a
contingency that results from this 'dignity of causality' as finite creatures
do not necessarily cause the best results by their actions.

Divine providence imposes a necessity on some things, but not
on all as was previously believed by some people. Providence
involves ordering things towards an end. The main good for all
things (after divine goodness, which is the ultimate purpose of

1. *Summa*, 1.22.2.
2. *Summa*, 1.22.3.

everything) is the perfection of the universe, which could not exist unless creation contained all grades of being. Divine providence must therefore produce every grade of being. As a result, divine providence prepared necessary causes for some things, so that they happen necessarily, and contingent causes for other things, so that they happen contingently, depending on the nature of their immediate causes.[1]

Aquinas holds to a high view of the providence of God in the ultimate direction of all things, but through the concept of government that involves creation in causation he does not see that God is responsible for evil as part of the working out of His plan for creation. This idea is built on later in Book One as Aquinas returns to providence and the government of God.

We can consider the ordering of divine providence in two ways: generally, as it proceeds from the governing cause of all things; and, in the particular, when it proceeds from a particular cause that carries out the order of divine government. In terms of the first way, nothing can resist the order of divine government as can be proved in two ways: firstly, because the order of divine government is completely directed towards the good and, therefore, everything in its own operation and work only tends towards the good . . . secondly, because, as was said above, every inclination of anything, whether natural or voluntary, is merely the result of an impression from the first mover, as the arrow is directed at a target purely due to the impulse received from the archer. Therefore, every agent, whether natural or free, achieves its divinely appointed end as though of its own accord. It is for this reason that God is said 'to order all things sweetly'.[2]

Aquinas next considers predestination, which he believes is a part of providence. The first Article therefore looks at this relationship.

It is right that God should predestine people because everything is subject to his providence, as was shown above, and providence directs things towards their end, as was also shown. God directs created things towards a twofold end. One of these exceeds all extent and faculty of any created nature, which end is life eternal. This consists in seeing God, which is above the nature of every creature, as shown above. The second end, however, is proportionate to the created nature, and any created being can attain this end according

---

1. *Summa*, 1.22.4.
2. *Summa*, 1.103.8.

to the power of its nature. If something cannot attain something through the power of its nature, it needs another to direct it to this, as an archer directs an arrow towards the target. Properly speaking, a rational creature that is capable of eternal life is led or directed towards this by God. The reason for such direction pre-exists in God, since the type of the order of everything towards an end is in him, and this we showed above to be providence. . . . The type of the aforementioned direction of a rational creature towards an end of life eternal is called predestination, since to destine is to direct or to send. Therefore, it is clear that predestination is a part of providence in terms of its purpose.[1]

We looked at predestination in the previous chapter on grace as part of the activity of God towards humankind. In this context, we focus on how this relates to the free will and activity of God, with the implications for human free will a secondary factor.

Predestination is not something in the predestined, but only in the one who predestines. Predestination is a part of providence, which is not something in that which receives provision . . . The working out of providence, which is called government, is passive in what is governed and active in the one governing. From this it is clear that predestination is a type of ordering in which some persons are directed towards eternal salvation, and this exists in the divine mind. The working out of this order is active in God, but passive in the predestined.[2]

Here we see the will of God free in its action to direct or not direct people towards salvation, while as the subject of predestination the human will is passive in needing to be granted this grace. The later Articles on predestination in the *Summa* were covered in the previous chapter on grace and here we need only repeat a short, most explicit comment on the relationship between predestination and will.

There can be no distinction between what results from free will and what from predestination, since there can be no distinction between what results from a secondary cause and what from a first cause. The providence of God produces effects through secondary causes, as was shown above, and so that which results from free will is also from predestination.[3]

---

1. *Summa*, 1.23.1.
2. *Summa*, 1.23.2.
3. *Summa*, 1.23.5.

What comes through again here is the paramount importance of the will, direction and action of God far above the temporary, created will of humankind. The will of God, linked into his infinite nature, is thus the supreme factor in all that occurs in creation, although, because it is worked out in and through created beings, it does contain contingencies that allow evil to occur and the effects of this evil to affect creation. There is an element of freedom to God's will, but it is not a free will as we would naturally use the term and this will then affect the nature of the free will of created beings.

Angels and Free Will

As with sin, when considering the will and its freedom, Aquinas chooses to look at God, then angels, and only then humankind since this is the order of being. That angels have a will is necessarily admitted because Aquinas holds that there is a link between intellect and will, as shown above in the section on God. If there is a will in the angels, is it free? The initial response is clear in the 'On the contrary' section of the relevant Article:

> Free will is part of the dignity of humankind, but the dignity of angels is far greater than that of humans. Therefore, since humans have free will, it is highly reasonable to say that angels have free will.[1]

This is then expanded on in the main response.

> There are some things that do not act based on any previous judgement, but seem to be moved and made to act by others, as an archer aims an arrow at the target. Others such as irrational animals act with some kind of judgement, but not from a free will. For example, a sheep flees from a wolf due to a judgement that seeks to avoid hurt to itself. This kind of judgement is not free, but rather one implanted in their nature. Only a being that has an intellect can act through a free judgement insofar as this comprehends the notion of goodness, from which the intellect can assess whether one or another thing is good. Therefore, whatever has an intellect has free will. It is therefore clear that, because the angels have intellect, so also they have free will, and this to a greater level of perfection than it is in humans.[2]

1. *Summa*, 1.59.3. On the contrary.
2. *Summa*, 1.59.3.

This is one of the Articles in which Aquinas disagrees to some extent with Aristotle, who is usually an authority for him in understanding nature and being. However, Aristotle had taught that the act of a free will is choice, which does not seem to be present in angels. Aquinas allows Aristotle's definition to apply to humankind but redefines choice in relation to angels: 'There is choice in the angels, but this does not involve a considered inquiry of options, but rather an immediate acceptance of the truth.'[1]

The one exception to this teaching is the moment after creation, highlighted in the chapter above on sin, in which there is the single choice to follow the natural good, which the devil refused:

> The will of an angel is inflexible after making its first choice, and therefore if the devil had not immediately placed a barrier to the blessed state after the first moment of his existence, when he had a natural movement to the good, he would have been confirmed in goodness.[2]

This is obviously a very brief treatment, but it is important background material on the nature of a created will and the fact that a right will does not need the option to choose evil to have a freedom. This understanding acts as a bridge between the will of God and the will of humankind.

Pre-Fall Human Will

In dealing with the human will, Aquinas looks first at the nature of the will in itself before questioning whether it can be considered free. There is a link in the first Article on the will in that it asks whether the will can desire something necessarily.

> The word 'necessity' can be used in many ways, since whatever must be is necessary. Now in order that a thing must be may be due to an intrinsic principle, either from its matter, so we say that a thing composed of different parts is necessarily corruptible; or from its form, as the three angles of a triangle are necessarily equal to two right angles. These are 'natural' and 'absolutely necessary'. Alternatively, a thing must be because of something outside its nature, either the end or an agent. In terms of the end, it may be necessary if, without it, the end could not to be achieved, or not so well attained. For example, food is necessary for life and a horse

1. *Summa*, 1.59.3. Reply to 1.
2. *Summa*, 1.63.6. Reply to 3.

is necessary for a journey. This is called 'necessity of end', and sometimes also 'utility'. In terms of an agent, something must be when an agent forces someone such that they cannot do anything else. This is called the 'necessity of coercion'. This necessity is completely hateful to the will because this violence goes against something's natural inclination. . . . Just as it is impossible for something to be both violent and natural, so it is impossible for something to be absolutely coerced or violent and at the same time voluntary.[1]

Later in this first Question on the will is a brief and useful summary of the work of the will as Aquinas understands it: 'The will as an agent moves all the soul's powers to carry out their respective work, excepting only the natural powers of our biological self, which are not subject to our will.'[2]

After clarifying that humankind has will, which must be linked to the intellect as we saw with God and the angels, Aquinas then discusses whether this will is free. It is important to note that there is an important change in the Latin here, with the previous Question dealing with '*voluntas*' (will at the core of the person) and this next Question moving onto '*liberum arbitrium*' (literally, 'free choice' or 'free judgement'). We are still not yet at the surface, decision part of humanity but this free judgement has a greater activity than the pure will that was just looked at. The first point that Aquinas makes is that rationality implies a free judgement.

Humans have free judgement as otherwise advice, encouragement, commands, prohibitions, rewards and punishments would be pointless. . . . Humans act on judgements, since they apprehend a situation and then judge whether something should be avoided or sought. Because such a judgement for a particular act is not the result of natural instincts but through reason engaging in an act of comparison, people act through their free judgement and retain the ability to be inclined to different things. The use of reason in such unclear circumstances may lead to different courses of action, as we can see in disputing syllogisms and rhetorical arguments. . . . Therefore, because humans are rational, is it necessary that they have free judgement.[3]

1. *Summa*, 1.82.1.
2. *Summa*, 1.82.4.
3. *Summa*, 1.83.1.

In the next Article, Thomas develops his understanding of where this judgement sits in this middle place between being and action, discussing whether it is a power or a habit.

> Although free judgement strictly denotes an action, we are accustomed to call free judgement the principle of the action through which a person judges freely. This principle of an action in us is both power and habit . . . Therefore, free judgement must be either a power or a habit, or a power with a habit, but it can clearly be proved that it is neither a habit nor a power with a habit . . . The free judgement is indifferent to good and evil choices, and so it is impossible that free judgement is a habit and therefore it is a power.[1]

In the final Article on free judgement, Aquinas shows that he understands this as closely related to the will that he had previously described.

> It is clear that the relationship of the intellect to the reason is mirrored by that of the will to the power of choice ['*electio*', another Latin word for choice], which is free judgement. It has been shown above that same power both understands and reasons, just as the same power can be at rest and be in movement. In this way, the same power both wills and chooses, and thus the will and free judgement are not two powers, but one.[2]

This is the end of the initial presentation of will, with the next Question moving onto the relationship of soul and body in comprehension. For modern discussions on free will, it is noteworthy that Aquinas doesn't engage deeply with the choices that we make, concentrating more on the nature of the self that is realised in those choices.

We saw in the chapter on sin some of the results of this teaching in the initial, pre-Fall state of humankind when in submission to God the will and therefore judgement were completely free and incapable of being deceived. It is interesting that when discussing the will of Adam (Book One, Question 95), the focus is on grace and righteousness rather than freedom.

The last sections that are relevant in the basic nature of the human will and its freedom come in the last treatise of Book One of the *Summa* concerning the government of creatures. In these Questions, Aquinas looks at how the human will is impacted by various external factors:

---

1. *Summa*, 1.83.2.
2. *Summa*, 1.83.4.

God, angels, demons and fate. In considering how God interacts with creatures, Aquinas considers whether this includes moving the will, concluding that God as the creator of the will naturally moves it from first and secondary causes but not through force, given that his work is always towards the intended purpose of the will.

> The will is moved by its purpose, which is good, and by the one who creates the power of willing. Now, while the will can be moved by the good that it is seeking, God alone can move it sufficiently and effectively. . . . While every created good is particular, God alone is the universal good. Therefore, he alone fills the capacity of the will and moves it sufficiently as the object of the will. In the same way, God alone causes the power of willing because willing is nothing but an inclination towards the object of the will, which is universal good. This inclination towards the universal good belongs to the first mover . . . Therefore, in both ways it is right that God moves the will, but especially in the second way through an internal inclination of the will.[1]

God thus moves the will in creating it and as the end that the will should seek. However, does this mean that the will is forced by God? Aquinas thinks not.

> Something is forced to move by another if this goes against its natural inclination, but if the other moves it to the proper and natural inclination, it is not forced. . . . God does not force the will when he moves it because he is giving the will its natural inclination.[2]

For our independent minds, even this level of engagement of God with the will may seem restrictive of human nature, but Aquinas has sought to show that this is the natural result of the Christian doctrine of God and creation. A few Questions later, Aquinas discusses the extent to which angels may be said to move the will.

> The will can be changed in two ways. Firstly, from within, in which the movement of the will is only inclining it to what is willed and, therefore, only God can change the will in this way because he gives the power for such an inclination to the intellectual nature. . . . Secondly, the will is moved from outside and, regarding an angel, this can only be in one way as the intellect is made aware of

---

1. *Summa*, 1.105.4.
2. *Summa*, 1.105.4. Reply to 1.

the good. . . . An angel or a person can move the will by persuasion, as above explained. . . . In this manner the angels, being able to stir human desires, can move the will, but not by necessity because the will always remains free to consent to or to resist a desire.[1]

In dealing with demons and the devil and their effect on the human will, Aquinas first distinguishes between their influence and that of angels, the latter wholly directed to the service of God while the demons work their own separate will.

> We can consider two things in the attack of the demons: the attack itself and the ordering of the attack. The attack itself come from the evil will of the demons, whose envy seeks to prevent human progress and whose pride takes on an aspect of divine power by assigning certain ministers to attack people, just as the angels of God in their various offices minister to people's salvation. However, the ordering of the attack is from God who knows that he can use evil well by directing it to a good end. On the other hand, both the guardianship and ordering of angels are the work of God as first author.[2]

Given this distinction, to what extent are the devil and demons responsible for human sin? Aquinas' answer is that the devil is behind all sin, but humans are primarily responsible for the sins they commit, and may be solely responsible. However, the devil and demons may also play a role.

> One thing can cause another in two ways: directly and indirectly. It is indirect when an agent causes one to be disposed to a certain action, and then it is an occasional and indirect cause of that action. For example, we might say that the person who dries the wood is the cause of the wood burning. In this sense, we say that the devil is the cause of all our sins because he encouraged the first man to sin, from whose sin resulted a tendency to sin in the whole human race. . . . But something is the direct cause of another when its work leads directly to that action. In this sense the devil is not the cause of every sin because all sins are not the result of the devil's encouragement, but some result from free judgement and the corruption of the flesh. As Origen says, even if the devil did not exist, people would still desire food and love and such pleasures and many disorders arise from these unless those desires

---

1. *Summa*, 1.111.2.
2. *Summa*, 1.114.1.

are restrained by reason, especially if we presuppose the corruption of our nature. It is within the power of the free judgement to restrain the appetite and keep it in order. Therefore, there is no need for all sins to be the result of the work of the devil.[1]

The external nature of the influence of angels and demons is emphasised indirectly in the discussion of fate when Aquinas repeats that the only effective influence on the human will comes from God.

Nothing prevents what happens here by accident, luck or chance, because everything results from an ordering cause that comes from the intellect, especially the divine intellect since only God can change the will, as shown above. Therefore, the ordering of human actions, which result from the will, must only be the result of God's work. Therefore, since everything that happens here on earth is subject to divine providence, because it is pre-ordained or foretold, we can admit the existence of fate. However, the holy doctors avoided the use of this word because of those who twisted its application to imply a degree of force in the position of the stars.[2]

This concludes the presentation of Aquinas' thought on the nature and freedom of the will in the created state that is foundational to all that follows. At times, as Aquinas develops this in the context of sin and grace, these original ideas come to the fore, while, at others, they fade somewhat due to the influence of the effects of sin and salvation on humankind.

Post-Fall Human Will

Aquinas returns to the matter of the human will in the first part of Book Two at the beginning of his consideration of human actions (which mainly covers the issues of passions, habits, virtues and vices presented in the chapter on sin). First, however, Aquinas has a basic Question on the voluntary and involuntary in humans, discussing the effects of various factors on the activity of the will, but beginning with a statement that there is a voluntary element in human action.

There must be something voluntary in human actions. In order to make this clear, we state that the principle of some actions or movements is inside the agent, or that which is moved, while

1. *Summa*, 1.114.3.
2. *Summa*, 1.116.1.

the principle of other movements or actions is external . . . But whatever has a knowledge of the result is said to move itself because there is a principle that leads to an action but also a desired result. Therefore, since both these elements are intrinsic, *i.e.* that they act and that they act for a purpose, such movements are said to be voluntary. The word 'voluntary' implies that movements and actions result from a person's inclination. . . . Therefore, since humans especially know the result of their work and move themselves, their actions are found to be voluntary[1].

This intrinsic nature of a voluntary action is highlighted when Thomas discusses violence and the will, holding that whatever is committed due to external force cannot be considered voluntary.

Violence is directly opposed to both what is voluntary and to what is natural. The voluntary and the natural are alike in that both result from an intrinsic principle. Violence, however, is from an extrinsic principle. Just as violence works against nature in beings without knowledge, so violence works against the will in beings endowed with knowledge. Whatever is against nature is called 'unnatural', and similarly whatever is against the will is called 'involuntary'. Therefore, violence causes involuntariness.[2]

This is the first of a series of Articles that seek to explore the extent to which various factors reduce the voluntary character of human actions. The next area to be discussed is fear.

Things that are done through fear 'are of a mixed character', being partly voluntary and partly involuntary. Something that is done through fear is not considered voluntary itself, but it becomes voluntary in this particular case, for instance to avoid the evil that is feared. . . . What is done through fear is voluntary in that it happens here and now, that is to say, in these circumstances it suffices to prevent the greater evil that was feared . . . therefore what is done through fear is essentially voluntary because the principle is within the person. But, if we consider what is done through fear outside this particular case, it is simply a consideration of the mind and such goes against the will. Therefore, what is done through fear is involuntary, considering the general aspect or what is outside the actual circumstances of any case.[3]

1. *Summa*, 2:1.6.1.
2. *Summa*, 2:1.6.5.
3. *Summa*, 2:1.6.6.

After fear Aquinas moves on to concupiscence, a loaded term theologically because of the work of Augustine who focuses on the desire as that for evil, although the Latin term is not necessarily negative. Aquinas at this point in the *Summa* actually grants it a positive aspect: 'Fear looks at evil but concupiscence looks at the good. Evil naturally goes against the will, whereas good harmonises with the will.'[1] Because desire rises within a person, Aquinas does not believe that it leads to involuntary action.

> Concupiscence does not cause involuntariness, but rather makes an action voluntary. Something is said to be voluntary because the will is moved to it, and concupiscence inclines the will to desire the object of concupiscence. Therefore, the effect of concupiscence is to make something voluntary rather than involuntary.[2]

Far more complex is the last of the potentially mitigating factors: ignorance.

> If ignorance causes involuntariness, this is because it deprives a person of the knowledge that is a necessary condition of voluntariness, as was declared above. However, not every ignorance deprives a person of this knowledge and so we note that ignorance has a threefold relationship to actions arising from the will: firstly, alongside the will, concomitantly; secondly, consequently; and thirdly, antecedently. Ignorance works alongside the will when there is ignorance of what is done but, even if a person had the knowledge, they would have done the thing anyway. In this case ignorance does not cause a person to wish to do something, but it just happens that something is done and not known at the same time. . . . Ignorance is consequent to an act of the will when ignorance itself is voluntary, which can happen happens in two ways . . . Firstly, when the will acts to cause the ignorance, such as when a person does not want the knowledge so that they have an excuse for a sin, or so that they are not restrained from sinning . . . and this is called 'affected ignorance'. Secondly, ignorance is said to be voluntary concerning something that one can and ought to know, and in this sense 'not acting' and 'not willing' are voluntary, as stated above. This kind of ignorance happens either, when someone does not actually consider what they can and ought to consider,

---

1. *Summa*, 2:1.6.7. Reply to 1.
2. *Summa*, 2:1.6.7.

which is called 'ignorance of evil choice', and results from a passion or habit; or, when someone does not take the trouble to acquire the knowledge they ought to have, and so ignorance of the general principles of law that a person ought to know is voluntary, resulting from negligence. If ignorance is the result of either of these ways, it is voluntary and cannot simply cause involuntariness. However, it does cause involuntariness in one respect since it precedes the movement of the will towards the action, and the will would not move if the person had knowledge. Ignorance is antecedent to an act of the will when it is not voluntary and yet causes a person to will what they would not otherwise will. In this sense, a person may be ignorant of some circumstance related to their action that they are not bound to know, with the result that they do what they would not have done if they had that knowledge. For example, even if a person took proper precautions before shooting an arrow, they may still not know that someone is coming along the road, and therefore kill that person. Such ignorance simply causes involuntariness.[1]

Again, it is Aquinas' method that comes through notably in this theology since the decision to act cannot be considered except as the manifestation of the knowledge and will (and even the will to have knowledge). The 'free' aspect of the will is shown in these examples to be far more complex than might at first appear. A couple of Questions later, Aquinas looks again at the will and agrees with Aristotle that the natural desire (or 'appetite') is for good, but that voluntary desire is only good insofar as this is perceived in the object rather than the existence behind the perception.

The will is the rational desire. Every desire is only for something good because it is simply the inclination of a person towards something that they want. . . . But we must note that every inclination results from a form, natural desires resulting from a form existing in the nature of things, while the desires of our senses (and intellectual or rational desires), which we call the will, result from the form as it is apprehended. Therefore, just as natural desires are for the good that exists in a thing, so animal or voluntary desires are for a good that is apprehended. Therefore, for the will to desire something, it is necessary that it is apprehended as good, not that it is good in truth.[2]

1. *Summa*, 2:1.6.8.
2. *Summa*, 2:1.8.1.

The Question that follows this returns to the question of what can move the will that was discussed in the Treatise on the government of creation. Here, Aquinas repeats that only God can immediately move the will, with a further Article that denies the possibility of heavenly bodies affecting the will building on the Question looking at fate. Following this, Aquinas considers whether the will is moved of necessity by its desires or by God. Regarding the former, he does allow that sometimes our will can be consumed by circumstances.

> The passion of the desires of our senses moves the will . . . in two ways. Firstly, so that the reason is completely bound and a person does not have the use of their reason. This happens in people who become furious or insane because of a violent excess of anger or concupiscence. . . . Such are like irrational animals, which necessarily follow the impulse of their passions; in them there is no movement of reason, and therefore no movement of will. Sometimes, however, reason is not entirely consumed by a passion and the judgement of reason retains a freedom, to a certain extent, and then the movement of the will remains to that degree. Therefore, the extent to which the reason remains free and is not controlled by the passion, the will's movement that remains does not necessarily move towards the passion's inclination. Consequently, there is either no movement of the will in a person, and only the passion is at work, or there is a movement of the will in which case it does not necessarily follow the passion.[1]

Regarding God moving the will, Aquinas repeats his position that this is sometimes necessary and sometimes contingent, the latter depending on the circumstances and the relationship between these and the will.

> Since the will is an active principle and is not determined to one end, having diverse relations to many things, God moves it so that he does not determine it necessarily to one end; rather the will's movement remains contingent and not determined, except for those things to which it is moved naturally.[2]

The extent of the difficulty in assessing free will is then shown in the next five Questions that discuss elements of the human experience associated with the will: intention, choice, counsel, consent and use. Something of the complexity of these Questions can be seen in that on choice, as an

1. *Summa*, 2:1.10.3.
2. *Summa*, 2:1.10.4.

example, which Aquinas holds is 'materially an act of the will but formally an act of the reason'.[1] Since the will is a product of the reason and the choice stems from this, choice in its substance is an act of the will. This is developed in a later Article that discusses whether choice is necessary.

> People do not choose from necessity because whatever can not be is not necessary. The reason why people can not choose or choose can be seen in a twofold power of people, in which we can will and not will, act and not act. Again, we can will this or that, and do this or that. The reason for this is found in the power of the reason because the will can move towards whatever the reason apprehends as good.[2]

These discussions form the basis for the examinations highlighted in the chapter on sin on good and evil in human actions, both the inner attitudes and thoughts and external acts. The extent of evil in an action is thus not solely based on the nature of the action itself, but is affected by the state of reason, the relevant knowledge and the ability of the will to move itself freely, among other things.

Free Will after Judgement

This short final section of the chapter looks at the concept of free will in those who are redeemed and those who are damned in Aquinas' thought. In terms of the redeemed, we must look at the Article on free will in Christ, since this is linked into the state of free will in the blessed. In the 'Treatise on the Last Things', found in the Supplement, there is no Article dealing with the nature of the will.

In examining the nature of Christ's will, Aquinas states that there is one human will in Christ but that the will in acting can be discerned as both 'nature' and 'reason'; the first is the 'simple will' and concerns those things that were necessary in themselves (like health); the second concerns anything that is desirable for a good end (like medicines).[3] Aquinas builds on this to state that there was free will in Christ.

> Simple will is the same as the 'will as nature', but choice is the same as the 'will as reason', which is the proper act of free will as we saw above. Therefore because 'will as reason' is in Christ, we must also say that Christ had choice and therefore free will, whose act is choice.[4]

1. *Summa*, 2:1.12.1.
2. *Summa*, 2:1.12.6.
3. *Summa*, 3.18.3.
4. *Summa*, 3.18.4.

One of the Objections initially raised in this Question is whether Christ could have free will, given that his will could only be for good things. Aquinas replies:

> The will of Christ, although it is determined to good, is not determined to any particular good. Therefore Christ, as is the case with the blessed, is able to choose with a free will that is confirmed in goodness.[1]

In terms of the damned, the nature of the will that they will have is discussed in the first Article of the Question concerning their will and intellect.

> A twofold will can be considered in the damned: the deliberating will and the natural will. Their natural will is not their own but comes from the author of nature, who gave human nature this inclination that is called the natural will. Therefore, since they retain their human nature, it follows that their natural will can be good. However, their deliberating will is truly their own since it is in their power to be turned by their affections to this or to that. This deliberating will is always evil in them because they are completely turned away from the final end of a right will, and a will cannot be good unless something directs it to that end. Therefore, although they will some good, they do not will it well and one cannot call their will good on that basis.[2]

This is the final, logical end of the corrupted human will that, as we saw in the chapter on grace, needed a work of God to turn it towards a consideration of the good, before further grace was needed to achieve what the awakened will desired. With grace no longer operating, the damned can no longer be raised to consider the good in their deliberations.

Conclusion

Some of the key teaching on the extent of freedom of the human will has already been covered in chapters four and five, above, on sin and grace and their relationship to human nature in its fallen state, and these sections have not been repeated here. Ordering these three chapters in considering Aquinas' thought is particularly difficult because he integrates his thinking and considers concepts at times in their finest

1. *Summa*, 3.18.4. Reply to 3.
2. *Summa*, Supplement.98.1.

nuances, and some of the discussions in this chapter become foundational for material found in the previous two chapters. One feels that to gain an appreciation of Aquinas, one must go in circles of understanding ideas in order to spiral towards a height of appreciation, with each stage needing careful concentration to grasp details that become important as terms and concepts are used in different contexts.

Aquinas' concept of free will and its inter-relationship with sin and grace, and the location of the will in intellect and reason, worked out in judgements, choices, intentions, temptations, thoughts and actions, is very complex and thus is perhaps not as great an issue to other writers. The result is that to answer the question of whether humans have free will in any given context requires pages of consideration, as we see in the Questions that look at particular sins and those examining the receipt of grace. Perhaps more than any other writer, Aquinas therefore calls us to a hesitancy in answering questions about free will without first considering what we mean when we use the term.

As in the previous chapter, the reader is directed to the conclusion of chapter four on Aquinas and sin for links to the *Summa Theologiae* and a couple of useful secondary sources.

7.
Martin Luther

Martin Luther (1483-1546) was perhaps the figure that I approached with most trepidation in this series because of the effects of his life and work and the lack of a single clear source from which to glean his significant theology on sin, grace and free will. The sheer scope of Luther's writings is difficult to conceive; volume 79 of the major American series *Luther's Works* was published in 2016 and this shows the extent of the task of reading – let alone summarising – Luther's thought in any area.

An additional issue that becomes apparent when reading Luther is that the standard dichotomy that places Luther on one side of the initial Reformation debates and the Catholic Church on the other side is severely misguided. For a start, there are two quite separate groups in the then existing scheme of things which Luther targets: the institutional Church and the papacy for abuses such as indulgences and claims to doctrinal authority; and the medieval Scholastic system and the humanism of Desiderius Erasmus (c.1466-1536).

In addition, Luther's Reformation in Wittenberg was taken over while Luther was in hiding in Wartburg Castle by Andreas von Karlstadt, a fellow defendant at the Leipzig Disputation of 1519 who later broke with Luther on issues related to both the Lord's Supper and infant baptism. Karlstadt was ultimately expelled from Saxony in 1524. He is one example of a 'Radical Reformer' who, in Luther's view, went far beyond the goal of reforming the faith. Because of the immediacy of many of these radical reform groups in the German lands, they are as often the subject of Luther's writings as the Catholics, with some works directed specifically at parts of the existing the Catholic Church and others at radical groups such as the Anabaptists (literally, the 'rebaptisers').

Luther thus sits more in a middle position seeking to highlight a right faith for the Church against various forces – ecclesial, philosophical, fanatical – that would seek to distort it for their own ends. Many of

Luther's theological works are therefore a reaction against certain teachings, such as his book *On the Bondage of the Will* written in response to Erasmus' promotion of human free will. There would thus be a great need for wisdom if one wished to build a constructive 'Theology of Martin Luther'. Fortunately for this volume, this is not the task at hand which is rather to present the thought of Luther in relation to sin, grace and free will across his works, not systematic position at the end.

The presentation will look in succession at sin, grace and free will – although there will be an extra section on the sacraments after looking at grace as there are several works in this area and their teaching cuts across both sin and grace. In addition to his works on the sacraments, the other most significant works presenting his teaching on sin, grace and free will are *Explanation of the 95 Theses* that has extensive passages on sin, *Table Talk*, which summarises a series of discussions with various people on several different theological issues, and *On the Bondage of the Will* that is the most thorough examination of the concept of free will in the Lutheran corpus. *On the Freedom of a Christian* and *A Treatise on Good Works* both have some useful material, while there will be some quotations from academic Disputations that Luther either prepared or was involved in.

One of the most interesting passages that defied categorisation in any one section of this chapter comes from *Table Talk* in which Luther reveals his view of the inherent inter-relatedness of our three major themes:

> We conclude in general that a person who is without the Holy Spirit and God's grace can do nothing but sin; in this they simply go on from sin to sin and fall from one sin into another. If a person will not listen to good doctrine, but rather condemns the saving word and resists the Holy Spirit, then they become the enemy of God through the effects and strength of their free will. They blaspheme the Holy Spirit and follow the lusts and desires of their own hearts, as examples throughout history clearly show. But we must carefully consider the words that the Holy Spirit spoke through Moses: 'the very inclination of the thoughts of the human heart was only evil all the time' (Gen. 6:5). We see through the greatest care that what a person can conceive with their thoughts, understanding and free will is evil, and not once or twice, but always evil. Without the Holy Spirit, a person's reason, will and understanding are without the knowledge of God; and to be without the knowledge of God means nothing else than being ungodly, walking in darkness and holding as best that which is actually worst.[1]

---

1. Luther, *Table Talk*, 8.261. References to *Table Talk* are by theme and then by

Perhaps with Luther more than any other writer in this series, it is
important here to go beyond the immediate quotations back to the
specific source because of the different motivation for each source.
These will be indicated as far as possible below. It must always be
borne in mind, however, as each section is read, that the collections of
thought on, for example, original sin are brought together from quite
disparate works and the nuances of each can only be fully appreciated
in their original context. This chapter will thus save the reader from
trawling through all the volumes of Luther's works but, if there
is content of interest, then there is further work to be done to fully
appreciate Luther's ideas.

Sin

Before considering certain aspects of sin, there are a couple of more
general passages that are worth noting. At the beginning of *A Treatise on
Good Works*, Luther makes two points on sin: firstly, that sin is to do that
which God has forbidden; and, secondly, that sins are those works that
do not proceed from faith. Both relate to whether Christians have to or
ought to carry out good works and what this would mean.

> We ought first to know that there are no good works except those
> which God has commanded, even as there is no sin except that
> which God has forbidden. Therefore, whoever wishes to know
> and to do good works needs nothing else than to know God's
> commandments. . . . The first and highest, the most precious of
> all good works is faith in Christ. . . . Now all these works are done
> outside of faith, therefore they are nothing and altogether dead.
> For as their conscience stands towards God and as it believes, so
> also are the works which grow out of it. Now they have no faith,
> no good conscience towards God, therefore the works lack their
> head, and all their life and goodness is nothing. Hence it comes
> that when I exalt faith and reject such works done without faith,
> they accuse me of forbidding good works, when in truth I am
> trying hard to teach real good works of faith.[1]

In a related idea, Luther elsewhere centres the nature of sinful actions
on a rejection of God's word, which is so vital to his ideas on the faith
that motivates the Christian.

---

section, the latter progressing cumulatively through the work.
1. Luther, *On Good Works*, 1.1-2.

We have within us many sins against our Lord God, and which justly displease him, such as anger, impatience, covetousness, greediness, incontinence, hatred, malice *etc*. These are great sins, which everywhere in the world go on with power and get the upper hand. Yet these are nothing in comparison with condemning God's word; indeed, none of these would be committed if we only loved and reverenced the word. But, unfortunately, the whole world is drowned in this sin. No one cares anything for the gospel, but all rage at it and persecute it, believing that this is not a sin. I see with wonder that of those listening in the church, one looks this way and another that; that among so many people, few have come to hear the sermon. This sin is so common that people will not confess that it is like other sins; everyone believes that it is a minor thing to hear a sermon without paying attention, not diligently seeking to understand, learn and inwardly digest it. It is the same with other sins such as murder, adultery, theft *etc*. After these sins, in due time there follows grief, sorrow of heart and remorse. But people are not concerned if they do not hear God's word with care, even condemning and persecuting it.[1]

We will now proceed to look at some themes within the concept of sin, looking at its nature and the relationship with God and the devil, and then at Luther's thought on original sin, all of which form the basis for discussions of grace and free will where some of the effects of sin will be apparent.

The Nature of Sin

The first point to look at is sin's relationship to God and how Luther, as other writers before him, sought to distance God from any connection with the existence of sin. In two works, Luther considers occasions when the Bible seems to consider God as active in evil, for example, when God hardens Pharaoh's heart. In *Table Talk*, this comes from a discussion with Philip Melanchthon (1497-1560), a key figure in Luther's reformation.

Melanchthon asked Luther if this word, hardened, ('hardens whom he will') should be understood directly as it sounded, or in a figurative sense. Luther answered: we must understand it specially and not operatively because God does not work evil. Through his almighty power he works all in all; and as he finds a person, so he works in them even as he did in Pharaoh, who was evil by nature. This was not God's fault, but his own fault. Pharaoh continually went on in his wickedness, doing evil; he was hardened because

---

1. *Table Talk*, 7.247.

God with his Spirit and grace did not prevent his ungodly work, but allowed him to continue and to have his own way. Why God did not prevent or restrain him, we should not inquire.[1]

A similar idea can be found in *On the Bondage of the Will*.

No one should think that when God is said to harden someone or to work evil in us (since hardening is to do evil) he does the evil as though he created a new evil in us . . . When people hear us say that God works both good and evil in us, and that we necessarily submit passively to the work of God, they imagine that a person who is good (or not evil) is passive while God works evil in them. This does not recognise that God is not inactive in any of his creatures, and never allows any of them to have a holiday from him. Whoever wishes to understand these things needs to think in this way: that God works evil in us, meaning by us; not as God's fault, but as the fault of evil in us. That is, since we are evil by nature, God, who is truly good, carries us along by his own action according to the nature of his omnipotence; therefore he cannot do anything but evil through us, his instruments, although he himself is good. However, he overrules that evil well through his wisdom to his own glory and for our salvation.[2]

In *On Good Works*, Luther claims that God does sometime allow a person to sin greatly for his own overall purposes.

God frequently allows a person to fall into or to remain in a serious sin in order that they may be put to shame in their own eyes and in the eyes of all people, because otherwise they would have fallen into the great evil of pride in their own honour and fame if they had remained faithful in using their great gifts and virtues. God must keep them from this sin by allowing other serious sins in order that his name alone is honoured. In this case, one sin becomes a medicine to prevent another because of our corrupting wickedness that not only does evil, but even misuses everything that is good.[3]

In the *Heidelberg Disputation*, Luther used an interesting phrase in thesis four about the work of God: 'Although the works of God are always unattractive and appear evil, they are nevertheless in reality

---

1. Ibid., 2.109.
2. Luther, *On the Bondage of the Will*, 86.
3. *On Good Works*, 2.24.

eternal merits.'[1] The following discussion shows that God highlights sins in order that people find their identity in God rather than their own works.

> The Lord humbles and frightens us through the law and the sight of our sins so that we seem in the eyes of others, and in our own eyes, as nothing, foolish and wicked, which in truth we are. As we acknowledge and confess this, there is no form of beauty in us, but our life is hidden in God, in a simple confidence in his mercy, and we find in ourselves nothing but sin, foolishness, death and hell . . . This depravity, however, comes to exist in us either when God punishes us or when we accuse ourselves . . . In this way, consequently, the unattractive works which God does in us, in those who are humble and devout, are really eternal, for humility and fear of God are our entire worth.[2]

Returning to the work *On the Bondage of the Will*, shortly before the passage quoted above there is material on a similar line that links God and evil to Satan, who will appear in the next set of quotations.

> Since God moves and does all in all, he must move and do all in both Satan and wicked people. But he does this in them as they are and as he finds them; that is, because they are sinful and evil, when they carried along by the work of the divine omnipotence, they can only do what is sinful and evil. . . . Here then you see that, when God works in and by evil people, the evils themselves are worked in them, yet God cannot do evil although he does work evils by evil men . . . The fault, therefore, is in the instruments that God allows not to remain passive, given that the evils are done as God moves people.[3]

There is some extensive discussion of the work of the devil in *Table Talk*. The first passage highlights Luther's belief that the power of the devil is limited for Christians by the ultimate victory of God won by Christ on the cross.

> The devil must be our enemy because we are against him with God's word, with which we destroy his kingdom. He is a prince and god of the world, and has a greater power than all the kings, potentates and princes on earth. Therefore he would have his

---

1. Luther, *Heidelberg Disputation*, 4.
2. Ibid.
3. *On the Bondage of the Will*, 84.

revenge against us, and continually assaults us as we both see and feel. But we have a great advantage against the devil: powerful, wicked and cunning as he is, he cannot hurt us because we have sinned against God, not against him. . . . We know, through God's grace, that we have a gracious God and a merciful Father in heaven; Christ Jesus, our only Lord and Saviour, has appeased the wrath he has against us through his precious blood. Now, since through Christ we have remission of sins and peace with God, the envious devil must be content to leave us alone, in peace, since from this point he can neither condemn us nor hit us in the teeth concerning our sins against God's laws, because Christ has cancelled and torn in pieces the writing of our consciences, which witnessed against us, and nailed these to his cross.[1]

The danger that does still exist is if we meet the devil on his own terms, which we would if we relied on our own merits or works.

Whoever disputes with the devil concerning sin and the law without a word of grace and prayer will lose; therefore, let stop this immediately. The devil is armed against us with Goliath's sword, with his spear and weapons; he has the testimony of our own consciences on his side to help him; this witnesses against us that we have transgressed all of God's commandments. Therefore, the devil can have a very great advantage against us.[2]

The final comment here on the devil – there is more good material in this section of *Table Talk* for those interested – concerns a report given to Luther of one attacked in his conscience by his sins who felt that he blasphemed against Christ when he prayed. Luther replied:

Blaspheming against God is twofold: one, in which we are active or operative, when one wilfully seeks occasions to blaspheme God; the other, a constrained blaspheming of God, which is passive, when the devil possesses us with evil thoughts against our will and we want to resist. In such cases, God would have us work so that we do not lie snoring in laziness, but strive and pray against the attacks. By these means, such things will eventually vanish away and cease, especially at our last end, because the Holy Spirit is present with Christians, stands by them, drives away the devil and creates a sweet, quiet and peaceful conscience. Therefore, let this man take this medicine for his disease: that he does not

1. *Table Talk*, 24.589.
2. Ibid., 25.629.

trouble himself about anything, but is encouraged, trusts in God and holds on to the word; then the devil will soon cease of his own accord from stirring up such temptations.[1]

Moving on from this to the sin that then confronts humankind, Luther describes three armies of sin that attack the Christian in *On Good Works*.

Even if none of these attacks [of the devil] force us to call on God's name and trust him, sin alone is more than sufficient to train and to urge us on in this work. Sin has surrounded us with three strong, mighty armies. The first is our own flesh, the second is the world and the third is the evil spirit, by which three we are constantly oppressed and troubled. Therefore, God gives us reason to constantly do good works, which are to fight against these enemies and sins. The flesh seeks pleasure and peace; the world seeks riches, favour, power and honour; the evil spirit seeks pride, glory, that a person should be well thought of and other people be despised.[2]

There is another threefold description on sin in *Table Talk* that examines the types of people that result from the effects of sin:

There are three sorts of people. The first are the common people, who live secure without any remorse in their consciences, failing to acknowledge their corrupt actions and natures, unaware of God's anger against their sins and even careless of this. The second are those who are scared because of the law, who feel God's anger and who work and wrestle with despair. The third are those that acknowledge their sins and God's righteous anger, know that they are conceived and born in sin and are therefore worthy of destruction, but still listen keenly to the Gospel and believe that God graciously forgives sins for the sake of Jesus Christ; such are justified before God and afterwards show the fruits of their faith through all kinds of good works.[3]

The distinction between the three kinds of people is not so clear as this might indicate, according to Luther, since there are some who may appear forgiven and on this basis engage in good works but who yet remain in sin.

---

1. Ibid., 25.682.
2. *On Good Works*, 2.27.
3. *Table Talk*, 3.144.

Not all are horribly stained by open sins so that we could fittingly
confront them in public with any one particular sin or transgression.
Although many covetous people, adulterers and others are among
us, they live so carefully and in this can hide their sins so that we
cannot detect them. However, although such people are with us in
the church, in the Christian assembly, hearing sermons and God's
word and receiving the holy sacrament with righteous and godly
Christians, yet because of their nature they are excommunicated
by God because they live in sin against their own consciences and
do not change their lives. Such sinners may deceive people, but
they cannot deceive God. At the Day of Judgement he will cause
his angels to gather all sinners together and will cast them into the
unquenchable fire.[1]

The corruption present in humankind from sin has further effects,
highlighted in the Heidelberg Disputation, that even those works that
ook good are in fact evil: 'Although the works of people always seem
attractive and good, they are nevertheless likely to be mortal sins.'[2]
Luther expounds this idea in his commentary on the thesis.

Human works appear attractive outwardly, but in themselves they
are filthy . . . They appear good and beautiful to the agent and
to others, but God does not judge according to appearances . . .
Without grace and faith it is impossible to have a pure heart . . .
The works of people are works of the law, and the resulting curse
will not be placed upon venial sins. Therefore, they are mortal
sins.[3]

This is particularly shown in the motivation behind actions, which
Luther discusses in the thesis that 'Human works are much more mortal
sins when they are done without fear and in pure, evil self-security.'[4]
He unpacks this in the following: 'Where is no fear, there is no
humility; where there is no humility, there is pride; and where there is
pride, there are the wrath and judgement of God.'[5]
   The last point on the nature of sin is a recognition of degrees of sin, that
some sins are worse than others. Luther presents this in characteristically
direct fashion in *Table Talk*.

---

1. Ibid., 15.386.
2. *Heidelberg Disputation*, 3.
3. Ibid.
4. Ibid., 8.
5. Ibid.

The sins of ordinary, untutored people are nothing when compared with the sins committed by great and high persons who are in spiritual and temporal offices. What are the sins done by a poor wretch, that according to law and justice is hanged, or the offences of a poor strumpet, compared with the sins of a false teacher, who daily makes away with many poor people, and kills them both body and soul?[1]

The ultimate sin described in the Bible is the sin of blasphemy against the Holy Spirit, the sin that can never be forgiven. There are myriad interpretations of what this might be through the history of the Church. Luther's version certainly has the benefit of being concise.

Sins against the Holy Spirit are: first, presumption; second, despair; third, opposition to and condemnation of a truth that is known; fourth, to resent a brother or neighbour experiencing the grace of God rather than wishing them well; fifth, to be hardened; sixth, to be impenitent.[2]

Original Sin

We move on now to look at some of the elements of Luther's teaching on sin, beginning with original sin. All that follows is, of course, inter-related, however, breaking the overall topic of sin down into these sections will, I hope, help to present Luther's views. Readers are encouraged, as always, to go back to the sources and investigate individual points/quotations in their original context.

The clearest overlap on the topic of original sin in Luther is with his theology of baptism and, therefore, this section will be rather brief, bearing in mind that we shall return to discuss original sin in greater detail when looking at the sacraments. In the *Disputation Concerning Justification*, Luther makes clear that, whatever is understood as part of the effect of baptism, original sin still affects all people throughout their lives.

Original sin, which is inherited and evil, always clings to us and makes us guilty to eternal death. It lasts as long as we live and can be called an innate disposition. . . . They [Scholastic thinkers] think that original sin is removed in baptism, so that there are no sins in you after you have been baptised. When you fall after this, your baptism pardons you again. Against this we say that, although forgiveness is imputed and sin removed so that it is not imputed,

---

1. *Table Talk*, 7.255.
2. Ibid., 7.245.

original sin is still not substantially or essentially destroyed except by the conflagration of fire in which the whole world and our bodies will be completely purified on the last day. When we have been reduced to dust, only then will sins be entirely destroyed. In the meantime, while we live, original sin also lives, as can be seen even in the saints until their last breath. But we also say that our sins have been forgiven.[1]

In this position, Luther rejects what he sees in Scholastic thought that concentrates too greatly on the effects of original sin in humanity in Augustine's idea of 'concupiscence', the natural tendency of every thought to evil. Luther argues that this attribute is merely a manifestation of a continuing corruption in a person.

The Scholastics were ignorant of original sin. They said that it is only concupiscence but this definition is inadequate and not strong enough. The definition of original sin as a lack of original righteousness that ought to be in us is too weak. Although it is very excellent, yet we cannot know where original sin comes from or what it is because it is not itself distinct. Original sin is not only a lack of righteousness, but an innate evil, as we said before, which makes us guilty of sin and subject to eternal death, to divine wrath. It remains in us even after baptism and resists the law of God and the Holy Spirit.[2]

In *Table Talk*, Luther takes his criticism further back to the Church Fathers, holding that there was no concept of original sin before Augustine – something that Volume One of this series shows is not quite correct, since there were plenty of references to the concept, although its application was certainly different before Augustine.

None of the Fathers of the Church mentioned original sin until Augustine came and he differentiated between original and actual sin – that original sin is to covet, lust and desire, which are then the root and cause of actual sin. God forgives this kind of lust and desire in the faithful, not imputing it for the sake of Christ, seeing that they resist by the help of the Holy Spirit. . . . We are all sinners by nature, conceived and born in sin. Sin has poisoned our entire nature. We receive a will from Adam that is always set against God unless the Holy Spirit renews and changes it.[3]

1. Luther, *Disputation Concerning Justification*, 6.
2. Ibid., 26.
3. *Table Talk*, 7.244.

Even while it is being renewed, original sin is still present in Christians.

After rebirth, original sin is like a wound that begins to heal. Although it is a wound, it is still in the healing process, but it still runs and is sore. Original sin thus remains in Christians until they die, but it is mortified and is continually dying. Its head is crushed into pieces so that it cannot condemn us.[1]

The result of the universal effects of original sin is the corruption of everything in creation.

There is no doubt that all created things have degenerated due to original sin. The serpent was initially a high and noble animal, eating fearlessly from Eve's hand; after it was cursed, it lost its feet and was made to crawl and eat on the ground. It was precisely because the serpent was then the most beautiful of creatures that Satan chose it for his work, because he likes beauty and knows that beauty attracts people to do evil. . . . Consider the bodies of children, and how much sweeter, purer and more beautiful they are than those of adults. This is because childhood is nearer to the state of innocence in which Adam lived before his fall. In our sad condition, our only consolation is the expectation of another life; here below, everything is incomprehensible.[2]

This affects not only humankind, but all species of life on earth.

As a result of original sin, many wild beasts hurt humankind – lions, wolves, bears, snakes, adders and others – but the mercy of God has so limited the punishments we deserve that there are many more animals that exist for our good and well-being than those that hurt us. There are many more sheep than wolves, oxen than lions, cows than bears, deer than foxes, lobsters than scorpions, ducks, geese and hens than ravens and kites; more good creatures than evil, more that benefit us than that hurt or hinder us.[3]

We shall be returning to the theme of sin regularly in the rest of this presentation of Luther's thought, in the response of grace both itself and in the sacraments and then in the effects of sin in the human will and its freedom.

---

1. Ibid., 7.256.
2. Ibid., 2.132.
3. Ibid., 2.103.

Grace

The results of Luther's general teaching on the roots and nature of sin mean that there is a very great role for grace in the restoration of humanity, particularly, given a consistent thread in his thought that human works in themselves are dead. This is stated clearly early in the theses of the *Heidelberg Disputation*.

> The law of God, which is holy, unstained, true and just, is given by God to humankind as an aid beyond their natural power as a light to move them to do good; yet the opposite takes place, in that they become more wicked. How then can we be led to do good through own power and without such aid? If a person cannot do good even with external help, they will do even less in their own strength. Therefore, the Apostle calls all people corrupt and impotent (Rom. 3:10-12), neither understanding nor seeking God because all, he says, have gone astray.[1]

The result should be a desire not so seek one's own justification or to despair, but to turn to God in repentance in order to seek his grace as is stated in *On Good Works*.

> If you want to be cured of sin, you should not withdraw from God but run to him and pray with far more confidence than you would if you suffered something in your body. God is not an enemy to sinners, but only to unbelievers, to those who do not recognise their sins and lament or seek help from God, but rather in their own presumption want to purify themselves, being unwilling to require his grace, and do not allow him to be a God who gives to everyone and takes nothing in return.[2]

Slightly earlier in *On Good Works* there is a similar call to a reliance on grace.

> You see for yourself that all who do not constantly trust God, who do not trust in his blessing, grace and good will in all of their works or sufferings, in life and death, but rather seek to gain his favour through other things or in themselves, do not keep this commandment [the First Commandment] but practice real idolatry, even if they were to obey all of the other commandments, and in addition did all of the combined saints' prayers, fasting, obedience, patience, chastity and innocence. . . . All who wish to make God favourable to themselves

1. *Heidelberg Disputation*, 2.
2. *On Good Works*, 3.10.

by their many good works are in this condition, seeking to buy God's grace from him . . . They are the most perverse people on earth, who will only with difficulty or never be converted to the right way. The same holds for those who run here and there in hard times, seeking counsel and help everywhere except from God, from whom they are most urgently commanded to seek it.[1]

The Nature of Grace

In 1517, Luther published a series of theses against Scholastic theology, a significant number of these introduce the reader, in a punchy style, to some of Luther's key teachings in relation to grace. Here is a selection from this document:

29. The best, infallible preparation for grace and the only active force moving towards grace is the eternal election and predestination of God.
30. In people, nothing precedes grace except obstinacy and even a rebellion against grace.
33. It is false to state that, by doing everything that one can, it is possible to remove the obstacles to grace.
55. The grace of God is never present in such a way that it is inactive, but rather it is a living, active and effective Spirit. It is also not possible that an act of friendship may occur through the absolute power of God without the presence of the grace of God.
56. It is not true to say that God can accept a person without his justifying grace.
57. It is dangerous to say that the law commands that one must obey a commandment through the grace of God.
58. From this it would follow that 'having the grace of God' is in fact a new requirement that extends beyond the law.
59. It would also follow that one could fulfil the law without the grace of God.
60. Likewise it would follow that the grace of God is more hateful than the law itself.
61. We do not need to believe that the law should be followed and fulfilled in the grace of God.
65. It is impossible not to become angry or lustful outside the grace of God, so that even in grace it is impossible to fulfil the law perfectly.

---

1. Ibid., 1.10.

68. Therefore it is impossible to fulfil the law in any way without the grace of God.
71. Law and will are two implacable enemies without the grace of God.
75. The grace of God leads to justice through Jesus Christ because it causes a person to be pleased with the law.
76. Every deed of the law has the appearance of good without the grace of God, but inwardly it is a sin.[1]

The *Heidelberg Disputation* also contains some theses on the nature of grace, this time with some exposition of the ideas.

Whoever believes that they can obtain grace by their own efforts adds sin to sin and becomes doubly guilty. On this basis, it is clear that a person working in their own strength sins and is completely self-seeking. If they suppose that by sinning they can become worthy of or prepared for grace, they add great arrogance to the sin and do not believe that sin is sin and evil is evil . . . You may ask: what then shall we do? Should we go on in our strength indifferent to God because we can only sin? I would reply: by no means! Rather, when we hear this, we should fall down, pray for grace and place our hope in Christ who is our salvation, life and resurrection.

Speaking like this does not give us cause for despair, but inspires a desire to humble ourselves and seek the grace of Christ. . . . One cannot be humble unless one recognises that they are condemned, that the smell of their sin rises up to high heaven. Sin is only recognised through the law. It is clear that hope is preached when we are told that we are sinners, not despair. Preaching like this about sin is a preparation for grace, or rather the recognition of sin and faith in this preaching. When we recognise sin, we begin to desire grace. . . . We do not make people despair when we say that we are nothing and that we constantly sin even when we do our best, unless we are fools; rather, we make them concerned about the grace of our Lord Jesus Christ.

It is certain that a person must utterly despair of their own strength before they are prepared to receive the grace of Christ. . . . One who simply acts on the basis of their own ability and believes that they are doing something good in this does not think they are nothing or despair of their own strength. Rather they are so presumptuous that they try to gain grace by relying on their own strength.[2]

---

1. Luther, *Disputation Against Scholastic Theology*.
2. *Heidleberg Disputation*, 16–18.

Finally, in this section, we will look at a couple of passages that speak of the communication of grace in looking at the roles of the Son and the Spirit. As with earlier thinkers, the focus in the realisation of grace in the person is on the work of the Spirit that flows from the Christ event.

> In order to examine more deeply the grace that our inner self has in Christ, we must realise that in the Old Testament God consecrated all first-born males to himself. . . . The first-born brother was a priest and lord over all the others and a type of Christ, the true and only first-born of God the Father and the Virgin Mary, true king and true priest, but not in a human or worldly manner . . . His priesthood does not consist in the outer splendour of robes and postures like the human priesthood of Aaron or our present-day Church; rather it consists of spiritual things through which he invisibly intercedes for us in heaven before God, offering himself there as a sacrifice and doing all the things that a priest should . . . He does not only pray and intercede for us, but teaches us inwardly through the living instruction of his Spirit; in this way he performs the two real functions of a priest, of which the prayers and preaching of human priests are visible types.[1]

This last work of Christ in communicating grace by the Spirit is picked up in *Table Talk*.

> The Holy Spirit has two works: firstly, he is a Spirit of grace who makes God gracious towards us and receives us as his acceptable children, for Christ's sake; secondly, he is a Spirit of prayer who prays for us and for the whole world in order that we may be protected from all evil and that we would experience goodness. The Spirit of grace teaches people; the Spirit of prayer prays.[2]

Connected to this is a passage against the radical reformation, the Anabaptists, whom Luther roundly condemns in *Concerning Rebaptism*. Despite his issues with their doctrine of baptism, Luther recognises that God by his grace does work through the Anabaptists.

> We must acknowledge that the fanatics have the Scriptures and the word of God in other doctrines [other than baptism]. Whoever hears this from them and believes will be saved, even though they

---

1. Luther, *On the Freedom of a Christian*. This short pamphlet has no sections to divide it and, therefore, to find the context for this passage, the easiest route is to access a digital translation and search for a key phrase such as 'Virgin Mary'.
2. *Table Talk*, 6.241.

themselves are unrighteous heretics and blaspheme Christ. It is not a minor grace that God gives his word even through such evil and godless people. In fact, it is in some respects more dangerous when God proclaims his word through holy rather than through unholy people, since those who are thoughtless are tempted to devote themselves to the holiness of the people rather than to the word of God.[1]

Grace and Faith

One theme that receives some significant attention in Luther's work is the relationship between grace and faith, an understanding of this can help explain his teaching on 'faith alone' as the means of salvation. This will feature heavily when we look at the teaching on the sacraments below. However, there are a couple of passages worth highlighting here that concern the experience of grace more widely.

The first passage highlights the difference between the grace work of God in salvation and the faith response of the Christian.

> Christ is full of grace, life and salvation; the soul is full of sin, death and condemnation. When faith comes between Christ and the soul, sin, death and condemnation becomes Christ's, while grace, life and salvation belong to the soul. If Christ is a bridegroom, he must take on himself everything that belongs to his bride and give her whatever is his. If he gives her his body and his whole self, must he not also give her everything that is his?[2]

The next quotes all look at the relationship between faith and works and emphasise the quality of the latter in light of the nature of the former. This is perhaps most clear in the following passage from *On the Freedom of a Christian.*

> As a person is, whether they are a believer or an unbeliever, so is their work; good if done in faith, wicked if done in unbelief. However, the opposite is not true, that a work can make a person either a believer or an unbeliever. Because works do not make a person into a believer, so they cannot make a person righteous. However, faith does make a person a believer and therefore righteous, and so faith does good works. Therefore, because works do not justify anyone, and a person must be righteous before they can do a good work, it is very clear that faith alone, because of the

---

1. Luther, *Concerning Rebaptism.*
2. *On the Freedom of a Christian.*

pure mercy of God through Christ and in his word, is right and sufficient to justify and save a person. A Christian does not need any work or law in order to be saved, since they are free through faith from every law and do everything from a pure liberty and freely. They do not seek any benefit or any salvation because they are already complete in all things, being saved through the grace of God and in faith seeking only to please God.[1]

Luther is consistently clear that works are a part of a Christian's life but that they must be the result of the work of grace and a response in faith, rather than a means of receiving grace in an absence of faith. Early in *On Good Works*, Luther puts this somewhat vaguely in stating that all people know that what they do is good or bad.

Everyone can see and tell themselves whether what they do is good or not good. If their heart is confident that it pleases God, then the work is good even if it is as small a thing as picking up a piece of straw. If there is no confidence or some doubt, then the work is not good even if it is to raise all the dead and the person gives themselves up to be burned. . . . Faith as the main work – and no other work – gives us the name 'believers in Christ'. A pagan, Jew, Turk or sinner can do any other work; but only a Christian is able to trust firmly that they please God, being enlightened and strengthened by grace.[2]

Later, he stresses more strongly the necessity of faith in the quality of a work.

I have often spoken against the display, magnificence and multitude of these works [religious practices] and rejected them because it is very clear that they are not performed in doubt or without faith, and there is not one person in a thousand who does not place their confidence in these works, expecting to earn God's favour through them and to anticipate his grace. Therefore people make a great deal of showing off these works, something that God cannot abide, having promised his grace freely and willing that we begin by trusting in his grace, performing all works through that grace, whatever they may be.[3]

Shortly after this in the same work, Luther again shows that the nature of the works is derived from their source rather than having a quality in themselves.

---

1. Ibid.
2. *On Good Works*, 1.4.
3. Ibid., 1.11.

We can see that works are forgiven, without guilt and good, not because of their own nature, but because of the mercy and grace of God, because of a faith that trusts in the mercy of God. Therefore, works should lead us to fear, but we are comforted because of the grace of God . . . we are children and also sinners; we are acceptable and yet do not do enough. All of this is the work of faith, firmly grounded in God's grace.[1]

As indicated above, we shall return to grace and faith in the following section on the sacraments, many passages of which also look at the role of works in relation to these concepts.

Sacraments and Grace

There is a choice in presenting Luther's views on the sacraments between taking the chronology of his writings, which would mean starting with Penance as the focus of *the 95 Theses*, or looking at them more in the order of the sacraments, which then means beginning with Baptism. Given the work we have already seen on original sin, we will take the latter approach here and move from Baptism to the Lord's Supper, before dealing with Penance.

Luther begins by stating what is being signified in Baptism: 'Baptism signifies that the old person and the birth in sinful body and blood will be completely drowned by the grace of God.'[2] Shortly afterwards, Luther shows that this is not merely symbolic in his view, but a change in the nature of a person: 'Through the spiritual birth of Baptism, a person becomes a child of grace and justified. Therefore, sins are drowned in baptism, and righteousness is produced as a result.'[3]

Given this effect of Baptism, and given that Luther strongly supports the baptism of infants, one major consideration for Luther is whether there can remain any sin after baptism.

When a person rises out of baptism, they are truly pure, without sin and completely without guilt. But there are many people who do not understand this correctly. They think that sin is no longer present in them and so become careless and negligent in the extent to which they kill their sinful nature . . . So long as we live here, our bodies are wicked and sinful by nature.[4]

---

1. Ibid., 1.16.
2. Luther, *Sacrament of Baptism*, 1.
3. Ibid., 3.
4. Ibid., 7.

There is thus a 'now-and-not-yet' work completed in baptism, that there will be a complete destruction of sin for the life to come but a continual battle with the ongoing sinful nature in this life.

> Someone who has been baptised is sacramentally completely pure and without guilt, all of which means that they have the sign of God. This means that the baptism shows that their sins will all be dead and that they will also die in grace, rising again on the last day to everlasting life as pure, sinless and guiltless. In sacramental terms, it is therefore true that they are without sin and guilt; but because the destruction of sin is not finished and a person still lives in sinful flesh, they are not without sin.[1]

Baptism is not therefore the completed salvation event, but only the beginning from which the grace of Christ through the Spirit and the perseverance of the believer together prepare a person for the promised new life.

> You give yourself to the sacrament of Baptism and what it signifies. That means that you desire to die together with your sins, and to be made new on the last day. . . . From that time God begins to form you into a new person. He pours his grace and the Holy Spirit into you, who begins to kill your sinful nature and sin and prepares you for death and resurrection at the last day.
>
> Secondly, you commit yourself to continuing in this desire and to killing your sinful nature more and more for as long as you live, even until your dying day. . . . When we do not suffer and are not tested, then our evil nature gains influence so that a person invalidates his baptism, falls into sin and remains the same old person that they were before.[2]

The grace that is received is therefore not wholly comforting. Rather, 'through baptism we come under the judgement of grace and mercy, which does not condemn our sins but does drive them out through many trials.'[3] This moves us onto the faith that justifies us as we place it in our God and in this context in the sacrament of Baptism.

> Faith means that a person firmly believes all this . . . but also that they must begin and achieve this. Faith means that baptism establishes a covenant between us and God to the effect that we

---

1. Ibid., 8.
2. Ibid., 9.
3. Ibid., 11.

shall fight against sin and kill our sinful nature until our dying breath, while God for his part will be merciful to us, deal graciously with us and – because we cannot be sinless in this life, but only when purified by death – not judge us with severity.[1]

Luther's concept of faith thus cannot be confused too closely with belief or mental assent, rather his is a living and active faith that seeks to destroy the sinful nature that remains after the grace of salvation has been received. If this book were to have faith as a major theme, this is where Luther's theology of childhood would come in with his teaching on the purity of childlike faith in contrast to the wrestles with faith and belief of an adult.

Luther has no room for mere passivity in the Christian life, since this in his view would negate any previous work of grace.

> Therefore, people are greatly mistaken if they think that they become completely pure through baptism. They continue in ignorance and do not seek to destroy their sin; indeed, they do not even admit that it is sin. They simply persist in it, and in this they make their baptism ineffectual.
>
> Sin and evil inclinations must be recognised as being truly sin. However, these do not harm us because of the grace of God. He will only not count our sins against us if we keep on working against it through many trials, tasks and sufferings, and finally destroy it at our death. For those who will not do this, God will not forgive their sins.[2]

This puts suffering into a new perspective, since the work of destroying sin in us – putting it to death – necessarily involves us in suffering. If there is no hardship in this life, where is the evidence of us seeking to destroy sin and evil in ourselves?

> Baptism, therefore, makes all suffering, and especially death, profitable and helpful to us in that we simply have to help baptism to do its work, which is the destruction of sin. It cannot be otherwise. Anyone who wants to fulfil the work and purpose of his baptism and be rid of sin must die. But sin does not like to die and, therefore, it makes death so bitter and horrible. Such is the grace and power of God that sin, which has brought death, is itself driven out by its own work, namely by death itself.[3]

---

1. Ibid., 12.
2. Ibid., 13.
3. Ibid., 16.

Luther then raises what he sees as an error resulting from this and evident in the Church of his day, namely, that, in the necessity to cooperate with the Holy Spirit in the destruction of our sinful nature, such effort has gained a meritorious nature to gain grace, rather than a result of and a work with the grace of God.

> The whole world was – and still is – full of baptism and the grace of God. But we have been led astray into performing our own anxious works, and then into indulgences and other false comforts. We have understood that we should not trust God until we are righteous and have made satisfaction for our sins, as if we could buy God's grace from him or pay him for it.[1]

The continuing fight against sin that is promised in baptism is picked up in Luther's description of the sacrament of the Lord's Supper.

> There is sin that remains in our bodies after baptism: the inclination to anger, hatred, pride, lust and so on. This sin attacks us for as long as we live. In this life, we do not only need the help of the community of saints and Christ, so that they can fight with us against these sins, but it is also necessary that Christ and his saints intercede for us before God so that our sins are not charged to our account by God's strict judgement. Therefore, to strengthen and encourage us against these sins, God gives us this sacrament [the Lord's Supper] in order to say: 'Look, many kinds of sin are attacking you. Take this sign in which I promise you that these sins are not only attacking you, but also my Son, Christ, and all his saints in heaven and on earth. Therefore, take heart and be bold: you are not fighting alone; there is great help and support all around you.'[2]

The Lord's Supper is therefore not simply about the individual Christian and God, but about their place in the body of Christ, the Church:

> The immeasurable grace and mercy of God are given to us in this sacrament in order that we might take our misery and trials from ourselves and lay them on the community of saints and especially on Christ.[3]

---

1. Ibid., 19.
2. Luther, *Sacrament of the Body of Christ*, 7.
3. Ibid., 8.

This then has ramifications for anyone willing to take the sacrament, since in this union with God's people there is not only the benefit of laying our cares on others and receiving their support, but also a necessity to support others in turn.

> There are indeed some who would gladly share in the profits of this sacrament, but not in the costs. That is, they like to hear that this sacrament promises them the help, fellowship and support of all the saints, which they then receive. However, they are unwilling in their turn to belong to this fellowship. They will not help the poor, put up with sinners, care for those in sorrow, suffer with the suffering, pray for others, defend the truth and seek the good of the church and all Christians at the risk of their lives, properties and honour. . . . They are selfish people and this sacrament does not benefit them.[1]

Turning to the sacrament of Penance, we shall look first at some brief excerpts from Luther's work specifically on this topic, before going to his *Explanation of the 95 Theses* where there is further relevant material.

> There are three elements to the holy sacrament of Penance. The first is absolution, which are the words of the priest that show, tell and proclaim to you that you are free and that your sins are forgiven by God . . . The second is grace, the forgiveness of sins, the peace and comfort of the conscience . . . The third is faith, which firmly believes that the absolution and words of the priest are true . . . It is not the sacrament that removes sin, but the faith that believes the sacrament.[2]

These latter two elements are vitally important for Luther, who rejected Penance as a full sacrament of the Church but taught that a practice of confession and receiving absolution was important for the Christian to express their faith and to receive comfort in their consciences that supports their faith. This latter idea comes across later in the same work.

> Since by God's grace we are commanded to believe and hope that our sins are forgiven, how much more ought we to believe this when God gives us a sign through another person! There is no greater sin than rejecting this article of 'the forgiveness of sins'

---

1. Ibid., 13.
2. Luther, *On the Sacrament of Penance*, 6.

that we pray every day in the Creed. This sin is called the sin against the Holy Spirit, strengthening all other sins and making them eternally unforgiveable.[1]

This does not mean that another's role is essential to forgiveness (as may appear from above and from further quotations below) but rather it recognises that on one's own it can be difficult to know the sufficiency of the grace of God to overcome sin.

> You should not debate at all whether or not your contrition is sufficient. Rather you should be assured that, after all your efforts, your contrition is not sufficient. This is why you must throw yourself on the grace of God, hear his sufficiently sure word in the sacrament, accept this in free and joyful faith and never doubt that you are under grace – not because of your own merits or contrition, but by his gracious and divine mercy . . . in this way you learn to glory and trust not in yourself or your own actions, but in the grace and mercy of your dear Father in heaven.[2]

This idea is strongly developed as Luther explains the 95 Theses.

> Faith is necessary everywhere; you receive as much as you believe. This is what I understand when our teachers say that the sacraments are effective signs of grace, not simply because the sacrament is performed but because people believe in it, as St Augustine argued and as I have said previously. The same is true here. Absolution is effective not simply because it takes place, regardless of who performs it and whether they are right or wrong, but because people believe in it. No reservation of certain cases [by the pope] can stop a person's faith from receiving absolution unless the faith itself is clearly undeserving or despises the absolution offered. I therefore say that a person who is so under sin that they are worried and disturbed by their conscience that, in their own opinion, they believe that everything they do is evil, such a person is certainly close to justification and has the beginnings of grace. Therefore they ought to flee for safety to the comfort of the keys in order to find rest in the authority of the priest, obtain peace and attain a confidence that they are participating in all of the benefits of Christ and the Church. If anyone does not believe that this person participates in the benefits of Christ

1. Ibid., 11.
2. Ibid., 12.

and the Church through this work of absolution by the priest, or if they have doubts about it, they are led astray not by an error of the keys but by an error of their own faithlessness. They inflict on their soul a great condemnation and commit an injustice against God and his word through the greatest irreverence. It would be much better for that person not to go to absolution at all if they do not believe that they are absolved, rather than to go without faith.[1]

The seventh of the theses states that, 'God removes no one's guilt unless they humble themselves in everything and submit to his vicar, the priest.' In defending this thesis, Luther begins by highlighting several passages that indicate a forgiveness of sins on earth before sins are forgiven in heaven – the Lord's Prayer, for instance, asks God to forgive our sins *as we forgive* those who sin against us. Luther concludes that,

> A person is right to ask how these things can take place before an infusion of grace, before God forgives sin, since a person cannot have their guilt forgiven or a desire to seek forgiveness without first having the grace of God that forgives.[2]

Luther argues that seeking any comfort that sins are forgiven in one's own mind will lead to despair because of the awareness of sin so that there will be an imbalance between the work of forgiveness and the experience of being forgiven.

> As long as a person remains in this wretched, perplexed state of conscience, they can have neither peace nor comfort unless they run to the power of the Church and seek solace and relief from their sins and wretchedness that have been revealed in confession. Neither by a person's own counsel or strength will they be able to find peace; rather their sadness will ultimately turn into despair. When the priest sees this humility and anguish, they shall free the repentant person with complete confidence in the power they have been given to show compassion and will declare them free, thereby giving peace to the conscience. . . . Anyone who seeks peace in another way, for example, internally through their own experience, certainly seems to tempt God and desires to have peace in fact, rather than in faith.[3]

1. Luther, *Explanation of the 95 Theses*, 38.
2. Ibid., 7.
3. Ibid.

Luther later clarifies that the priest does not create grace in a person, since this is the work of God, but does realise the effects of this in a person's life.

> Therefore, God's forgiveness effects grace, but the priest's forgiveness brings peace, which is both the grace and a gift of God because it is faith in actual forgiveness and grace. I believe that this grace is what our teachers declare is given effectively through the sacraments of the Church.... Therefore, Peter did not forgive people's sins before Christ did, but he declared and disclosed the forgiveness given by Christ. Whoever believes this confidently has truly obtained peace and forgiveness from God (that is, they are sure that they are pardoned), not by any certainty in the process but by a certainty from faith.[1]

The problem for Luther is that the effective power in grace seems to have been transferred by the Church of his time from Christ to the priest so that people seek forgiveness in the Church first and foremost, rather than in Christ.

> More recent theologians, however, give far too much power to the torment of conscience by discussing and teaching about the sacrament of Penance in such a way that people learn to trust in the delusion that it is possible to have their sins forgiven by their own sorrow and satisfactions.... The people must first be taught faith in Christ, the one who graciously grants forgiveness. Then they must be persuaded to despair of their own sorrow and works so that, when they have been strengthened by a confidence and joy in their hearts about the compassion of Christ, they can finally despise sin cheerfully, become contrite and make satisfaction.[2]

In concluding this discussion, Luther returns to the link between grace and faith and asserts the necessity of the later for the receipt of the former.

> Indeed, the sin would remain if a person did not believe that it was forgiven. The forgiveness of sin and the gift of grace are not enough; one must also believe that one's sins have been forgiven. This is the witness that the Spirit of God gives to our spirit, that we are children of God (Rom. 8:18). It is such a great mystery to be a child of God, when we seem to ourselves to be enemies of God, that if we do not believe this to be so, it cannot be so.[3]

---

1. Ibid.
2. Ibid.
3. Ibid.

One final point on the sacrament of Penance (there is much more material present in the original sources than there is space to convey here) builds on much of that above expressing Luther's teaching that a Christian should act on their sorrow for their sins in order to devote themselves to God and to conquer the power of sin in their lives. These outward works are not meritorious in deserving grace, but they are the necessary fruit of the work of the Spirit in a person.

> The three parts of satisfaction (fasting, prayer and almsgiving) are not related to sacramental penance in terms of the essence of actions because all are commanded by Christ. However, they do relate to sacramental penance in terms of the exact manner and timing of these satisfactions (which the Church prescribes for this penance), in terms of how long one should pray, fast and give alms, and how much one must give to charity. Since these satisfactions are related to evangelical penance, fasting includes all mortification of the flesh, in addition to the choice of food or a difference in clothing; prayer includes every pursuit of the soul in meditation, reading, listening and praying; the giving of alms includes every service towards one's neighbour. In this way, through fasting, a Christian can serve themselves, by prayer they can serve God and by giving alms they can serve their neighbours. Through fasting, they can conquer the desires of the flesh and live soberly and purely; through prayer, they can conquer a pride in life and live in a godly manner; through giving alms, they can conquer the desire of the eyes and live righteously in this world. Therefore, all mortifications that a conscience-stricken person brings on themselves are fruits of an inner penance, whether they are vigils, work, hardship, study, prayers or abstaining from sex and pleasures, insofar as they minister to the spirit. . . . Without doubt, good works are the outward fruits of inner penance and of the work of the Spirit, although the Spirit makes no sound except that of the turtledove, which is the groaning of the heart that is at the root of good works.[1]

It should now be clear that, while Luther had a great aversion to the late-medieval Catholic Church's teaching on grace, primarily that humans have a role to play in earning grace, he was not in favour of removing the experience of grace to the individual and out of the Church because of the dangers that he saw in this approach.

---

1. Ibid., 3.

Free Will

The bulk of the material in this section will come from Luther's work *On the Bondage of the Will*, which works extensively with the concept of the freedom of the will, largely in light of (and opposed to) Erasmus' positive role for the human will. These quotations will focus on looking at the limitations of the will without a work of grace, as well as the work that grace is able to do in freeing the will. Before that, as a backdrop to the major work, we shall glance briefly at some other documents where free will is discussed.

In the section of sin some of the theses of the *Disputation Against Scholastic Theology* were presented as a starting point and we shall follow the same approach here with the following statements.

4. It is true that humankind, being a bad tree, can only will and do evil.
5. It is false to state that a person's will is free to choose between either of two opposites. Indeed, the will is not free, but captive.
6. It is false to state that the will can by its own nature conform to correct teaching.
7. In fact, without the grace of God the will produces an act that is perverse and evil.
8. However, it does not follow that the will is evil by nature, that it is essentially evil, as the Manichaeans teach.
9. It is, nevertheless, innately and inevitably evil and corrupt.
10. One must admit that the will is not free to work towards whatever is declared to be good.
11. Nor is it able to will or not to will whatever is commanded.
12. Nor does one contradict St Augustine in saying that nothing is so much in the power of the will as the will itself.
13. It is absurd to conclude that fallen people can love a creature above all things and therefore also God.
14. Nor is it surprising that the will can conform to incorrect and not to correct teachings.
15. Indeed, it is peculiar to the will that it can only conform to incorrect and not to correct teachings.
16. One ought rather to conclude: since fallen humankind can love a creature, it is impossible for it to love God.[1]

---

1. Luther, *Disputation Against Scholastic Theology*.

There is a similar tone shown in the *Heidelberg Disputation* in theses 13-15, which state:

> 13. Free will exists after the Fall in name only. Whenever it does what it can do, it commits a mortal sin.
> 14. After the Fall, free will has the power to do good only passively but it can always be active in doing evil.
> 15. Free will could not actively remain in a state of innocence, much less do any good, but only passively.[1]

In *Table Talk*, Luther makes a distinction between the use of the will in temporal matters compared to its use in eternal matters, recognising that the human will has achieved much in this world but that this does not relate to knowledge of God.

> When we divines speak of free will, we ask what a person's free will is able to accomplish in divine and spiritual matters, not in outward and temporal affairs. We conclude that humankind, without the Holy Spirit, is altogether wicked before God, even if it were fitted out and trimmed with all the virtues present in the world and had performed all the works possible. There are certainly some fair and glorious examples in the world of many virtues, of people who are modest, uncorrupted and generous; people who loved their country, their parents, spouses and children; people who were courageous and who behaved unselfishly and generously. But people's ideas about God, the true worship of God and God's will are all in complete blindness and darkness. The light of human wisdom, reason and understanding, which alone are given to humankind, only understand what is good and profitable externally. Although we can see some pagan philosophers occasionally teaching about God and his wisdom very pertinently, so that some people have sought to make prophets of Socrates, Xenophon, Plato *etc.*, yet because they did not know that God sent his Son Christ to save sinners, such fair, glorious and apparently wise speeches and teachings are nothing but simple blindness and ignorance.[2]

Luther wants to be very careful about the application of free will, therefore, while not totally denying its existence.

> For my part, I admit that God gave people a free will, but the question is whether this freedom lies in our power and strength or not? We may rightly call it a subverted, perverse, fickle and

---

1. Luther, *Heidelberg*, 13-15.
2. Luther, *Table Talk*, 8.261.

wavering will, because it is only God who works in us and we must suffer and be subject to his pleasure. Even as a potter makes a pot or a vessel out of clay as they desire, so our free will must suffer and not work. It does not exist in our strength because we are unable to do anything good in divine matters.[1]

Later in *Table Talk*, Luther produces a litany of the effects of free will that pushes beyond humanity as it was created to the devil and then goes on to a final stage in the establishment of the papacy.

The devil produced darkness; darkness produced ignorance; ignorance produced error and his brothers; error produced free will and presumption; free will produced merit; merit produced a forgetfulness of God; forgetfulness produced transgression; transgression produced superstition; superstition produced satisfaction for sins; satisfaction produced the Mass offering; the Mass offering produced the priest; the priest produced unbelief; unbelief produced King Hypocrisy; hypocrisy produced the selling of offerings for profit; the selling of offerings for profit produced purgatory; purgatory produced the annual solemn vigils; the annual vigils produced Church livings; Church livings produced greed; greed produced an increase in wealth; an increase in wealth produced self-sufficiency; self-sufficiency produced anger; anger produced authority; authority produced empire and domination; domination produced pride; pride produced ambition; ambition produced the selling of grace; the selling of grace produced the Pope and his brothers about the time of the Babylonian captivity.[2]

We move to *On the Bondage of the Will* and its vast amount of material related to the will, often written in reaction to the ideas of Erasmus at whom the work is primarily directed. This presentation will seek to draw out Luther's more constructive ideas, beginning with the definitions in the opening passages of his discussion after a lengthy amount of work on what Erasmus has written. Luther starts by ascribing true free will only to God.

I have shown before that 'free will' cannot be applied to anyone, but only to God. It is possible that you may correctly assign humankind some kind of will, but to grant them free will in divine things is going too far. All who hear the term 'free will' understand it to mean that which can and does do whatever it pleases in honour of God, unrestrained by any law or command. However,

---

1. Ibid., 8.259.
2. Ibid., 17.426.

you cannot call a person free who is a servant acting under the power of the Lord. How much less, then, can we correctly call people or angels free who live so much under the all-controlling command of God (to say nothing of sin and death) that they cannot exist one moment through their own power?[1]

Luther suggests that Erasmus, by granting free will to humankind, seems to be ascribing divinity to people.

If the human will can will and not will, it can also love and hate; and if it can love and hate, it can, to a certain degree, obey the law and believe in the Gospel. It is impossible for one who can will and not will to be unable through that will to begin some kind of work, even though someone may hinder the work so that you are unable to perfect it. Therefore, because God has numbered all his works that lead to salvation, death, the cross and all the evils of the world, the human will can will its own death and destruction. Indeed, it can will anything if it can will one to embrace the word and work of God. What is there that can exist anywhere beneath, above, within or without the word and work of God except God Himself? What is left in this understanding to grace and to the Holy Spirit? This clearly includes divinity as a part of free will, since the will to embrace the law and the Gospel and not to will sin and death belongs to the power of God alone.[2]

Denying this power to people, Luther denies free will to those who are without grace: 'Free will without grace, when it has lost its freedom, is forced to serve sin and cannot will good.'[3] Thus humans are unable to merit anything from God, but only receive the ability to do good from grace.

Respecting merit or reward, you must speak either of worthiness or of consequences. If you speak of worthiness, there is no merit or reward because free will cannot will good on its own, but by grace alone (we are speaking of free will apart from grace and inquiring into the power that properly belongs to each person). It is then clear that good will, merit and reward belong to grace alone.[4]

Salvation is thus not any work of the will of humankind but is from the will of God and comes under his sovereignty.

---

1. Luther, *On the Bondage of the Will*, 41.
2. Ibid., 44.
3. Ibid., 48.
4. Ibid., 70.

God has promised his certain grace to the humble, to those who hate themselves and despair. However, a person cannot be completely humble until they know that salvation is utterly beyond their own power, counsel, endeavour, will and works, but is absolutely dependent on the will, counsel, pleasure and work of another, of God alone. As long as anyone is persuaded that they can do even the least thing towards their own salvation, they will retain a confidence in themselves and not utterly despair. They will not be humble before God, but will propose some place, time or work whereby they may ultimately attain to salvation. But whoever does not hesitate but depends solely on the good will of God, they totally despair of themselves, choose nothing for themselves, but wait for God to work in them. Such a person is near to grace and might be saved.[1]

The human will, according to Luther, is constrained by its existing state in sin so that it cannot move itself towards a desire for good without some external pressure.

Since it is not we who work salvation in us, but only God, it must follow that we do nothing contributing towards salvation before God works in us. By necessity, I do not mean compulsion but what is called the necessity of immutability . . . a person cannot in their own power end, hold back or change their will and desire to do evil, because it still goes on desiring and craving. Even if they should be compelled by force to perform some work against this, the evil will inside them remains an enemy of that which forces it or resists it, and rises in indignation against that power. The will would not rise in indignation if it were changed, and made willing to yield to a constraining power. This is what we mean by the necessity of immutability, that the will cannot change itself or give itself another direction. . . . This would not be the case if the will were free, or if we had a free will.[2]

Luther then goes on to demonstrate to Erasmus why humans have no free will, working with Erasmus' own definition of the free will as a degree of power which, without God's grace, is ineffective.

If the grace of God is lacking, or if it is removed from that small degree of power, what can the will do on its own? 'It is ineffective [you say] and can do nothing good.' Therefore, it cannot do what

1. Ibid., 24.
2. Ibid., 25.

God or his grace wills. Why? Because we have now separated it from the grace of God, and what is not done by the grace of God is not good. It follows from this that free will, without the grace of God, is absolutely not free, but the unchanging servant and slave of evil because it cannot turn itself to will any good.... Therefore, it stands as confirmed even by your own testimony that we do everything from necessity, not from free will, given that the power of free will is nothing. It does nothing good, nor can it do any good, without grace.[1]

Luther therefore holds that the term 'free will' in a theological sense must be restricted only to the being of God, whilst allowing again that it could be used philosophically or sociologically to refer to the temporal works of people.

If we do not want to lose this term altogether (which would be most safe and also most religious), we may with a good conscience teach that it can be used to refer to human free will regarding only those things below us, not regarding those things that are above us. That is, we may be allowed to know that we have a right to use our goods and possessions, acting or not according to our free will. However, even then our free will is overruled by the free will of God alone, just as He pleases. For things regarding God, or those that pertain to salvation or damnation, people have no free will, but are captives, slaves and servants, either to the will of God or to the will of Satan.[2]

Much of this thought arises from Luther's doctrine of God and his sovereignty. In his early survey of Erasmus' work, Luther highlights the fact of God's absolute foreknowledge and (in contrast to Anselm) holds that this negates any real idea of human free will.

God foreknows nothing by contingency [dependence on events], but foresees, purposes and realises everything according to his immutable, eternal and infallible will. By this thunderbolt, free will is thrown down and is completely dashed to pieces. Therefore, any who would assert free will must either deny this thunderbolt, pretend not to see it or push it away from them.[3]

This creates two realities, one that is absolute from God's perspective and one that is transitory and how we experience things.

---

1. Ibid., 26.
2. Ibid.
3. Ibid., 9.

It undoubtedly follows from this that everything that we do, although it may appear to us to be done through choice and as a result of our will (it may even be done by us in this dependent way), is in reality done necessarily and immutably with respect to the will of God. The will of God is effective and cannot be changed, because the very power of God is natural to him and his wisdom is such that he cannot be deceived. Because will cannot be changed, his work cannot be altered from being done in the place, at the time, in the measure and by whom he foresees and wills.[1]

Luther does recognise that the term 'necessity' when applied to the human will is not ideal and expresses a desire for some other term that does not have the harsh overtones that this conveys. He defines the core ideas that must be held as 'the immutable will of God and the impotence of the fallen human will'.[2] Upholding the foreknowledge of God is vital for Luther because of what it means for salvation, after all, how could humankind depend on the promises of God if he does not know what awaits us?

If you doubt or reject the knowledge that God foreknows and wills all things, not dependent on external factors but necessarily and immutably, how can you confidently believe, trust in and depend on his promises? When he promises, it is necessary that you should be certain that he knows, is able and wills to perform what he promises. Otherwise, you will not hold him to be true or faithful, which is unbelief, the greatest wickedness and a denial of the Most High God! How could you be certain and secure unless you were persuaded that he knows and wills certainly, infallibly, immutably and necessarily, and will do what he promises?[3]

Such a view of the sovereign relation of God to creation is behind a later discussion on election and salvation. Luther addresses the age-old question of why some are saved and not others.

If free will were of one and the same nature and impotence in all people, no reason can be given why it might attain grace in one and not in another . . . God could not elect anyone, nor would there be any place left for election but only for free will, choosing or refusing

1. Ibid.
2. Ibid., 10.
3. Ibid., 12.

the patience and anger of God. If God is robbed of his power and wisdom in election, what remains but the idol Fortune, under the name of which everything is said to take place at random.[1]

This idea that things might happen outside the knowledge or will of God is ridiculous for Luther, and leads to another demonstration of his demolition of free will.

Natural Reason herself is forced to confess that the living and true God must be able, in his own freedom, to impose a necessity on us. It would be a ridiculous God, or rather an idol, who did not certainly foreknow the future or could be deceived in events, since even the Gentiles ascribed an inevitable fate to their gods. He would be equally ridiculous if he could not do and did not do all things, or if anything could be done without him. If the foreknowledge and omnipotence of God is granted, it naturally follows as an inevitable consequence that we were not made by ourselves, nor live by ourselves, nor can do anything by ourselves, but all this only through his omnipotence. Since at the beginning God foreknew that we should be as we are, and since he has made us what we are, moving and ruling over us, I would ask how we could pretend that there is any freedom in us to do anything other than he foreknew in the beginning and now proceeds in action? Therefore the foreknowledge and omnipotence of God directly oppose our free will. It must be that either God is deceived in his foreknowledge and his action is wrong (which is impossible), or we act and are acted on according to his foreknowledge and power. By the omnipotence of God, I do not mean the power by which he does not do many things that he could, but the actual power by which he powerfully works everything in all, which is the sense in which Scripture calls him omnipotent. I say that this omnipotence and foreknowledge of God completely abolishes the doctrine of free will.[2]

Later in *On the Bondage of the Will*, Luther turns to Satan and God and the dual forces at work on the human person.

If you place the human will in a free middle place, left to itself, in this you definitely create an endeavour that can exert itself either way. You place both God and the devil at a distance, as spectators only, of this mutable free will. You do not believe that they are

---

1. Ibid., 81.
2. Ibid., 93.

workers on and agitators of that bound will, most hostilely
opposed to each other. Even admitting only this part of your faith,
my teaching stands firmly established and free will lies prostrate,
as I have already shown. It must either be that the kingdom of
Satan in people is nothing at all, in which case Christ is made to
lie; or, if Satan's kingdom be that which Christ describes, free will
must be nothing but a beast of burden, a captive of Satan, which
cannot be freed unless the devil be first cast out by the finger of
God.[1]

Luther returns to the idea of a 'middle' place with some element of free
will, which Erasmus claims solves some of the apparent contradictions
in Scripture between the efficacious role of grace and commands for
humans to respond.

In this moderate medium, the matter is no better and there is no
advantage gained whatsoever. Unless you ascribe the whole and
everything to free will, as the Pelagians do, the 'contradictions' in
Scripture are not altered; merit and reward are entirely removed,
the mercy and justice of God are abolished and all the difficulties
that we try to avoid by allowing this 'certain little ineffective
power' to free will remain as they were before (as I have already
shown). Therefore, we must come to the plain extreme, deny free
will altogether and ascribe everything to God.[2]

Luther goes even further than this and states that believing in free will
involves a denial of Christ.

I would also condemn the advocates of free will here that, when
they assert free will, they deny Christ. If I obtain grace by my
own endeavours, why do I need the grace of Christ in order
to receive my grace? What do I want once I have received the
grace of God? . . . That the advocates of free will deny Christ
is not only proved by Scripture, but also by their own way of
life. In advocating free will, they have made Christ no longer a
sweet mediator for them, but a dreaded judge whom they strive
to please by prayers to the Virgin Mother and the Saints; and
by various invented works, rites, ordinances and vows. By all
of this they seek to appease Christ in order that he might give
them grace. But they do not believe that he intercedes before
God and obtains grace for them by his blood and grace . . . they

1. Ibid., 127.
2. Ibid., 133.

leave Christ, who is a Mediator and most merciful Saviour, and account his blood and grace of less value than the devoted efforts and endeavours of their free will.[1]

The final quotation from *On the Bondage of the Will* has a somewhat different tone as Luther reflects on his relationship to the existence of free will, concluding that he is pleased not to have a free will that would make his salvation in any way dependent on himself.

As to myself, I openly confess that I should not wish to be granted free will, even if it could be, nor have anything else left in my own hands by which I might work something towards my own salvation. This is not merely because, with so many opposing dangers and assaulting devils, I could not stand and hold fast (in which state no one could be saved, given that one devil is stronger than all humankind). Rather, even if there were no dangers, no conflicts and no devils, I should be compelled to live under a continual uncertainty and only beat the air. Even if I were to live and work for all eternity, my conscience would never come to a settled certainty about how much it ought to do in order to satisfy God. Whatever work would be done, there would still remain a doubt whether or not it pleased God, or whether he required something more. This is proved in the experience of all justices and, as I myself learned to my bitter cost, through so many years of my own experience.[2]

Luther's position on human free will is consistent, although the arguments he uses vary because he is determined to deny it on two fronts: in the face of a doctrine on indulgences that seeks to attribute merit to human works; and in the face of Erasmus' more philosophical approach that seeks to elevate the nature of humankind in contrast to the ideas received from St Augustine.

Conclusion

The task of reading through Luther's theological works is rather daunting, given their extent and the man's significance in the history of the Church. However, the more broadly one reads his various treatises, books and disputations, the more one appreciates Luther's desire to propose and defend the faith of the Christian Church, derived from the authority of Scripture, against any group or person who would seek to

1. Ibid., 157.
2. Ibid., 164.

corrupt or claim authority over that faith. At times, this certainly led Luther to use language that seems rather extreme to modern ears in his denunciations both of Catholics and Protestants. Nevertheless, this is evidence of his devotion to God and to the word. Because Luther reacts against many perceived false teachings, his diverse writings with their different targets can contrast strongly with each other; however, it does generally seem to be a contrast rather than a contradiction.

Luther's works are available at the Post-Reformation Digital Library (www.prdl.org), generally in the original language either Latin or German, but also with some translations. The quotations here are paraphrases from original sources aided by available translations, some of which can be found at www.ccel.org (*Concerning Christian Liberty, The Bondage of Will, First Principles of the Reformation or the 95 Theses and the Three Primary Works, Table Talk, A Treatise on Good Works*) or from the great translation project, which is the series of *Luther's Works* (Saint Louis, MO: Concordia Publishing House, 1958-) that currently has 79 volumes.

8.
Huldrych Zwingli

I like the fact that Carter Lindberg, in his book *The European Reformations*, begins his chapter on Huldrych Zwingli (1484-1531) by referring to the 'Affair of the Sausages' – that seems to be a sign of a writer who knows how to get his readers interested.[1] We shall have a look at that shortly[2] but note first some of Zwingli's background in Switzerland. The humanism that he encountered during his university studies gave him important critical tools that were developed in contact with Erasmus and in his study of the biblical languages, allowing him to break free from the Thomistic tradition in his theological education.

Zwingli's powerful preaching gained him renown, partly because one of his major topics was opposition to the work of Swiss mercenary forces and partly because of his method in devotion to Scripture and its meaning, rather than the received teaching of the Church. This method was central to Zwingli throughout his life and was evident in his approach to many issues of which the most important and consistent is the theme of salvation through Christ alone. The sausages mentioned above is another example. Zwingli was present in 1522 when these were consumed during the period of Lenten fast. Although Zwingli did not himself eat the sausages, he did defend those who had on the basis that Scripture did not prescribe this fast and people were therefore free to choose whether or not to observe the fast commanded by the Church. His method of prioritising Scripture did lead to some problems for Zwingli with the Anabaptists, a group that advocated rebaptism as adults since the baptism of infants is not

---

1. Carter Lindberg, *The European Reformations* (Chichester: Wiley-Blackwell, 2010), p.161.
2. Good readers will notice that I have followed Lindberg's lead, just in a slightly duplicitous fashion.

explicitly mentioned in Scripture. Zwingli showed in debate with the Anabaptists that he prioritised what he saw as the clear implication of the Bible, rather than simply the words themselves, as he defended the practice of baptising infants.

In terms of this volume, there are two notable areas of Zwingli's thought that will come through in the presentation of his work. The first is his view of providence, with a work on that topic being the final study in this chapter. In the background to this teaching is a significant event in Zwingli's life; there was an outbreak of plague in Zurich in 1519 during which Zwingli nearly died. For Zwingli, reflecting on this, the sovereignty of God was manifested in his survival when so many others had died. Another area of importance is Zwingli's teaching on the sacraments in which he emphasised their symbolic importance, rather than any idea of these as instruments of grace.

Zwingli's role as a reformer has not been emphasised to the same extent as that of Luther and Calvin. Luther's attack on Zwingli on the issue of the Lord's Supper, reinforced by the prominence of Luther in the beginnings of the Reformation, left something of a stain on Zwingli's reputation, in which Luther's language (accusing Zwingli of doing the devil's work) played some part. In terms of the Swiss Reformation and its stress on the sovereignty of God, Zwingli's project was overtaken by John Calvin, with the relative success of the Geneva experiment at the end of Calvin's life a notable difference to Zwingli's death in battle defending his reformation.

We shall begin with some brief passages from his *Short Christian Instruction*, written in 1523 around the time of his disputes with John Faber, a Catholic, followed by short extracts from Zwingli's *Exposition and Basis of the Conclusions or Articles Published by Huldrych Zwingli* (The 67 Articles) of the same year, and his *Commentary on True and False Religion* of 1525. Finally, the most extensive work will be drawn from his treatise *On Providence*, which focuses on issues of grace and free will. In working through Zwingli's work, it seems that this approach of looking at individual books rather than themes is the most helpful for acquainting the reader with Zwingli's thought.

Short Christian Instruction

The *Short Christian Instruction* was written by Zwingli on behalf of the leaders of Zurich to people throughout the canton encouraging them in the means and content of the faith to which they should hold. It

discusses sin (the major focus in this section), law, gospel, images and
the mass as Zwingli believes these areas are taught in Scripture, which
is strongly affirmed as the authority for the faith, rather than and in
opposition to Catholic tradition and practice.

In writing about sin, Zwingli notes that it can be recognised in two
ways: from birth and in temptations. In terms of the first of these, the
fall of Adam into sin before there were children means that all people
'inherit this weakness from him'.[1] This is defended on the basis of like
reproducing like, so that as fallen people cannot give birth to an angel, so
fallen humans cannot produce an unblemished person. Zwingli lists the
results of sin for humankind:

> a loss of the grace and friendship of God, a loss of the indwelling,
> ruling or leading of the Spirit of God, a loss of the perfection of
> human nature and a fall into sin.[2]

The practical outworking of this is that 'Adam and all his descendants
are incapable of doing anything good because they are sinful', and that as
the grace of God has been lost, 'there is no salvation, but only complete
despair'.[3]

Secondly, the weakness that results from sin in human nature will
result in 'evil fruit forever and ever', as the corrupted desires that led to
the first sin manifest in every generation that follows.[4] Humans are now
naturally selfish and ambitious with insatiable desires:

> Each believes that the work of other people should serve them
> and works to achieve this. If a person does not destroy something,
> it is the result of the power of God rather than human power. . . .
> Human nature is always to look out for oneself and to think of
> oneself first.[5]

There is little of great note in this expression of sin beyond an
affirmation of a strong view of original sin in line with the main late-
Augustinian position. As we shall continue to see as we go through
Zwingli's relevant works, the doctrine of sin sets up the need for humans
to depend solely on God's grace for salvation.

---

1. Zwingli, *Short Christian Instruction*, 3.
2. Ibid.
3. Ibid.
4. Ibid.
5. Ibid.

The 67 Articles

The 67 Articles or Theses of the faith were the basis of the proposed
reformed church in Zurich, written by Zwingli and defended by him
before the city council. The first sixteen Articles concern the essence of
the Gospel and its authority in Scripture, with the remainder outlining
the nature of the reforms proposed in terms of the nature and practice
of Roman Christianity as it existed at that time. These do not therefore
comprise Zwingli's systematic theology as such, and finding explicit,
developed teaching on sin, grace and free will is difficult. Free will as
a concept is largely absent, not being a term that is found much in the
Bible; grace is mainly found in direct quotations from the Bible, with
the dominant applications being to grace and salvation and grace and
the law. For this work, there will only be a few quotations from a couple
of the early Articles that most clearly indicate something of Zwingli's
belief about the nature of sin.

Article 5 concerns the Gospel and there are a few passages here that
expand slightly on points noted above in the *Short Christian Instruction*.
The first concerns the effects of sin on humanity and looks also at the
role of grace in revival.

> If Adam and his descendants are dead, who will call them back to
> life? No person can because they are all on the side of death. No
> one who is dead can bring themselves back to life and, if everyone
> is dead in Adam, then all are incapable of bringing themselves
> back to life. They remain dead until the grace of God's Spirit
> makes them alive again, as it did at the beginning.[1]

This role of grace is developed later in the Article, broadening the
work from the revival of the person to their purification.

> Although the believer knows that they are not without traces
> of sin, faith nevertheless brings us goodness so that we discover
> through this process how utterly nothing we are. The more that
> this happens, the more God's Spirit and grace elevate and protect
> us from sinning; the more our trust in ourselves diminishes, the
> more our trust in God grows; and the more trust we have in God,
> the more presence also of the Spirit of God; the more grace, the
> less sin.[2]

---

1. Zwingli, *Exposition and Basis of the Conclusions or Articles Published by Huldrych Zwingli*, 5.
2. Ibid.

One great strength in the exposition of this Article is the work on defining sin, initially in the context of a susceptibility to sin.

> We ought to note in this context that the term 'sin' is sometimes taken to mean 'weakness' or 'fallen nature', which again and again tempts us to give in to the temptations of the flesh and is generally referred to as 'infirmity'.[1]

This idea of infirmity is included then in a reflection on the ways in which sin is related to unbelief, which begins Zwingli's conclusion of the whole matter of the Gospel.

> Sin is taken to mean unbelief. Firstly, in that anyone found in sin will not be saved. Secondly, sin is the infirmity and defect that results from fallen nature because of which we are incapable of doing anything in ourselves, since we are children of wrath although we have knowledge of the one true God . . . Thirdly, [sin is taken to mean] the works that grow out of sin like branches . . . Fourthly, sin sometimes indicates the sacrifice that was customarily made for sin.[2]

In the commentary on Article 16 about the inability of human teaching to contribute towards salvation, there is the following passage on the effects of sin on the human will that show Zwingli following Augustine closely in the corruption of the will.

> Theologians have attempted to reason from the term 'tend toward' the fact that we merely have an inclination towards evil rather than that we are evil, proud and useless by nature, which was broken in Adam. From this source, strong opinions have arisen about our free will, our abilities and the light of our understanding, which were followed by human teaching, laws, the sale of good works and every other hypocrisy. This was because all could fool themselves from the phrase 'tend toward' that they had overcome this tendency, despite knowing full well how they really were in themselves, in their inner being. If the concept that 'human feeling and desires are evil' had been taught clearly and without any doubt, no one would have dared to pride themselves on the basis of such obvious hypocrisy because they would have known that all our intentions are evil.[3]

---

1. Ibid.
2. Ibid.
3. Ibid., 16.

As with the *Short Christian Instruction*, we see in the Articles and their explanation the core of the Gospel message rather than deep theological considerations of topics, as is appropriate given the role of the Articles in the ongoing reformation in Zurich.

On True and False Religion

This 'commentary' is more systematic, written as it was as a response to a request that Zwingli's religious views be presented in Latin for consideration.[1] In terms of the structure of the book, the first sections are devoted to central theological topics – God, humankind, gospel, sin – while the last two-thirds move on to discuss aspects of Catholic religion, most notably looking through sacramental theology, and highlighting why Zwingli categorises these as 'false'. The focus here will be on the earlier sections, although the last quotation will come from the work on merit where free will is mentioned in relation to providence, an important note before we look at the book *On Providence*.

The first quotations come from Zwingli's teaching on humankind and show the corruption of human nature that began in and stems from the sin of Adam. On the first sin, Zwingli writes,

> The devil was envious of this happy condition of humankind and persuaded Adam's spouse that God told them not to eat from the tree because he feared for his dominion . . . Our first parent, who hoped to become a god as a result of the knowledge of good and evil, actually learned nothing but his disgrace and found eternal death.[2]

Zwingli develops the link between sin and death in considering death in its manifestation in the character of people rather purely as the end of life.

> Therefore, because humankind has become guilty of a love of self and stands convicted on that account, it is clear that death as sin, in terms of its character, consists in people always loving themselves, pleasing themselves, trusting themselves, taking the credit for everything, thinking that they can see what is straight and what is crooked and believing that what they approve all should approve, even the creator.[3]

---

1. This is not a commentary in the modern, biblical sense, but rather a full communication of views to friends.
2. Zwingli, *Commentary on True and False Religion*, 4.
3. Ibid.

The effects of this self-deception include a resistance to the idea of the total corruption of humanity that results from sin.

> Few people achieve such a high level of contempt for themselves that they claim that there is nothing good in them and openly confess the evil desires of their innermost heart. Therefore, people cannot be convinced that their whole heart is evil and admit to this. Persistently denying this, people even go so far in their boldness that they will change, or rather corrupt, the word of God to suit their views.[1]

The section that follows on from a discussion of humankind is on religion, which Zwingli believes in its true form is simply a complete devotion to God, whereas false religion gives part of its devotion to human reason or constructs. Zwingli seeks to show the need for complete dependence on God in order to move away from the exaltation of ourselves.

> Does it seem likely that Adam would have ever willingly come back to ask for grace on his own? You must admit that there is no reason to suppose it likely that one so determined to run away and hide that he could hardly be dragged out would have returned unless the Lord followed him in his flight . . . Let us suppose that God had let Adam be; Adam would never return to the one from whom he had fled. Let us suppose that God lets humankind be; we will never seek the one who created us. Everyone is a God to themselves and this is made plain by a worship of ourselves.[2]

The need to depend simply on God and his grace rather than any human merit or reason leads to a challenging idea in the section on Christian religion – certainly for a theologian – as Zwingli advocates a simple faith and questions the role of theologians in seeming to complicate the faith for their benefit.

> If people had widely started to rely on Christ – that is, on God's grace that is received from Christ and confirmed through Christ – who would have continued to pay them [the theologians] so much for looking after their salvation?[3]

The section on sin begins with a twofold definition of sin and shows how these inter-relate.

1. Ibid.
2. Ibid., 5.
3. Ibid., 6.

There is a twofold sense of sin in the teachings of the Gospel. Firstly, it is that disease which we contract from the author of our race, as a result of which we are handed over to a love of ourselves . . . Secondly, sin is that which is contrary to the law because a knowledge of sin comes from the law (Rom. 7:7). Therefore, any course of action that is contrary to the law is called sin. Let us now see how these two senses are related to each other, sin as disease and sin as a transgression of the law. A disease does not know that it is a disease and thinks that it is able to do whatever it likes. God does not think this and, when the disease tries to get everything for itself and thinks that all things were made to serve it and to minister to its greed, God prunes this rich growth using the sickle of the law.[1]

There is no separate section on grace in this work, but grace does appear in the section on sin in its work against the effects of sin. Zwingli has apparently been accused by some of encouraging too great a freedom for Christians in the supreme work of grace in salvation, and he seeks in this section to respond to these critics.

People argued that magnifying the grace that comes through Christ could make Christians become frivolous and immoral. I answer this by saying that anyone who trusts in Christ becomes a new person. How? Do they take off their original body and put on a new body? By no means! The original body remains. Therefore, does the disease that has been inherited remain in them? Yes. What is made new in us therefore? The heart. How? It happens in this way. Before the heart did not know God, and wherever there is no knowledge of God, there is only flesh, sin and selfishness; after God is known, a person sees their inner self to their heart and rejects themselves as they are then known. The result is that a person sees that all their works have no value, even those they had always thought were good. Therefore, when heavenly grace gives light to the heart and it comes to know God, a person is made new because where before they had trusted in their own wisdom, works, abilities or strength, they now put their hope in God alone.[2]

The section that follows the teaching on sin looks specifically at the sin against the Holy Spirit, that unforgiveable sin mentioned in Scripture without clarification about what precisely this entails. There have been many attempts to define what it might be, and Zwingli reduces it to a lack of faith.

---

1. Ibid., 10.
2. Ibid.

Where there is faith, although you always remain a sinner, you will never stop hating the unfortunate inclination to sin and are therefore always trying to renew yourself. On the other hand, where there is no faith, no account is kept either of sin or of the fear of God . . . Therefore, it is the greatest blasphemy against God not to trust in him . . . And so, it is only a lack of faith, which we call unfaithfulness or unbelief, that is never forgiven because this never takes hold of or worships God, never fears him, never puts itself in line with his will, never avoids sin so that he is not offended.[1]

As was mentioned above, the last quotation comes from a much later section on merit in which the supremacy of grace in Zwingli's thought is again made manifest in the inability of humans to help themselves.

It would be strange if the supreme good knew everything before it happened and yet was not able to plan and to order everything. In the same way, it would be ungenerous and mean if God could control all things, and had all knowledge and all power, and yet did not control everything; and it would be impious to accuse the supreme deity of this. The providence of God therefore completely removes free will and merit because, if it orders everything, what part do we play that allows us to think highly of anything that we have done ourselves? Since everything is done through his activity, how can we have any merit?[2]

Given that the sections in the *Commentary on True and False Religion* are fairly short and generally deal with quite large topics, the work is very useful for gaining an insight into Zwingli's theology without getting overly profound in its exploration of specific ideas. The last of the works examined in this chapter is far deeper in its engagement with our main themes and thus receives a more significant amount of space.

On Providence

This work is far more specific in its focus and thus achieves greater depth of insight. Published in 1530, it is dedicated to Landgrave Philip of Hesse (who commissioned it) and is based on Zwingli's recollection of a sermon on Divine Providence, delivered at the Landgrave's castle in Marburg the previous year. In the introduction, Zwingli apologises

---

1. Ibid., 11.
2. Ibid., 24.

that he cannot remember every word and thus writes this short treatise, which at over a hundred pages in most translations is, I hope, extended well beyond the original sermon that Philip listened to.

In the opening chapter, Zwingli asserts the importance of holding to the providence of God as part of the sovereign nature of God in relationship to creation.

> We will see that providence must exist and that it both cares for and regulates everything. It is in the nature of supreme truth to see everything clearly, since whatever is divine must see everything; it is in the nature of supreme might to do what it sees, or rather to do everything; and finally, it is in the nature of the supreme good to will in its goodness to do what it clearly sees and what it can do; from these it follows that he who can do everything must provide for everything.[1]

This view of God means that the history of creation is unalterable from the perspective of such a supreme being, which necessarily affects the extent to which the human will can be called free.

> I called the direction and regulation [of everything] unchangeable in order to show that the opinion of those who declare that the human will is free is not completely well-founded. The wisdom of the supreme deity is too certain to allow the possibility of anything happening without its knowledge that might force that wisdom to later change its designs.[2]

When looking at human action and influence that might be seen to cause things to happen, Zwingli turns to a line of thought that is very similar to aspects of Aquinas' thought in attributing primary causation to God and secondary causation to created factors.

> Any means or instruments that are called causes are not correctly named except figuratively, in that they derive this ability to cause from the one first cause of all that exists. It is the same as anything that is attributed to an angel, which does not belong to the angel but to the God who sent the angel.[3]

To allow primary causation in anything other than God, for Zwingli, denies the very existence of God because it does not allow for the absolute supremacy of God in all things.

---

1. Zwingli, *On Providence*, 1.
2. Ibid., 2.
3. Ibid., 3.

If anything happens by chance or randomly, if anything exists of itself and is independent of God, then everything is random and drifts along by chance; in this case, all wisdom, thought and reason of all intelligent beings is empty and meaningless . . . Everything will act according to its own pleasing will, everything will only obey chance and fortune and nothing will follow intelligence, reason or thought. In this case, there will simply be no deity.[1]

This is clearly a very black and white understanding of intellect as derived from God and is the logical conclusion of the kind of providence that Zwingli initially establishes that he understands from the Bible.

The next chapter goes on to discuss the dignity of humankind and establishes a governing position for humans over creation as God governs humankind. The uniqueness of humanity is that it might have fellowship with God. At this point, Zwingli seems to move into strongly dualist language regarding humankind, elevating spirit over body first in the creation when 'an intelligent spirit was planted in a dull body'.[2] The result is that the human mind continues to seek God, while the body seeks its own delight.

The human mind is an unblemished, clear stream that flows forth from the Godhead itself. This is why it is so eager for truth and right and is so devoted to these that if you considered it alone, separated from the dark mass of the body, like the angels exist, you would find nothing low, disturbing or corrupt in it.

The mind seeks light, purity and goodness because its nature is light, its substance is pure and is devoted to what is right, since its origin comes from the Godhead; the body inclines to idleness, laziness, darkness and dullness, because its nature is lazy and sluggish, without reason or intelligence, since it consists of earth.

The mind groans for God and expects to receive everything from his riches, not from its own worth; the flesh, while it thunders and roars, declares that it is owed everything.[3]

The unity of the human person is indicated in the judgement that is given by God.

---

1. Ibid.
2. Ibid., 4.
3. Ibid.

Why is the soul damned if sin comes from the desires of the impetuous nature of the flesh? I answer briefly because the person has sinned against the law. The law was given so that sins would not be committed; where there is no law, there is no transgression.[1]

Even with this extension of punishment to the whole person, the dualism present in the earlier passages, the continuing purity of the 'mind' – which clearly has spiritual overtones, being that which is received from God – set against the corruption of the body, is surprising to find in a writer of Zwingli's time, with its clear echoes of Gnosticism and the spiritualist 'Fanatics' around at the time from whom the major reformers sought to distance themselves in their theology.

The next chapter moves on to creation and the existence of evil in the creation of a good God from whom only goodness can proceed – one of the classic questions of theology to which these volumes have already seen multiple responses. Early in this discussion, Zwingli shows the role of evil in revealing the righteousness of God.

How can we recognise righteousness if there is no unrighteousness? . . . We cannot know what good is unless there is evil, and through comparing and judging these we understand the notion of goodness . . . Because the deity could not demonstrate unrighteousness in himself, because he is perfectly true, holy and good in his nature, he produced an example of unrighteousness through a created being. This was not the created being producing unrighteousness of itself, since it cannot have being, life or work without the deity, but rather the deity himself is the author of that which is unrighteousness for us, although it is not this in any way for him.[2]

This is a line of thought that Zwingli will follow in further presentations, that that which is evil for the creation of God is not evil for him because there can be no evil in God. There does seem to be a contrast drawn here between the being and action of God. He describes the creation of angels and humankind in righteousness but with a law to follow, and then states: 'Both sinned because both had to know what righteousness and integrity are; as soon as they had sinned, they saw the face of righteousness.'[3] This is slightly strange in the case of angels, at least, since those angels that did not fall only knew of righteousness because of other angels who fell. However, Zwingli continues the idea:

---

1. Ibid.
2. Ibid., 5.
3. Ibid.

The angel was cast out of the home of the blessed and was handed over to eternal fire; humankind was cast out of their happy home but was saved by the mercy of God, in the same way that one who may be killed by the laws of war could be spared and made a slave. God made both of these things happen, but used an instigator as an instrument for his purposes: in the angel, this was his ambitious spirit; in humankind, it was their flesh and the devil. However, God himself is not unrighteous and what he did is not unrighteousness for him because he is not under the law . . . Therefore, when God makes the angel and human sinners, he is still not shown to be a sinner himself because the law does not apply to him. Therefore what God did was not sin, but for humans and the angel it was sin because the law pursues them and accuses them. God is free to deal with his creatures as he sees fit, just as a person is free with his property or a potter with his clay.[1]

In creating humans with the capacity for sin, there was thus no sin in God in Zwingli's opinion because the Fall demonstrated the glory of God: 'In creating humankind so that they could fall, God showed his goodness because the Fall made clear the splendour of divine righteousness.'[2] There is thus a more active agency of God for Zwingli in the Fall of the angels and humankind than has generally been seen in previous writings examined in these surveys of thought.

Following the Fall, humankind remain the instruments of God's will because nothing can happen outside that will (as we saw in earlier sections of *On Providence*). This means that ongoing sin can still be considered as the indirect work of God, still causing guilt and punishment for those who commit the sin without staining the character of the God who directs all things.

Because the law was given to people, they always sin when they act against the law; however, it is true that people do not exist, live or do any work except in God, of God and through God. What God brings about through the work of people is imputed as a crime to them, but not also to God, because one is under the law while the other is the free spirit and the mind behind the law. When we say therefore that divine providence did this or that evil, which one person or another has carried out, we do not speak correctly because, insofar as God does it, it is not a sin because it is not against the law . . . Therefore, the same deed, be it adultery

1. Ibid.
2. Ibid.

or murder, insofar as God is the author, mover and instigator, is an act but not a crime; but as it concerns the person acting, it is a crime and is wicked.[1]

Zwingli gives the example of King David's adultery and how he views this in relation to God.

God does everything freely, not influenced by any evil emotion, and therefore without any sin. David's adultery, as God is the author of it, is no more a sin for God than when a bull covers and impregnates a whole herd.[2]

The result of this for the nature of humankind in relation to God is that we are pictured as tools to be used for his glory.

Therefore, the same action that is committed through the instigation and under the direction of God brings honour to him, while it is at the same time a crime and a sin for a person . . . In this, God does no wrong to the instrument because everything is his, more than a craftsman's tools are his own. The craftsman does no wrong if he chooses to turn a file into a hammer or a hammer into a file.[3]

Before considering salvation and the role of humanity in this, Zwingli highlights the absurdity – in his view – of asserting the freedom of the human will, given that everything is created by and continues under the direction of God.

How can we claim the credit for anything ourselves, since we do not even exist, much less live or act, without God? Therefore, since nothing can be or exist by its own power – and cannot live, act, understand or deliberate, because the present power of God does all these – how could the human will be considered free?[4]

His thought on salvation, that follows, shows the absolute supremacy of the work of God in saving humans, and the role of the human will as described in Scripture must therefore be subject to this overarching understanding of the relationship between God and creature.

Therefore, free will or merit cannot be upheld in reality, although no one can deny that they are named and discussed in the Holy Scriptures. However, this can certainly only be the naming of

1. Ibid., 6.
2. Ibid.
3. Ibid.
4. Ibid.

things that belong to God alone, which are given to people as a gracious gift to our natures, proving God's friendship; or a kind of loan given to people because everything is of God and to God.[1]

In moving towards a summary of this extensive chapter, Zwingli reiterates that all things related to humankind have their source and their end in God.

The conclusion of all this is that everything that concerns humankind, related to their body or to their soul, is so completely from God as the only real cause that not even an action of sin is from any source other than God – although it is not a sin in him, as I said earlier in this discussion.[2]

Zwingli moves on to talk of the election of God, a topic concerning which this prior work has removed many of the potential complications, and Zwingli begins by restating that election is not due to any human worth. A case study that Zwingli uses relates to infants, who are declared to be part of the elect because of the work of Christ, if, as we shall see, they are born to believing parents:

Anyone who has once been elected, always remains elect. If this were not so, those who die in infancy and are not part of the elect are sentenced to eternal punishment without having deserved this because they have been saved from original sin through the mediation of Christ, and they have themselves done no wrong.[3]

Those who continue to live and fall away show that they are not part of the elect by their profligate life. Zwingli therefore holds to his concept of original sin and original grace through Christ for the children of believing parents.

No one's election is more sure than those children who are taken away while young, while they are still without the law. People's lives are sometimes not really righteous, but only in appearance; but there can be no stain of sin in children who are born of believing parents. This is because original sin has been atoned for by Christ (because as in Adam we all die, so in Christ we are all restored to life, that is those who believe or are in his Church according to the promise) and no stain of wicked deeds can corrupt them because they are not yet under the law. Therefore, since only sin

1. Ibid.
2. Ibid.
3. Ibid.

can separate a person from God and these infants are without any
sin, it is clear that no one is so incontrovertibly known to be one
of the elect as those children who end their days while they are
young.[1]

In the Epilogue to this work, Zwingli continues to assert the
sovereignty of God, the certainty of his election and returns to the idea
that the Fall was caused by God ultimately for the benefit of humankind
although it was itself evil.

> Because the Fall brought disaster for humankind, it was clearly
> not a blessing itself, nor can the disaster that followed from it be
> called a blessing. However, when we think about what humankind
> learned as a consequence of the Fall – namely a knowledge of
> righteousness that we could not learn except by looking at the face
> of unrighteousness, which God could not display himself – we can
> see that the Fall was imposed on the human race for their good,
> that we might learn from the Fall and from sinning what we could
> not have learnt through honest work and endeavour.[2]

Conclusion

The most eye-catching of Zwingli's theology in terms of sin, grace and
free will is clearly found in *On Providence* where distinctive positions on
the origin and nature of sin appear, with connections to the supremacy of
grace and the limitations when talking about human free will. As such,
these have formed the longest section of this chapter. What is noticeable
when reading through the corpus of Zwingli's works is how surprising
some of these statements appear, when the remainder of his work is so
bound to Scripture and its immediate implications that there is little of
great note to extract for its profound wisdom or as points for contention.

The quotations here are my own from the works that are available
(for those that can read them in the original language) at the Post-
Reformation Digital Library (www.prdl.org). For a long time, Zwingli's
work was not easily available in English, although Samuel Macauley
Jackson had arranged the translation of many over a century ago. There
are several recent publications generally from this origin, including
On Providence and Other Essays (Durham, NC: The Labyrinth Press,
1922) that was reprinted in 1983 and the *Commentary on True and
False Religion* (Durham, NC: The Labyrinth Press, 1923) reprinted in

---

1. Ibid.
2. Ibid., Epilogue.

1981. E.J. Furcha has translated and published two volumes of *Huldrych Zwingli Writings* (Allison Park, PA: Pickwick Publications, 1984) in which the 67 Articles, with many other Zwingli texts, are expounded.

For secondary literature on Zwingli, the major books on the Reformation such as Lindberg's *The European Reformations* (mentioned in the introduction to the chapter) or Alistair McGrath's *Reformation Thought: An Introduction* (Oxford: Blackwell, 1999) are good for setting Zwingli in the context of other contemporary debates. There are still not many works dedicated to Zwingli, but if you want some real depth then G.R. Potter's *Zwingli* (Cambridge: Cambridge University Press, 1976) remains an excellent source.

9.
John Calvin

Presenting Calvin's thought is a significant task given both the extent and depth of his thought, and his impact on and relation to churches and theologies that claim a connection to the reformer. What becomes clear as one reads Calvin himself is the distance that there often is between the original source and the systems of thought that have developed from this beginning.

John Calvin (1509-1564) was born in France and trained as a lawyer before leaving the Roman Catholic Church and fleeing France for the Swiss lands. He then travelled around Europe and engaged with many different Protestant voices, arriving in Geneva in 1536. He intended to stay only a short time but was convinced by a great preacher named Guillaume Farel (1489-1565) to stay and organise the reformation of religion in that city. Calvin famously records that Farel threatened Calvin with a curse if he did not stay and the fear this engendered led Calvin to remain in Geneva. Barring a short exile in Strasbourg, Geneva would be the centre of Calvin's work for the remainder of his life. The reforms that Calvin brought to the religious and civic life of that city have been the study of a large number of books, with the theme of morality – excessive, ideal or otherwise – often at the centre of discussions.

In terms of his theological project, Calvin sits in a different time and thus has a different method of argument to that of Luther and Zwingli. They experienced the first battles with the Catholic Church and there is a strong reactionary element to their writings as they confront issues that arise both with the Catholics and, particularly in Luther's case, with the Fanatics or Radical Reformers. Calvin can be more considered and constructive in his theology, most notably in his *Institutes of the Christian Religion*, which was first published in 1536 and went through various editions until the final version was published in 1559. This is a great systematic theology that clearly bears in mind issues with the Catholic

Church as well as disagreements within emerging Protestantism. Nevertheless, it builds its own theology from the authority of the Scriptures and the teachings of the church.

The *Institutes* comprises four books on the knowledge of God the creator, the knowledge of God the redeemer in Christ, the mode of obtaining the grace of Christ and on the Holy Catholic Church – the last clearly considering the Catholic Church from the theology developed in the first three books. The *Institutes* will form the major basis of this presentation, with some additional material brought in from Calvin's *On the Bondage and Liberation of the Will.* This work is a response to Albert Pighius (c.1490-1542) who had written ten books on free choice and predestination arguing for a strong role of the human will in salvation. Much of the work involves Calvin clarifying the tradition of the Church in this area against Pighius' misuse of historical sources and is an interesting commentary on texts that have been presented in earlier chapters of this volume and in Volume One of this series. This clarifies Calvin's task in his theology as the recovery of the faith of the Church based on the authority of the Bible rather than a new theology for his time.

The decision not to use commentaries or sermons as sources in this series of studies cuts out a large number of Calvin's works. However, these two major works are sufficient for an extended presentation of Calvin's views on our three key themes of sin, grace and free will.

God

We must look first at some of Calvin's main concepts of God that relate to sin, grace and free will. Calvin starts by recognising the distance that exists between us and God as a result of sin, which means that God will always be beyond our comprehension and that his values, actions and purposes cannot be judged from any human perspective.

> The miserable ruin that the rebellion of the first human plunged us into forces us to turn our eyes upwards, not only that we can request of God what we want when hungry and famishing, but also that we may learn humility as we are made fearful. Just as humans have something like a world of misery in them, and ever since we were stripped of our divine clothing, our naked shame shows us a great range of disgraceful attributes, every person as they are convicted by a consciousness of their own unhappiness necessarily obtains from this at least some knowledge of God.

Therefore our sense of our ignorance, pride, desires, weaknesses, in short our depravity and corruption, remind us that the true light of wisdom, solid virtue and exuberant goodness dwell only in the Lord and in no one else. We are therefore urged by our own evil to consider the good things of God, and indeed we cannot earnestly seek him until we have begun to be displeased with ourselves.[1]

The purity of God that we see when we turn from ourselves to contemplate him shows us that even what we had considered good in ourselves is dirty in light of his glorious holiness.

But when we begin to raise our thoughts to God and reflect on what kind of being he is – how absolute is the perfection of his righteousness, wisdom and virtue, to which we are called to be conformed as our standard – what had formerly delighted us in its false appearance of righteousness will be seen as polluted with the greatest evil; what had been strangely imposed on us as wisdom will disgust us in its extreme foolishness; and what had presented the appearance of virtuous energy will stand condemned as the most miserable impotence. This is how far even those qualities which seem most perfect in us are from corresponding to the divine purity.[2]

Both the above quotations focus on the standards of God and effect the view of human nature and sin that will be developed. Another key aspect of Calvin's doctrine of God is his sovereignty in all things, something that he clarifies in relation to the Stoics.

We do not agree with the Stoics who imagine a necessity that consists of a perpetual chain of causes, a kind of related series of events contained in nature, but we believe that God is the disposer and ruler of all things, that from the remotest eternity he decreed what he would do according to his own wisdom and now executes this through his power. Therefore we maintain that all things are governed by his providence, not only heaven and earth and inanimate creatures but also human counsels and wills so that they move exactly in the course that he has destined. You will then ask, does anything happen fortuitously or contingently? I answer that Basil the Great truly said that fortune and chance are pagan terms, and pious minds should not contemplate their

1. Calvin, *Institutes of the Christian Religion*, 1.1.1 (*i.e.* book.chapter.section).
2. Ibid., 1.1.2.

meaning. Since all success is a blessing from God and all disaster or adversity are his curse, there can be no place left in human affairs for fortune and chance.[1]

Here we must begin by correcting one important misconception about Calvin's work, namely, that predestination is the foundational concept of the *Institutes*. In fact, it is the providence of God that provides the basis, with predestination left until much later. Certainly, Calvin teaches a strong view of predestination, but it develops from this earlier concept. The discussion of the relation of providence to the nature and will of humans will be presented below, but here we shall focus on this aspect of the doctrine of God. Calvin continues to explore the idea in relation to what appears to us as an open future.

> In terms of our ability to discern, all these things appear to be fortuitous. How should the Christian feel about this? Although they will consider that every circumstance related to a person's death was indeed fortuitous in nature, they will also have no doubt that the providence of God overruled in all this and guided fortune to his own end. The same idea holds in the case of future contingencies. All future events are uncertain for us, and there is suspense as if they are ready to take either direction. However, the impression remains seated in our hearts that nothing will happen that the Lord has not provided. It is in this sense that the term 'event' is repeatedly used in Ecclesiastes because, at first glance, people do not see through to the primary cause that lies hidden. However, what is taught in Scripture about the secret providence of God has never been completely removed from the human heart, and so some sparks continue to shine in the darkness.
>
> What seems to us to be contingence, faith recognises as the secret work of God. The reason for this work is not always equally apparent, but we must hold that all changes that take place in the world are produced by the secret agency of the hand of God. At the same time, that which God has determined is not in its own nature necessary, although it must come to pass.[2]

---

1. Ibid., 1.16.8.
2. Ibid., 1.16.9.

The Devil

This section will seek to establish some foundational understanding of spiritual realities in the nature of the devil and the relationship between God and the devil that affect the main themes. Calvin (unlike, for example, Thomas Aquinas) is more focused on humanity than on hypothesising about the spiritual dimension, except as it is revealed in Scripture and relevant to human life.

Calvin affirms that God created the devil as good and that the fall of the devil was the result of his rebellion rather than the action of God.

> Since the devil was created by God, we must remember that the evil that we attribute to his nature is not from his creation, but from his depravation. Everything that is damnable in him he brought upon himself through his revolt and fall. Scripture reminds us of this to prevent us from believing that he was created evil at first, and thus ascribe to God what is most foreign to his nature. For this reason, Christ declares (John 8:44) that Satan, when he lies, 'speaks from himself', and states that the reason is 'because he did not live in the truth'. By saying that he did not live in the truth, Christ certainly implies that the devil was at one point in the truth; and by calling the devil the father of lies, Christ removes from the devil the power to charge God with the depravity that he himself was the cause of. Although these expressions are brief and not very explicit, they are certainly sufficient to vindicate the majesty of God from every blame. What concern is it of ours to know more about devils? Some argue that we seek more because Scripture does not in the various passages give a clear and regular exposition of Satan's fall, its cause, mode, date and nature. But these things are of no concern to us, and so it is better at least to deal with them only lightly, if not to pass over them entirely in silence. The Holy Spirit did not choose to feed curiosity with idle, unprofitable histories. We see that it was the Lord's purpose to deliver nothing in his sacred oracles from which we might not learn to build ourselves up. Therefore, instead of dwelling on superfluous matters, it should be enough for us simply to hold in regard to the nature of devils that at their first creation they were angels of God, but as a result of their revolt they both ruined themselves and became the instruments of destruction for others.[1]

---

1. Ibid., 1.14.16.

While there may not be great detail as to the nature or formation of the devils in Scripture, Calvin does highlight that they continue to come under the authority of God even in their fallen state.

> It is clear that Satan is under the power of God and is so ruled by his authority that he must submit in obedience to it. In addition, although we say that Satan resists God and performs works that differ from God's works, at the same time we maintain that this difference and opposition depend on the permission of God. I am now speaking only about the result of Satan's work, not about Satan's will and endeavour. Because the will of the devil is evil, he has no inclination whatsoever to obey the divine will; on the contrary, his will is wholly bent on stubbornness and rebellion. Therefore, from himself and his own evil he eagerly and with set purpose opposes God, aiming at those things which he considers most to work against the will of God. However, since God holds him bound and fettered by the limits set by his power, the devil only executes those things for which permission has been given to him. He therefore obeys his creator, however unwillingly, being forced to serve him whenever he is required.[1]

Later in Book One, Calvin makes the same point rather more succinctly: 'Therefore, whatever humans or Satan himself plan, God holds the helm and makes all their efforts contribute to the execution of his judgements.'[2] This control of God is important in considering the extent to which Satan is active in temptation in view of certain passages in Scripture.

> Nothing can be clearer than the many passages which declare that Satan blinds the minds of men, punishes them with instability, intoxicates them with a spirit of laziness, makes them infatuated and hardens their hearts. Many would limit even these expressions to permission as if, by deserting the reprobate, God allowed them to be blinded by Satan. But since the Holy Spirit distinctly says that blindness and infatuation are inflicted as the just judgement of God, this solution is completely inadmissible . . . I would admit that God often acts in the reprobate through the agency of Satan, but in such a manner that Satan himself performs his part only as he is impelled and succeeds only insofar as he is permitted.[3]

---

1. Ibid., 1.14.17.
2. Ibid., 1.18.1.
3. Ibid., 1.18.2.

We shall return to the devil later in dealing with sin and free will. Nevertheless, we must bear in mind this concept for Calvin that the Satan remains under the control of God and only acts in accordance with the will of God as an agent of his justice.

The Origin of Sin

We turn now to humanity in its created state and the change of that nature to evil in the Fall. In considering this, Calvin upholds the free will possessed by humans in their first state that led to the first sin.

> In their righteous [created] state, humans possessed freedom of the will by which, if they had chosen, they were able to obtain eternal life. This is not the time to ask the question about the secret predestination of God because we are not considering what might or might not have happened, but only what was the true nature of humanity. Adam, therefore, might have stood if he had so chosen, since he fell only by his own will; but he fell so easily because his will was pliable in either direction and he had not yet received steadfastness that he might persevere. Adam had a free choice of good and evil; not only this, but there was the greatest righteousness in the mind and will, and all the organic parts were duly framed to obedience until Adam corrupted his good properties and destroyed himself.[1]

Calvin discusses briefly why humanity was not given a stronger nature to resist temptation in this first state but does not conclude anything beyond the right of God to create as he saw fit.

> At present, it is only necessary to remember that humankind, at their first creation, was very different from all their descendants who, deriving their origin from Adam after he was corrupted, received a hereditary defect. In the first state, every aspect of the soul was formed for righteousness; there was soundness of mind and freedom of will to choose the good. If anyone objects that humans were, so to speak, placed in a slippery position because their power was weak, I answer that the nature conferred was sufficient to remove any excuse. Surely the deity cannot be tied down to a condition that he should make humans so that they either could not or would not sin. Such a nature might have been more excellent, but to argue with God as if it were his duty

1. Ibid., 1.15.8.

to confer such a nature on humans is more than unjust, seeing
that God had full right to determine how much or how little
he would give. Why God did not sustain Adam by the virtue
of perseverance is hidden in his counsel; we must keep within
the bounds of sobriety. Humans received the power to do good,
if they maintained the will; but they did not have the will that
would have given them the power because such a will would
have been followed by perseverance. Having received so much,
there is no excuse for Adam having spontaneously brought
death upon himself. There was no necessity for God to give
Adam more than an intermediate and even temporary will, so
that he might extract materials for his own glory out of the fall
of humankind.[1]

It is in Book Two that the sin of Adam is discussed in terms of its
nature.

Since the action that God punished so severely cannot have been
a trivial fault, but must have been a heinous crime, it is necessary
to look at the peculiar nature of the sin that produced Adam's fall
and that provoked God to inflict such fearful vengeance on the
whole human race. The common idea of a lack of sensual control
is childish. The substance and totality of all virtue could not
consist in abstaining from a single fruit amid a general abundance
of every delicacy that could be desired, the earth in its happy
fertility yielding not only abundance but also endless variety. We
must therefore look deeper than a lack of sensual control. The
command not to touch the tree of the knowledge of good and evil
was a trial of obedience, so that Adam would prove his willing
submission to the command of God by his obedience. . . . At the
same time, we can observe that the first man revolted against the
authority of God not only in allowing himself to be tempted by
the plots of the devil, but also by despising the truth and turning
aside to lies. Assuredly, when the word of God is despised, all
reverence for him is gone.[2]

Before looking at fallen human nature and its relationship to sin, it
is worth highlighting a passage on Adam that has indications for the
results of the first sin on humankind. Shortly after the previous quotation,
Calvin makes this explicit:

---

1. Ibid.
2. Ibid., 2.1.4.

After the heavenly image was destroyed in Adam, he was not only punished himself by the withdrawal of the ornaments in which he had been arrayed (wisdom, virtue, justice, truth and holiness) and the substitution in their place of those evil characteristics (blindness, impotence, vanity, impurity and unrighteousness), but he also involved his posterity and plunged them into the same wretchedness. This is the hereditary corruption that the early Christian writers called 'original sin', meaning by this the depravation of a nature formerly good and pure . . . All of us therefore, because we are descended from an impure seed, come into the world tainted with the disease of sin. Even before we see the light of the sun we are defiled and polluted in God's sight.[1]

There is a similar teaching on the fall of humanity and its effects in *On the Bondage and Liberation of the Will*:

Already I have it on Pighius' own admission that we ascribe the fact that man is evil not to nature nor to the origin of the first man, but only to his wrongdoing by which he brought this wretchedness on himself. For we do not deny that man was created with free choice, endowed as he was with sound intelligence of mind and uprightness of will. We do declare that our choice is now held captive under bondage to sin, but how did this come about except by Adam's misuse of free choice when he had it?[2]

Later in the same work, Calvin writes:

But surely it is the native philosophy of Christians that our first ancestor corrupted not only himself but all his offspring at the same time, and that it is from this that we derive the habit which resides in our nature.[3]

From this basis, we now turn to look at human nature as we receive it, looking first at its sinfulness before moving on to see the effects on the human will and the possibility for receiving grace.

---

1. Ibid., 2.1.5.
2. Calvin, *On the Bondage and Liberation of the Will*, Book Two, p.47 (page numbers are included from the translation volume because the work is not broken up beyond the book level, so this will allow readers to locate quotations from the book).
3. Ibid., Book Four, p.150.

Sin and Human Nature

In this section we examine passages that show Calvin's views on the corruption of human nature by the sin received from Adam. This is indicated in the following passage from the *Institutes of the Christian Religion* that looks back before sin and ahead to the restored human nature.

> Therefore, just as the image of God constitutes the entire excellence of human nature as it shone in Adam before his fall, but was afterwards corrupted and almost destroyed, with nothing remaining but a ruin – confused, mutilated and tainted with impurity – so it is now partly seen in the elect to the extent that they are regenerated by the Spirit. However, its full brightness will be displayed in heaven.[1]

The theme is picked up in Book Two, which deals extensively with sin and its effects as necessary for our understanding and knowledge of the redemption of God.

> We see that the impurity of parents is transmitted to their children so that all, without exception, are depraved in their origins. The beginning of this depravity will not be found until we reach the first parent of all as the fountainhead. We must therefore believe for certain that Adam was not merely the first parent from whom human nature was derived, but a kind of root that, on account of his corruption, the whole human race was deservedly corrupted.[2]

Calvin writes on this theme in *On the Bondage and Liberation of the Will.*

> We say that man has inborn in him a perversity derived from inherited corruption, so that he should blame himself whenever he sins and not fix the blame elsewhere when he finds the root of evil in his own self.[3]

Later in the same work, Calvin writes:

> We say that he [man] is evil because he comes from an evil descent, like a bad branch from a bad, corrupt root. Therefore, as long as he continues in his own nature, he cannot will and act except in

---

1. *Institutes of the Christian Religion*, 1.15.4.
2. Ibid., 2.1.6.
3. *On the Bondage and Liberation of the Will*, 2, p.39.

an evil way. Indeed we deny that it is in his power to abandon his wickedness and turn to the good. Since, then, he can of himself be nothing but evil, we determine that there is necessity in his case. And that not indeed without qualification, but insofar as he originates from an evil root and maintains his original character, that is, for as long as he is not led by the Spirit of God.[1]

This sets the scene for a lengthy definition and development of the concept of original sin in Calvin's understanding.

Original sin may be defined as the hereditary corruption and depravity of our nature that extends to every part of the soul, which first makes us hateful and under the wrath of God and then produces in us works which Scripture terms 'works of the flesh'. This corruption Paul repeatedly designates as 'sin' (Gal. 5:19), while the works that proceed from it – adultery, fornication, theft, hatred, murder, orgies – he calls the 'fruits of sin' (although in various passages of Scripture, and even by Paul himself, they are also termed sins). . . . We are thus perverted and corrupted in every part of our nature and, simply because of this corruption, we are deservedly condemned by God for whom nothing is acceptable except righteousness, innocence and purity. However, this is not a liability for another's fault. When it is said that the sin of Adam has made us hateful to the justice of God, the meaning is not that we who are ourselves innocent and blameless are bearing his guilt, but that his sin has placed us all under the curse and therefore he has left us under an obligation to God. Through Adam we have not only derived punishment, but have a pollution instilled in us for which punishment is justly due.

Therefore, even infants who bring their condemnation with them from their mother's womb do not suffer for another but for their own inherent defect. Although they have not yet produced the fruits of their own unrighteousness, they have the seed for these implanted in them. Indeed, their whole nature is a kind of seed-bed of sin, and therefore must be hateful and abominable to God. It therefore follows that human nature is rightly deemed sinful in the sight of God, because there can be no condemnation without guilt.

Our nature is not only completely devoid of goodness, but so prolific in all kinds of evil that it can never be idle. Those who term this 'concupiscence' use a word that is quite appropriate

1. Ibid., 4, p.149-50.

provided it is added (which many would in no way allow) that everything in a person, from the intellect to the will, from the soul even to the flesh, is defiled and pervaded with this concupiscence. Alternatively, to express this more briefly, the whole person is in themselves nothing but concupiscence.[1]

The results of this for fallen human nature can be easily inferred, but it is worth highlighting a few passages where Calvin works this out. Shortly after the previous lengthy quotations, Calvin succinctly states:

Here I only wished briefly to observe that the whole person, from the crown of the head to the sole of the foot, is so deluged, as it were, that no part remains exempt from sin and, therefore, everything which proceeds from a person is imputed as sin.[2]

Earlier in Book One there were indications of a similar concept of humanity.

[Such is our innate pride that] we always seem to ourselves to be just, upright, wise and holy, until we are convinced by clear evidence of our injustice, evil nature, foolishness and impurity . . . Because we are all naturally prone to hypocrisy, any empty semblance of righteousness is quite enough to satisfy us instead of righteousness itself. And since nothing appears within us or around us that is not tainted with very great impurity, so long as we keep our minds within the confines of human pollution, anything that is in some small degree less defiled delights us as if it were most pure; just as an eye, to which nothing but black had been previously presented, deems an object of a whitish or even a brownish hue to be perfectly white.[3]

There is an additional element to this corruption of humankind through sin in the role of temptation and the spiritual forces that engage with people.

God turns the unclean spirits here and there at his pleasure, employing them in testing believers by warring against them, attacking them with temptations, urging them with solicitations, pressing close upon them, disturbing, alarming and occasionally wounding them, but never conquering or oppressing them. On the other hand, they hold the wicked in their power, exercising

---

1. *Institutes of the Christian Religion*, 2.1.8.
2. Ibid., 2.1.9.
3. Ibid., 1.1.2.

dominion over their minds and bodies and employing them as slaves in all kinds of evil. Since believers are disturbed by these enemies, they are addressed in exhortations such as these: 'Do not give a place to the devil'; 'Your enemy the devil is like a roaring lion, walking about and seeking whom he may devour; you should resist him steadfastly in the faith' (Eph. 4:27; 1 Pet. 5:8). Paul acknowledges that he was not exempt from this type of contest when he says that a messenger of Satan was sent to buffet him in order to subdue his pride (2 Cor. 12:7). This trial is therefore common to all the children of God, but because the promise of bruising Satan's head (Gen. 3:15) applies alike to Christ and to all his members, I deny that believers can ever be oppressed or conquered by Satan. They are certainly often thrown into alarm, but never so thoroughly that they cannot recover themselves. They fall from the violence of the blows, but they get up again; they are wounded, but not mortally. In conclusion, they labour on through the whole course of their lives so as to gain the ultimate victory, although they meet with occasional defeats on the way.[1]

The last part of this section links to the next in a couple of quotations that indicate that there can be a battle against this inherited sinful nature, such that the effects of its power over a person can be mitigated to some extent. The first indication is in Book One.

Although experience testifies that a seed of religion is divinely sown in all, scarcely one in a hundred is found who cherishes this in his heart, and there is not one in whom it grows to maturity because it is so far from yielding fruit in its season. Moreover, with some losing themselves in superstitious observances and others determined to wickedly revolt from God, the result is that all are so degenerate in regard to the true knowledge of him that in no part of the world can genuine godliness be found.[2]

The conclusion here shows that this is no optimistic view of humankind without grace, but there are indications that some cherish that seed to some extent. In Book Two there is a lengthier passage along similar lines, with a conclusion that there is some special grace at work here that would separate this from the passages that highlight a more common experience of grace in humankind.

---

1. Ibid., 1.14.15.
2. Ibid., 1.4.1.

In every age, there have been some who, under the guidance of nature, were devoted to virtue throughout their lives. It is of no consequence that many blots may be detected in their conduct; by the mere study of virtue, they showed that there was some purity in their nature. The value which virtues of this kind have in the sight of God will be considered more fully when we treat of the merit of works. Meanwhile, however, it is right to consider this here as it is necessary for the exposition of the subject in hand. Such examples seem to warn us against supposing that the nature of man is utterly vicious, since under the guidance of that nature some have not only excelled in illustrious deeds, but have conducted themselves most honourably through the whole course of their lives. But we ought to consider that, notwithstanding the corruption of our nature, there is some room for divine grace that, without purifying the nature, may lay it under internal restraint.

But in what way will such people be proofs of a virtuous nature? Must we not go back to the mind, and from it begin to reason this out? If a natural man possesses such integrity of manners, human nature is not without the ability to study virtue. But what if the mind was depraved and perverted and followed anything rather than righteousness? Such it undoubtedly was, if you grant that they were only a natural human. How then will you praise the power of human nature for good if, even where there is the highest demonstration of integrity, a corrupt bias is always detected? Therefore, just as you would not praise a person for their virtue when their vices appear to you as a show of virtue, so you will not attribute the power for choosing righteousness to the human will while it is rooted in depravity. The surest and easiest answer to the objection [that there are people who live good lives] is that those virtues are not common endowments of human nature, but rather special gifts of God that he distributes in various forms and in a definite measure to people who are otherwise sinful. For this reason, we do not hesitate to say in common speech that one has a good and another a vicious nature, although we do not stop believing that both come under the universal condition of human depravity. All we mean is that God has conferred on one a special grace that he has not seen fit to confer on the other.[1]

---

1. Ibid., 2.3.3.

The view of humankind has thus not changed through these studies of people who live good lives, since Calvin sees this as the fruit of a work of grace in those people. What has changed is the human perspective on others that is called to recognise where such grace is at work in changing a person so that their reality is not the absolutely depraved nature that Calvin sees as inherent to all.

This relates to what would later be known as 'common grace', although this is a somewhat loaded term. The principle that the grace of God remains present to some degree in human nature is established in a chapter in Book One on the knowledge of God in the world and his ongoing governance of creation: 'every person has within themselves undoubted evidence of the heavenly grace by which they live and move and have their being'.[1]

On the Bondage and Liberation of the Will has a similar teaching in a passage that contrasts the grace present in all with that present in the elect.

> We exist and move in one sense as human beings and in another as the sons of God. The former grace is the common possession of everyone, but the latter is granted specially to the elect. The former is in a certain way implanted in our nature, but the latter is given to man as a supernatural gift, so that he may cease to be what he was and begin to be what he has not yet become.[2]

The idea is expanded on in Book Two of the *Institutes of the Christian Religion*. In the chapter on the enslavement of the human will (which does sound rather pessimistic in terms of human nature) there are extensive sections demonstrating aspects of humanity, in which the grace of its creation remains evident. Calvin distinguishes between earthly things, such as economy, mechanics and liberal arts, in which the human mind is able from its nature to display its aptitude, and heavenly things, of which there is ignorance without a special work of grace. For the former, Calvin tends to use the language of 'endowments', 'gifts' or 'blessings' received from God that indicate aspects of grace even though the word itself is not stated. An example of this would be the following:

> If the Lord has been pleased to help us by the work and ministry of the ungodly in physics, dialectics, mathematics and other similar sciences, let us avail ourselves of this help in case, by neglecting the gifts of God spontaneously offered to us, we are rightly punished for our laziness.[3]

---

1. Ibid., 1.5.3.
2. *On the Bondage and Liberation of the Will*, 4, p.167.
3. *Institutes of the Christian Religion*, 2.2.16.

In concluding the positive contributions of humanity despite their fallen selves, Calvin writes:

> In that some excel in perceptiveness and some in judgement, while others are more ready to learn a peculiar art, God in this variety shows his favour towards us in case anyone should presume to claim for themselves that which flows from his simple generosity. For why is one more excellent than another, unless in a common nature the grace of God is specially displayed in passing by many and therefore proclaiming that it is under obligation to none?[1]

Such grace to act and think well can be present in any human, Christian or not, depending on the choice of God to show his kindness and majesty in these ways. In terms of the knowledge of heavenly things, however, human reason and ability is utterly powerless without grace. Calvin writes that we are 'blinder than moles' about the knowledge of God's fatherly kindness to us that is the cause of our salvation, although philosophers may have been able to gain some insight into the character of God in their writings.[2] Calvin summarises Paul's teaching on all that results from sin for all people.

> Firstly, he strips people of their righteousness, which is their integrity and purity; secondly, he strips them of sound intelligence, arguing that a defect of intelligence is proved by the rejection of God. To seek God is the beginning of wisdom, and therefore there must be a defect in all who have revolted from him. Paul adds that all have gone astray and become simply corrupted; there is no one who does good. He then lists the crimes of those who have given free rein to their wickedness that pollutes every part of their bodies. Lastly, he declares that they have no fear of God, according to whose guidance all our steps should be directed. If these are the hereditary properties of the human race, it is pointless to look for anything good in our nature. I accept that all of these evils do not break out in every individual. Yet it cannot be denied that the hydra lurks in every breast.[3]

The conclusion on fallen human nature is thus bleak for all the signs of goodness.

---

1. Ibid., 2.2.17.
2. Ibid., 2.2.18.
3. Ibid., 2.3.2.

The end of the natural law, therefore, is to render humankind inexcusable . . . the judgement of conscience distinguishing sufficiently between just and unjust and, in convicting people on their own testimony, it deprives them of any pretext for ignorance. So indulgent are people towards themselves that, while doing evil, they always endeavour as much as possible to suppress the idea of sin.[1]

Providence and the Human Will

Before dealing with the concept of free will, we shall follow Calvin's method and examine with him how the doctrine of the providence of God affects the nature of the will, before considering the extent to which any freedom could then be claimed for the will. There is some mention of the phrase 'free will' in the following quotations, but the chapters at this point in the *Institutes* are looking at the providence of God as their main theme; the next section in this chapter deals with later material in the *Institutes of the Christian Religion* that focus on free will.

We begin with Calvin on Augustine who does mention free will even in his later works, although Calvin qualifies how such references need to be understood within a wider theological view.

Although Augustine declares that everything happens partly by the free will of humankind and partly by the providence of God, he shortly after shows clearly that his meaning was that people are ruled by providence when he assumes that this is a principle, and so there cannot be a greater absurdity than to hold that anything is done without the ordination of God because it would happen at random. For this reason, he also excludes the idea that things are dependent on the human will, maintaining a little further on more clearly that no cause must be sought but the will of God. When he uses the term 'permission', the meaning attached to it best appears from a single passage [in *On the Trinity*, 3.4] where Augustine proves that the will of God is the supreme and primary cause of all things because nothing happens without his order or permission. He certainly does not picture God sitting idly in a watchtower when he chooses to permit anything. The will that he represents at work is, if I may so express it, actual and without this could not be regarded as a cause.[2]

1. Ibid., 2.2.22.
2. Ibid., 1.16.8.

On the Bondage and Liberation of the Will contains a passage highlighting one of the issues that opponents have with Calvin, based on this teaching of God's providence, which is that the necessity of things for God would seem to invalidate any concept of the voluntary for humankind. The result is a necessity for humankind yet without any coercion on the part of God – sin remains voluntary despite the overarching necessity that results from the nature of God.

> Our opponents want to force us to agree that being voluntary is inconsistent with being necessary. But we have shown that both are combined together in the goodness of God. They say that it is absurd that those things which people do in such a way that they are not able to do otherwise should be attributed to their fault or blame. We solve this contradiction by introducing the comparison. We do not argue that people are good or evil of necessity because God is good of necessity, but show by means of an example only that it is not contrary to reason for a quality which exists of necessity nevertheless to be deemed worthy of praise or censure.[1]

Calvin warns of the dangers of what 'puerile' people could do with God's providence in imputing to God the blame for crimes that are carried out by people. The following scathing passage shows that Calvin does not equate providence with a hard-line determinism that could in any way excuse people's acts on the basis of divine ordination.

> The ungodly make such a fuss with their foolish puerilities that they almost, as one might say, confound heaven and earth. If the Lord has marked the moment of our death, it cannot be escaped and so it is pointless to work or take precautions. Therefore, when one decides not to travel on a road that they hear is infested with robbers; when another calls in the doctor and disturbs themselves with drugs for the sake of their health; when a third abstains from richer foods so that they may not harm a sickly constitution; and when a fourth fears to live in a ruined house; when all, in short, devise and with great eagerness of mind take paths by which they may attain the objects of their desire; either all of these are pointless remedies that people choose to correct the will of God, or God's certain decree does not fix the limits of life and death, health and sickness, peace and war, and other matters that people work at studying in order to obtain or avoid, as far as they desire or hate them. Such meddlers even imply that the prayers of the faithful

---

1. *On the Bondage and Liberation of the Will*, 4, p.147.

are perverse, not to say superfluous, because they ask the Lord to make provision for things that he has decreed from eternity. Then, imputing whatever happens to the providence of God, they conspire with the person who is known to have expressly designed the action. Has an assassin killed an honest citizen? He has, they say, executed the counsel of God. Has someone committed theft or adultery? The deed has been provided and ordained by the Lord, and so the person is the minister of God's providence. Has a son waited with indifference for the death of his parent without trying to cure them? He could not oppose God, who had predetermined this death from eternity. In this way, all crimes receive the name of virtues because they happen in accordance with divine ordination.[1]

In response, Calvin works with a text from the book of Proverbs to show the continuing responsibility of humans in their lives despite the fact of God's providence.

Regarding future events, Solomon easily reconciles human deliberation with divine providence. While he derides the stupidity of those who presume to undertake any work without God, as if they were not ruled by his hand, he elsewhere expresses himself in these terms: 'A person's heart plans his ways but the Lord directs their steps' (Prov. 16:9). This implies that the eternal decrees of God by no means prevent us from proceeding, under his will, to provide for ourselves and to arrange all our affairs. The reason for this is clear. He who has fixed the boundaries of our life has at the same time entrusted us with the care of that life, he has provided us with the means of preserving it, he has forewarned us of the dangers to which we are exposed and he has supplied us with warnings and remedies so that we should not be caught unaware and overwhelmed. Our duty is then clear: since the Lord has committed to us the defence of our life, we should defend it; since he offers assistance, we should use this; since he forewarns us of danger, we should not rush headlong into it; and since he supplies remedies, we should not neglect them. But some would say that a danger that is not fatal will not hurt us, and one that is fatal cannot be resisted by any precautions. But what if dangers are not fatal simply because the Lord has given you the means of holding them off and overcoming them? See how far this reasoning agrees with the order of divine procedure? You infer that danger is not to be guarded against because, if it is not

---

1. *Institutes of the Christian Religion*, 1.17.3.

fatal, you will escape without any precaution; whereas the Lord
encourages you to guard against it because he wills that it should
not be fatal.[1]

After this considered analysis of why the position highlighted earlier
does not work with the natures of God and humankind as revealed in
Scripture, Calvin returns to more severe language in arguing against his
opponents.

> These insane jesters overlook what is plainly before their eyes, that
> the Lord has given people the faculties of deliberation and caution
> that they may employ these in obedience to his providence for the
> preservation of their lives; while, on the contrary, by neglect and
> laziness people heap evils on themselves as God has promised for
> these attitudes. How is it that a prudent person, thinking about
> their safety, is disentangled from impending evils, while a foolish
> person dies through unadvised boldness, unless it is that prudence
> and foolishness are the instruments of divine ordinance in each
> case? God has been pleased to hide all future events from us so
> that we may prepare for them as they are doubtful, and so that we
> will not stop applying the provided remedies until the dangers
> have either been overcome or have proved too much for all our
> care.[2]

Calvin therefore concludes that those who do evil are not doing the
will of God, despite his belief in the sovereign providence of God behind
all things.

> By the same type of people, past events are improperly and
> inconsiderately said to be the result of simple providence. Since all
> decisions depend on this, therefore no thefts, adulteries or murders
> are committed without a movement of the divine will. They then
> ask, why should a thief be punished for robbing someone who the
> Lord chose to discipline with poverty? Why should the murderer
> be punished for killing a person whose life the Lord had ended? If
> all such people serve the will of God, why should they be punished?
> I deny that they serve the will of God. For we cannot say that one
> carried away by a wicked mind performs a service on the order of
> God when they are only following their own evil desires. A person
> obeys God when, instructed in his will, they hasten in the direction
> that God calls them. But how can we be instructed except by his

1. Ibid., 1.17.4.
2. Ibid.

word? Therefore it is the will that God's word declares that we must keep in mind when acting; God requires nothing from us but what he commands. If we plan anything against his commands, it is not obedience but rebellion and transgression. But if God did not will something, we could not do it. I admit this. But do we act wickedly in order to be obedient to him? This he assuredly does not command. No, rather we rush on, not thinking of what he wishes but inflamed by our own passionate desires so that, with fixed purpose, we work against him. In this way, while we are acting wickedly, we serve his righteous ordination because in his boundless wisdom he knows how to use bad instruments for good purposes. See how absurd this kind of arguing is! They believe that the authors of crimes ought not to be punished because these are not committed without the planning of God. I concede more than this, that thieves, murderers and other evil-doers are instruments of divine providence because they are employed by the Lord himself to execute the judgments that he has resolved to inflict. But I deny that this gives any excuse for their evil deeds. How? Will they implicate God in the same evil with themselves, or will they hide their depravity by his righteousness? They cannot remove the blame from themselves because their own consciences condemn them; they cannot accuse God because they perceive that the whole wickedness is in themselves, while there is nothing in him except a legitimate use of their wickedness.[1]

The doctrine of providence therefore, regarding looking forwards, should not be used as an excuse against doing good or acting wisely since these are things that are commanded by God for us to do. Calvin moves on to look at how a Christian reflects on good and bad things, thanking God as the source of the former and confessing weakness in considering the latter.

Therefore, everything that turns out prosperous and according to their wish, the Christian will ascribe entirely to God, whether they have experienced his kindness through the work of people or been helped by inanimate creatures. They will think about it in this way: it is certain that the Lord disposed the minds of these people in my favour, attaching them to me in order to make them instruments of his kindness. In an abundant harvest they will think that it is the Lord who listens to the heaven in order that the heaven may listen to the earth, and the earth herself listen

---

1. Ibid., 1.17.5.

to her own offspring. In other cases, they will have no doubt
that they owe all their prosperity to divine blessing, and being
admonished by their many circumstances, will feel it impossible
to be ungrateful.[1]

If the Christian sustains any loss through negligence or
imprudence, they will believe that it was the Lord's will that
it should be so, but at the same time will take the blame on
themselves. If they had a duty to care for someone, but treated
them with neglect so that they die from a disease, although they
are aware that the person reached a limit beyond which it was
impossible to pass, they will not on that basis excuse their fault;
rather, because they neglected to do their duty faithfully towards
that person, they will feel as if the victim died through their guilty
negligence.[2]

In *On the Bondage and Liberation of the Will*, Calvin writes on this
theme:

> We do not say that the wicked sin of necessity in such a way as
> to imply that they sin without wilful and deliberate evil intent.
> The necessity comes from the fact that God accomplishes his
> work, which is sure and steadfast, through them. At the same
> time, however, the will and purpose to do evil which dwells
> within them makes them liable to censure. But, it is said, they are
> driven and forced to this by God. Indeed, but in such a way that
> in a single deed the action of God is one thing and their own
> action is another. For they gratify their evil and wicked desires,
> but God turns this wickedness so as to bring his judgements to
> execution.[3]

With regard to all that arises from the doctrine of providence for the
will of humankind, Calvin says:

> The conclusion of the whole is this: since the will of God is said
> to be the cause of all things, we must believe that all the counsels
> and actions of people are governed by his providence. Therefore,
> he not only works his power in the elect, who are guided by the
> Holy Spirit, but also forces the reprobate to do him service.[4]

1. Ibid., 1.17.7.
2. Ibid., 1.17.9.
3. *On the Bondage and Liberation of the Will*, 2, p.37.
4. *Institutes of the Christian Religion*, 1.18.2.

Free Will

The question of the freedom of the human will can only now be considered under this larger framework of the nature and action of God in relation to all existence and the will itself. Perhaps the clearer work simply on free will is found in *On the Bondage and Liberation of the Will* where it is treated slightly more directly, whereas in the *Institutes of the Christian Religion* it is part of a wider, developing theology. In *On the Bondage and Liberation of the Will*, Calvin discusses the relationship between freedom and coercion, recognising that it is not an easy matter of creating a simple dichotomy between the two concepts.

> If freedom is opposed to coercion, I both acknowledge and consistently maintain that choice is free, and I hold anyone who thinks otherwise to be a heretic. If, I say, it were called free in the sense of not being coerced nor forcibly moved by an external impulse, but moving of its own accord, I have no objection . . . [However, when people take it] to imply ability and power, one cannot prevent from entering the minds of most people, as soon as the will is called free, the illusion that it therefore has both good and evil within its power, so that it can by its own strength choose either one of them.
>
> Therefore, we describe [as coerced] the will which does not incline this way or that of its own accord or by an internal movement of decision, but is forcibly driven by an external impulse. We say that it is self-determined when of itself it directs itself in the direction in which it is led, when it is not taken by force or dragged unwillingly. A bound will, finally, is one which because of its corruptness is held captive under the authority of evil desires, so that it can choose nothing but evil, even if it does so of its own accord and gladly, without being driven by any external impulse.
>
> According to these definitions we allow that man has choice and that it is self-determined, so that if he does anything evil, it should be imputed to him and to his own voluntary choosing. We can do away with coercion and force, because this contradicts the nature of will and cannot coexist with it. We deny that choice is free, because through man's innate wickedness it is of necessity driven to what is evil and cannot seek anything but evil . . . For we do not say that man is dragged unwillingly into sinning, but that because his will is corrupt he is held captive under the yoke of sin and therefore of necessity wills in an evil way.[1]

---

1. *On the Bondage and Liberation of the Will*, 2, p.67, 69.

When Calvin approaches this early in Book Two of the *Institutes of the Christian Religion*, he begins with a guiding statement warning of certain dangers if one does not steer a careful course.

> The best way of avoiding error is to consider the dangers that face us on either side. Humankind is devoid of any uprightness and thus immediately decides from this to indulge in laziness; having no natural ability to study righteousness, they treat the whole subject as if it was of no concern. On the other hand, humans cannot claim anything for themselves without robbing God of his honour, and through rash confidence they subject themselves to a fall. In order to avoid both of these rocks, our proper course will, first, be to show that humans have no remaining good in them and are faced by the most miserable hardship on every side; and, secondly, to teach them to aspire to the goodness they lack and the freedom that they have been deprived of. This will provide a stronger stimulus to work than they would have if they imagined themselves possessed of the highest virtue.[1]

There follows in this chapter an extensive engagement with historical Christian sources on free will where Calvin shows the strengths and weaknesses of the various teachings; there is a similar and even longer engagement with these voices is *On the Bondage and Liberation of the Will*. The conclusion is that there is a freedom present in humankind, but it is limited and unworthy of so grand a title as 'free will'.

> In this way, then, humans are said to have free will not because they have a free choice of good and evil, but because they act voluntarily and are not forced. This is perfectly true, but why should so small a thing have been dignified with so proud a title? It is an admirable freedom that humans are not forced to be servants of sin, and yet they are voluntary slaves since their wills are bound by the chains of sin.[2]

In the following chapter, following on from some of the above material on the sinful nature, Calvin writes about the nature and role of the will in salvation.

> I say that the will is abolished, but not in that it is will, because in conversion everything that is essential to our original nature remains. I also say that it is created anew, not because the will then begins to exist but because it is turned from evil to good.[3]

---

1. *Institutes of the Christian Religion*, 2.2.1.
2. Ibid., 2.2.7.
3. Ibid., 2.3.6.

Where the human will is at work, it is not free to do what it wants and choose to do good except under the influence of God.

> The first part of a good work is the will; the second is a vigorous effort involved in doing the work. God is the author of both these. Therefore, we rob God when we claim anything for ourselves, either in the will or in the action. If it were said that God gives assistance to a weak will, then something might be left for us; but when it is said that God makes the will, everything that is good in it is placed outside us. Moreover, since even a good will is still weighed down by the burden of the flesh and is thus prevented from rising, we would add that God supplies the persevering effort to meet any difficulties in the work until the effect is obtained.[1]

The last quote on free will concerns those actions that do not affect salvation, where the will or choice would seem to have a greater freedom; certainly, Calvin attributes this view to some people. However, while Calvin sees some truth in this, for those things that are advantageous he still sees a work of God present in the will.

> In those actions that are neither good nor bad in themselves, and that concern the physical rather than the spiritual life, the freedom that humans possess has not yet been explained, although we have touched upon it above. Some have allowed that humans have a free choice in such actions, I suppose this is more because they were unwilling to debate a matter of no great importance than because they wished positively to assert what they were prepared to concede. While I would say that those who believe that people have no ability in themselves to do what is right believe what is most necessary to be known for salvation, I think we should not overlook that we are indebted to the special grace of God whenever we either choose what is for our advantage, and when our will inclines in that direction, or when with our heart and soul we reject what would otherwise do us harm.[2]

We can thus see that the idea of free will loses its importance for Calvin once we understand his concept of the providence of God and the impact that this and the corruption of sin have on the power of humans to make choices, particularly concerning that which is good.

---

1. Ibid., 2.3.9.
2. Ibid., 2.4.6.

Grace

Given the inability of fallen humankind to will or to act well for themselves, the work of God through His grace is necessarily an important part of Calvin's thoughts on creation and even more so on salvation. While the major concentration on this area comes in Book Two, there are already some clear indications present in Book One in the discussion on the Holy Spirit.

> In like manner, by means of the Spirit we become partakers of the divine nature, so that we can somehow feel his enlivening energy within us. Our justification is the Spirit's work; from him comes power, sanctification, truth, grace and every good thought, since it is from the Spirit alone that all good gifts proceed.[1]

The power of grace is shown in the contemplation of the providence of God as that which makes us aware of the work of God in order to worship him.

> While we can see how God has destined all things for our good and salvation, we at the same time feel his power and grace both in ourselves and in the great blessings that he has given to us; this stirs us up to have a confidence in him, to pray, praise and love God.[2]

This first move of God's grace in preparing a person for salvation is developed in *On the Bondage and Liberation of the Will* in a passage that emphases the role of grace in every stage of a person's turning to God.

> But all that we say amounts to this. First, that what a person is or has or is capable of is entirely empty and useless for the spiritual righteousness which God requires, unless one is directed to the good by the grace of God. Secondly, that the human will is of itself evil and therefore needs transformation and renewal so that it may begin to be good, but that grace itself is not merely a tool which can help someone if he is pleased to stretch out his hand to [take] it. That is, [God] does not merely offer it, leaving [to man] the choice between receiving it and rejecting it, but he steers the mind to choose what is right, he moves the will also effectively to obedience, he arouses and advances the endeavour until the actual

---

1. Ibid., 1.13.14.
2. Ibid., 1.14.22.

completion of the work is attained. Then again, that [grace] is not sufficient if it is just once conferred upon someone, unless it accompanies him without interruption.[1]

Early in the consideration of salvation, in the context of the limited human will that results from the corruption of sin, Calvin follows Augustine in holding to the primacy of the role of grace in allowing for a hope of salvation.

> I am pleased with the well-known saying that has been borrowed from the writing of Augustine, that people's natural gifts were corrupted by sin and their supernatural gifts withdrawn; supernatural gifts implying the light of faith and righteousness, which would have been sufficient for people to attain to heavenly life and everlasting joy. When humans withdrew their allegiance to God, they were deprived of the spiritual gifts by which they had been raised to the hope of eternal salvation. It therefore follows that they are now exiles from the kingdom of God, and thus everything that pertains to the blessed life of the soul are lost in them until they are recovered by the grace of regeneration.[2]

At the end of the chapter that establishes the human condition as requiring salvation, Calvin states that there can be no first move by people.

> We are all sinners by nature, and therefore we are held under the burden of sin. If our whole person is subject to the dominion of sin, surely the will that is the principal seat of that person must be bound with the closest chains. Therefore, if divine grace were preceded by any human will, Paul could not have said that 'it is God who works in us both to will and to do' (Phil. 2:13).[3]

If we are saved by grace, what is the result for a person after conversion? How cooperative is the ongoing experience of grace? Calvin sees this as the ongoing work of God.

> It must not be said that the legitimate use of the first grace is rewarded by subsequent measures of grace, as if people made the grace of God effective by their own work; nor must we think that there is any kind of reward that would cease to make it the

---

1. *On the Bondage and Liberation of the Will*, 3, p.114.
2. *Institutes of the Christian Religion*, 2.2.12.
3. Ibid., 2.2.27.

gratuitous grace of God. Therefore, I admit that believers may expect a blessing from God in that the better use they make of previous grace, the greater the supplies they will receive of future grace. But I say that even this use is from the Lord, and that this reward is given freely from simple good will.[1]

The need, then, is to rely solely on the grace of God that, as Calvin goes on to show, is the work of the Holy Spirit in the life of the believer.

Therefore, it seems that the grace of God (this phrase is used when we speak of regeneration) is the work of the Spirit in directing and governing the human will. He cannot govern without also correcting, reforming and renovating (hence we say that the beginning of regeneration consists in the destruction of what is ours). Similarly, he cannot govern without moving, impelling, urging and restraining. Therefore, all of the actions that are done afterwards are rightly said to be completely his . . . There is nothing to prevent us from saying that our will does what the Spirit does in us, although the will contributes nothing of itself without the help of grace. We must therefore remember what we quoted from Augustine, that some people labour in vain to find some good quality in the human will that rightly belongs to it. Yet any mixture that people attempt to make by joining the effort of their own will with divine grace is corruption, just as when unclean and muddy water is used to dilute wine. But although everything good in the will is entirely derived from the influence of the Spirit, yet because we naturally have an innate power of willing, we are not improperly said to do those things for which God claims all the praise. Firstly, this is because everything that his kindness produces in us is our own (only we must understand that it is not from ourselves); and secondly, because it is our mind, our will and our study that are guided by him to what is good.[2]

Calvin contrasts his position with that of Pighius in *On the Bondage and Liberation of the Will* in that his opponent allows God only the smallest role in the Christian's life through grace, whereas Calvin continues to see grace as fundamental to all that we are and do.

We agree that labour and striving are needed on both sides. Nor do we deny that the struggle is of such a kind as both to involve the utmost difficulty and to require the greatest efforts and the whole of a person's dedication. The question is only whether we

1. Ibid., 2.3.11.
2. Ibid., 2.5.15.

fight for God with our own strength, or he supplies from heaven the skill, the courage, the hands, the strength, and the weapons. Pighius grants a tiny part to the grace of God, but claims for us the greater role. I say that in us in fulfilled what God once promised to the people of Israel, namely that while we are at rest he fights for us. It is not that we ourselves do nothing or that we without any movement of our will are driven to act by pressure from him, but that we act while being acted upon by him. We will as he guides our heart, we endeavour as he rouses us, we succeed in our endeavour as he gives us strength, so that we are animate and living tools, while he is the leader and the finisher of the work.[1]

This work of the Holy Spirit results from the work of Christ, which is the main theme of Book Three, although there is a link provided near the end of Book Two.

Christ's obedience truly purchased and merited grace for us with the Father, as is accurately seen in several passages of Scripture. I take it for granted that if Christ provided satisfaction for our sins, if he paid the penalty due to us, if he appeased God by his obedience, in conclusion if he suffered as the just for the unjust, then salvation was obtained for us by his righteousness. This is simply equivalent to meriting salvation.[2]

The grace won by Christ has necessary effects on our lives in repentance, not that this is the cause of us receiving grace but a necessary effect of the work of grace.

Since pardon and forgiveness are offered through the preaching of the Gospel in order that the sinner, delivered from the tyranny of Satan, the burden of sin and miserable slavery to sin, may pass into the kingdom of God, it is certain that no one can embrace the grace of the Gospel without removing himself from the errors of his former life onto the right path and making it his whole study to practise repentance. Those who think that repentance precedes faith rather than flowing from or being produced by it, as the tree produces fruit, have never understood its nature and are moved to adopt such a view on very insufficient grounds.[3]

1. *On the Bondage and Liberation of the Will*, 4, p.152.
2. *Institutes of the Christian Religion*, 2.17.3.
3. Ibid., 3.3.1.

Calvin clarifies the work of God through the Holy Spirit that is present in the change made in an individual, that it is not a new self that is created but a restoration of the true self before it was corrupted by sin.

> I say that the will is evil not by nature (that is, by God's creation) but by the corruption of nature, and that it cannot be otherwise until it is changed to be good by the grace of the Holy Spirit. Nor do I imagine that a new product or a new creature is made in such a way that with the destruction of the former substance a new one takes its place. For I explicitly mention that the will remains in man just as it was originally implanted in him, and so the change takes place in the habit, not in the substance. By a renewal of such a kind I say that the heart is made different – David says that a new heart is created.[1]

In Book Three of the *Institutes*, Calvin turns to predestination and election and the theme of grace appears heavily in these passages.

> The Lord adding grace to grace, builds on a former experience to add a subsequent grace so that he does not lose any means of enriching his servants. As we experience this free kindness, God would still have us always see free election as the source and beginning. For although God loves the gifts that he daily gives to us, because they proceed from that fountain, still our duty is to hold fast by that gratuitous acceptance that alone can support our souls. In this way we connect the gifts of the Spirit, which he afterwards gives, with their primary cause so that we in no way detract from this.[2]

Calvin compares the grace received in the new covenant with that received by the children of Abraham in the Old Testament.

> In the adoption of the family of Abraham, God gave a generous display of favour that he denied to others; but in the body of Christ there is a far more excellent display of grace, because those grafted into him as their head never fail to obtain salvation.[3]

This grace is later developed further.

> The elect are called into the fold of Christ not from the womb nor all at the same time, but just as God sees fit to dispense his grace. Before they are gathered to the supreme shepherd they wander

---

1. *On the Bondage and Liberation of the Will*, 6, p.210.
2. *Institutes of the Christian Religion*, 3.14.21.
3. Ibid., 3.21.7.

dispersed in a common desert, and do not differ in any respect from others except that by the special mercy of God they are kept from rushing to their final destruction.[1]

The supreme role of grace in the creation and any continuation of goodness is the necessary result of Calvin's understanding of God and then the effects that sin has had on humankind, in particular, in their utter corruption.

Grace and Sacraments

Calvin devotes extensive sections to sacramental theology in Book Four of the *Institutes of the Christian Religion* and because of its relationship to grace this is a theme that needs to be presented here. Calvin clarifies at the beginning that he is not against the sacraments in themselves nor against their association with the communication of grace.

> Similarly to the preaching of the gospel, we have another help to our faith in the sacraments, regarding which I am concerned that some sure doctrine should be delivered, informing us both of the purpose for which they were instituted and their present use. First, we must look at what a sacrament is. It seems to me a simple and appropriate definition to say that a sacrament is an external sign by which the Lord seals on our consciences his promises of his good will toward us in order to sustain the weakness of our faith; and we in our turn bear witness to our devotion towards him, both before himself, before angels and before other people. We may also define a sacrament more briefly by calling it a testimony of divine favour towards us, confirmed by an external sign, with a corresponding witness of our faith towards him. You can make your choice of these definitions, which do not differ in meaning from that of Augustine, who defines a sacrament to be a visible sign of a sacred thing or a visible form of an invisible grace, but this is no better or surer explanation.[2]

The sacraments were an issue of contention in reforming groups, and Calvin addresses this and particularly those who would want to remove the work of grace associated with them.

---

1. Ibid., 3.24.10.
2. Ibid., 4.14.1.

It is irrational to argue that sacraments are not manifestations of divine grace toward us on the basis that they are given to the ungodly also, who rather than experiencing God to be more favourable towards them, only incur greater condemnation. By the same reasoning, the Gospel will be no manifestation of the grace of God because it is rejected by many who hear it; nor will Christ himself be a manifestation of grace because very few received him, although he was seen and known by many . . . It is certain, therefore, that the Lord offers us his mercy and a promise of his grace both in his sacred word and in the sacraments; but this is not received except by those who receive the word and sacraments with firm faith. In the same way Christ, although he is offered and held forth for salvation to all, yet is not acknowledged and received by all . . . We conclude, therefore, that the sacraments are truly termed evidences of divine grace, and a kind of seal of the good will that God has towards us. By sealing this to us, they sustain, nourish, confirm and increase our faith.[1]

Calvin is keen to reform the current use of the sacraments in which the instruments themselves were seen by many to contain power rather than God working through these. This is a restatement of the traditional position of the Medieval Church on the sacraments that we saw in the earlier chapters in this volume.

They do not of themselves grant any grace, but they announce and manifest it and, like earnests and badges, give a confirmation of the gifts that the divine kindness has given to us. The sacraments do not bring the Holy Spirit freely to all, but the Lord specially gives the Spirit to his people; the Holy Spirit brings the gifts of God along with him, makes way for the sacraments and causes them to bear fruit. But although we do not deny that God, by the immediate agency of his Spirit, confirms his own decree, preventing the administration of the sacraments that he has instituted from being fruitless and vain, we still maintain that the internal grace of the Spirit, as it is distinct from the external administration, ought to be viewed and considered separately.[2]

Calvin recognises that the grace conferred in the various sacraments differs in relation to the effect on the believer, their sinful past and their developing identity. On baptism, there is a clear effect on the sinful nature.

1. Ibid., 4.14.7.
2. Ibid., 4.15.1.

The first object [of baptism], for which it is appointed by the Lord, is to be a sign and evidence of our purification; or, to explain this better, it is a kind of sealed instrument by which God assures us that all our sins are so deleted, covered and removed that they will never come into his sight, never be mentioned, never imputed. For it is his will that all who have believed should be baptised for the remission of sins. Therefore, those who have thought that baptism is nothing more than the badge and mark by which we profess our religion before men – as soldiers witness their profession by bearing the insignia of their commander – have not recognised the principal thing in baptism, which is that we are to receive it in connection with the promise 'He who believes and is baptised shall be saved' (Mark 16:16).[1]

Despite this strong position on baptism, Calvin does not hold that baptism by water is essential to salvation since this would limit the grace of God. In explaining this there is the following interesting passage that includes unborn children as part of the adopted family of God – a rather strange idea given the earlier material on the effects of original sin.

God declares that he adopts our children before they are born for his own when he promises that he will be a God to us and to our seed after us. In this promise their salvation is included. No one will dare to offer such an insult to God as to deny that he is able to give effect to his promise. Few people recognise how much evil has been caused by the dogma, wrongly explained, that baptism is necessary to salvation, and therefore do not take due caution. For when the opinion prevails that all are lost who happen not to be dipped in water, our condition becomes worse than that of God's ancient people, as if his grace were more restrained now than under the law. In that case, Christ could be thought to have come not to fulfil but to abolish the promises, since the promise that was then effective in itself to grant salvation before the eighth day would not now be effective without the help of a sign.[2]

The importance of the communal promises given to families leads Calvin to advocate the baptism of infants as witness to the grace of God that is the only effective work in salvation.

The divine symbol [baptism] given to the child, like the impress of a seal, confirms the promise that is given to the godly parent and declares that the Lord will be a God not to the parent only,

---

1. Ibid., 4.15.1.
2. Ibid., 4.15.20.

but also to his seed; not merely visiting the parent with his grace and goodness, but their posterity also to the thousandth generation. When the infinite goodness of God is thus displayed, it provides abundant materials for proclaiming his glory and fills pious breasts with no ordinary joy, urging them more strongly to love their affectionate parent when they see that, on their account, he extends his care to their posterity.[1]

In the section on the sacraments, baptism is given by far the most explicit grace language, while the introduction to Calvin's sacramental theology shows that grace is present in all that he would deem to be sacraments, rightly understood.

Conclusion

Calvin's theology needs to be rediscovered for itself by the Church, including the Church that claims a descent from the great reformer. Although the modern Church will talk extensively about Calvin and predestination, it is the doctrine of providence based on the nature of God that is the basis of his resulting discussions on the nature and effects of sin on humankind, the primacy of grace in all aspects of Christian faith and the lack of any real free will in light of these twin 'powers'. If people will recognise their sinfulness and submit themselves to God and his work, then much of Calvin's project will be complete.

The *Institutes of the Christian Religion* are available in an old but reasonable translation at www.ccel.org. A great book for anyone seeking to understand this work is Tony Lane's *A Reader's Guide to Calvin's Institutes* (Grand Rapids: Baker Academic, 2009). For a wider appreciation of the man and his work, the *Cambridge Companion to John Calvin* (Cambridge: Cambridge University Press, 2004) is a useful book. (The Cambridge Companion series have titles on most of the writers looked at in these volumes.) For *On the Bondage and Liberation of the Will*, the first translation has been published by Graham Davies and edited by Tony Lane (Grand Rapids: Baker Books, 1996) and these gentlemen have kindly given me permission to quote directly from their work.

---

1. Ibid., 4.17.10.

IO.

The Council of Trent

The Council of Trent (1545-1563) is one of the most important councils in the history of the Catholic Church. It was called to discuss the doctrine of the Church, following the challenge of protesting voices across Europe, and to reform the morality of the Church, given concerns about practices that had arisen in various places that were not in accord with the Catholic faith. One of the most notable aspects of the *Canons and Decrees of the Council of Trent*, when looking through the various sessions, is that the balance overall is far more towards reform of the Church, rather than on the statements of faith both for and against the teachings of the reformers.

In the Bull of Indiction that set the background and gave purpose to the Council, Pope Paul III (under whom the Council opened, although two further popes would oversee various sessions due to the length of the Council) states its intention to collect Catholic authorities together to consider matters of the faith and to strengthen western Europe against the increasing threats from Muslim powers.

> We deemed it necessary that there should be one fold and one shepherd for the Lord's flock in order to maintain the integrity of the Christian religion and to confirm in us the hope of heavenly things; the unity of the Christian name was broken and nearly torn apart by schisms, dissensions and heresies.
>
> Therefore, with God going before us in our deliberations and holding the light of his own wisdom and truth before our minds, we may in this sacred ecumenical council, in a better and more seemly manner, consider and, with the charity of all working to one purpose, deliberate and discuss, execute and bring to the desired result speedily and happily, whatever concerns the integrity and truth of the Christian religion, the restoration of good and the

correction of evil practices, the peace, unity and harmony both of Christian princes and peoples, and whatever is needed for repelling the assaults of barbarians and infidels, through which they seek to overthrow all Christendom.[1]

There were twenty-five Sessions in total over the eighteen years of the Council, but for most of that time there were no Sessions in progress; thirteen of the Sessions simply acknowledged a delay in the ability to meet or moved the Council to a new venue – there were three main sessions at Trent and one period at Bologna. Over half of the more 'active' Sessions that dealt with doctrine concerned the sacraments both generally and each of the Catholic sacraments in themselves. For this work, it is disappointing that grace was not more explicitly discussed in the Decrees on the sacraments since it is implied throughout. There will be some quotations below from these Decrees but less than might be expected, given the material quoted in the previous chapters on Lombard and Aquinas, in particular.

The most noteworthy Session dealt with the theme of justification, Session Six, but in the preceding Session there were some important statements about original sin within which context the later pronouncements need to be understood. This brief presentation will go through the Canons and Decrees by Session rather than seeking to break things up thematically. The whole document is readily available online and, given the number of short Sessions, does not take a great deal of time to read through. The theology from the Council of Trent – Tridentine theology – became normative for the Catholic Church and generally continues to be highly influential today in a Catholic understanding of the Christian faith.

Session 5: Original Sin

The teaching on original sin begins, naturally, with Adam and the first sin that loses holiness and justice and puts Adam both under the judgement of God, leading to death, and the power of the devil, and sin. Following this, the effects of this on successive generations is made clear.

> If anyone claims that the sin of Adam only injured him and not his posterity, or that the God-given holiness and justice that he lost, he lost only for himself and not also for us, or that, being

---

1. *The Canons and Decrees of the Council of Trent*, Bull of Indiction.

corrupted by the sin of disobedience, he only passed on death and bodily pain to the whole human race, but not also sin, which is the death of the soul, let them be condemned.[1]

After the universality of sin received from Adam, the Council turned to discussing the remedy for sin, making it clear that this is only found in the work of Christ.

> If anyone claims that this sin of Adam (which has one origin and is then transfused into all by descent, not by imitation, and is in every person as their own) is taken away either by the power of human nature or by any other remedy than the merit of the one mediator, our Lord Jesus Christ, who has reconciled us to God through his own blood, and has given us justice, sanctification and redemption; or if they deny that this merit of Jesus Christ is applied, both to adults and to infants, by the sacrament of baptism rightly administered in the form of the church, let them be condemned.[2]

This point on baptism is followed up in recognising that this understanding of original sin requires an infant to be baptised to release it from the stain of sin with its consequences that is received from Adam, recognising a tradition going back to the earliest church.

> Even infants, who cannot yet commit any sin themselves, are for this reason truly baptised for the forgiveness of sins, so that what they have received through birth might be washed away by rebirth. For, unless a person is born again of water and the Holy Spirit, they cannot enter into the kingdom of God.[3]

Finally in this Session, the Council of Trent distinguished between the original sin and guilt that is received from Adam and that is washed away by the grace of Christ communicated through baptism, which means that 'nothing whatever can stop their entrance into heaven', and the sin committed after becoming a Christian that is labelled 'concupiscence', against which people must fight but that does not affect their ultimate salvation:

> This Holy Synod confesses and is aware that there remains in those baptised concupiscence, or an incentive to sin. While this is left to put us through trials, it cannot injure those who do not

1. Ibid., 5.2 (*i.e.* session.decree).
2. Ibid., 5.3.
3. Ibid., 5.4.

consent to it, but who resist steadfastly by the grace of Jesus Christ; indeed, those who will have strived lawfully shall be crowned. This concupiscence, which the Apostle sometimes calls sin, the Holy Synod declares that the Catholic Church has never understood it to be called sin, as being truly and properly sin in those who are born again, but because it is from sin and inclines to sin.[1]

This understanding of the nature and effects of original sin on both Adam and on humankind since Adam sets the basis for the next session that looks at justification.

Session 6: Justification

This begins by stating the inadequacy of humans, either through their own natural powers or through the Old Testament law, to save themselves from the punishments received from original sin.

> The Holy Synod declares firstly that, for a correct and sound understanding of the doctrine of Justification, it is necessary that everyone recognise and confess that, since all lost their innocence in the sin of Adam – having become unclean and, as the Apostle says, children of wrath by nature (as set forth in the decree on original sin) – they became the servants of sin and under the power of the devil and of death, so that neither the Gentiles purely by the force of nature, nor even the Jews by the very letter of the law of Moses, were able to be freed or rise out of this condition. However, free will, constricted as it was in its power and bent down, was by no means extinguished in them.[2]

The manner of justification is then clarified as through the grace of Christ communicated in baptism.

> A description of the justification of the sinful is indicated as being a translation from the state in which a person is born as a child of the first Adam to the state of grace, of adoption as the sons of God, through the second Adam, Jesus Christ, our Saviour. This translation, since the preaching of the Gospel, cannot be effected without the cleansing power of regeneration, or the desire for this, as it is written: unless a person is born again of water and the Holy Spirit, they cannot enter into the Kingdom of God.[3]

---

1. Ibid., 5.5.
2. Ibid., 6.1.
3. Ibid., 6.4.

The following Decree looks at the preparation for justification in adults, recognising a difference between these and infants who are brought to baptism by their parents.

> The Synod furthermore declares that the beginning of justification in adults is derived from the prevenient grace of God through Jesus Christ, that is to say, from his calling. In this, without any existing merit on their part, they are called so that they, who in their sinful nature were alienated from God, may be disposed through his life-giving and assisting grace to convert themselves to their own justification by freely assenting to and co-operating with that said grace. This happens so that, while God touches the heart of a person by the illumination of the Holy Spirit, that person is not completely unable to do anything while he receives that inspiration, since they are also able to reject it; but they are not able, through their own free will and without the grace of God, to move themselves to justice in God's sight.[1]

The Council continues on this theme of the priority of grace and the response of the person in the next Decree that looks at the manner of preparation.

> Adults are disposed towards this justice when, excited and assisted by divine grace, conceiving faith by hearing, they are freely moved towards God, believing those things to be true that God has revealed and promised, and especially that God justifies sinners by his grace through the redemption that is in Christ Jesus. When they understand themselves to be sinners, they turn from themselves in fear of divine justice, by which they are profitably concerned, and considering the mercy of God, they are raised to hope, being confident that God will be favourable to them for Christ's sake. They begin to love him as the fountain of all justice, and are therefore moved against their sins by a certain hatred and loathing, in other words by the penitence that must be performed before baptism.[2]

The results of this preparation are described in the Decree that looks at the effects of justification.

> Justification is not merely the forgiveness of sins, but also the sanctification and renewal of the inner person through the

---

1. Ibid., 6.5.
2. Ibid., 6.6.

voluntary reception of the grace and gifts by which an unjust
person becomes just, and an enemy becomes a friend, that so they
may be an heir according to hope of life everlasting.[1]

This same Decree also looks at the causes of justification, all of which
are attributed to the Godhead.

The causes of this justification are as follows. The final
cause is indeed the glory of God and of Jesus Christ, and life
everlasting. The efficient cause is a merciful God, who washes
and sanctifies graciously, signing and anointing a person with
the Holy Spirit of promise, who is the pledge of our inheritance.
The meritorious cause is his most beloved only-begotten Son,
our Lord Jesus Christ, who, when we were enemies, for the
exceeding love with which he loved us, merited justification
for us by his most holy passion on the wood of the cross, and
made satisfaction for us to God the Father. The instrumental
cause is the sacrament of baptism, which is the sacrament of
faith, without which [faith] no one was ever justified. Finally,
the sole formal cause is the justice of God, not that whereby
he himself is just, but that by which he makes us just, that
indeed which we are given him to be renewed in the spirit of
our mind, and through which we are not only reckoned, but
are truly called and are, just, receiving justice within us, each
one according to their own measure, which the Holy Spirit
distributes to everyone as he wills, and according to each one's
proper disposition and cooperation.[2]

The Council of Trent then considers salvation by grace through
faith.

We are therefore said to be justified by faith because faith is the
beginning of human salvation, the foundation and the root of all
justification. Without this, it is impossible to please God and to
come into the fellowship of his children. We are therefore said
to be justified freely because none of the things that precede
justification, whether faith or works, merit the grace itself of
justification. For if it is by grace, it is not now by works; otherwise,
as the same Apostle says, grace is no more grace.[3]

---

1. Ibid., 6.7.
2. Ibid.
3. Ibid., 6.8.

Concerning predestination, the Council affirms the position taught by Augustine in his work on that topic (see Volume One for details), that the predestined do not know that they are such unless they experience persevering grace to the end of their lives.

> No one, moreover, so long as they are in this mortal life, ought to presume so far regarding the secret mystery of divine predestination that they determine for certain that they are assuredly in the number of the predestined; nor is it true that a justified person either cannot sin any more, or if they do sin, that they ought to promise themselves an assured forgiveness. Except by special revelation, it cannot be known whom God has chosen for himself.[1]

Similarly, in the following Decree on perseverance, the Council follows Augustine's teaching that a Christian must persevere in grace rather than resting on the salvation once received.

> Regarding the gift of perseverance, of which it is written, 'Whoever perseveres to the end, they shall be saved', this gift cannot be gained from any other source but him who is able to establish the person that stands, will stand perseveringly, and to restore whoever falls. Let no one promise themselves in this anything as certain with an absolute certainty, although all ought to place and repose a most firm hope in God's help. For God, unless a person does not want his grace, as he has begun the good work, so will he perfect it, working to will and to accomplish this. Nevertheless, let those who want to stand take care in case they fall and, with fear and trembling, work out their salvation, in labours, in watchings, in almsdeeds, in prayers and oblations, in fasting and chastity. Knowing that they are born again to a hope of glory, but not as yet into glory, they ought to fear the combat that still remains with the flesh, with the world and with the devil, in which they cannot be victorious unless they are obedient to the Apostle with God's grace, who says, 'We are not in debt to the flesh, to live according to the flesh, for if you live according to the flesh, you shall die; but if by the Spirit you destroy the deeds of the flesh, you shall live.'[2]

At the end of the Decree there are several Canons dealing with (and condemning) very specific points related to the doctrine of justification. Those most relevant to this work are:

---

1. Ibid., 6.12.
2. Ibid., 6.13.

Canon I: If anyone says that a person may be justified before God by their own works, whether through the teaching of human nature or that of the law, without the grace of God through Jesus Christ, let them be condemned.

Canon II: If anyone says that the grace of God through Jesus Christ is only given that a person may be able more easily to live justly and to merit eternal life, as if they were able to do this by free will and without grace, even though this would be hard indeed and difficult, let them be condemned.

Canon IV: If anyone says that human free will, moved and excited by God, in assenting to God's exciting and calling, in no way co-operates towards disposing and preparing itself to obtain the grace of justification, that the will cannot refuse its consent even if it wanted to, but that, as something inanimate, it does nothing whatever and is merely passive, let them be condemned.

Canon V: If anyone says that, since Adam's sin, human free will is lost and extinguished, or that it is a thing in name only, a name without a reality, a figment, in conclusion something that was introduced into the Church by Satan, let them be condemned.[1]

Throughout the Decree on Justification, one can sense two forces at work: one an attempt to state the Catholic position clearly; and a second to refute teachings and potential spiritualities of reforming groups. In terms of the latter, there seems at times almost a wilful misunderstanding – none of the major reformers taught that a predestined person would cease to sin – and an overstating of the reformers' teaching in order to keep people in the Catholic Church. It is also clear here that the reformers' teaching that Catholic doctrine included salvation by works without grace or faith is similarly a misrepresentation, even if sometimes the communication of doctrine from the top down to the parish priest and through them to the congregation may have affected the teaching received.

---

1. Ibid., 6.Canons.

Sessions 7 Onwards: Sacramental Theology

As indicated above, there is a disappointing lack of explicit grace terminology in the definition and presentation of the sacraments, and sometimes when it is mentioned there is little significance in the use of the term. As a result, this section is rather brief, although the reader is, as always, encouraged to go back through the primary document to gain a sense of the wider understanding of grace in response to sin and sinful nature that is present in the Decrees of the Council.

Session Seven dealt with sacramental theology in a broad sense and here there are a few Canons that are worth highlighting for what they say about grace at this higher level.

Canon IV: If anyone says that the sacraments of the new law are not necessary for salvation, but superfluous, and that without them, or without a desire for them, people can obtain the grace of justification from God through faith alone (although all are not indeed necessary for every individual), let them be condemned.

Canon VI: If anyone says that the sacraments of the New Law do not contain the grace that they signify, or that they do not confer that grace on those who do not place an obstacle to the grace, as though they were merely outward signs of grace or justice received through faith and certain marks of the Christian profession, through which believers are distinguished from unbelievers, let them be condemned.

Canon VII: If anyone says that grace, as far as God's part is concerned, is not given through the said sacraments always and to all people, even though they receive them in a right manner, but sometimes and to some persons, let them be condemned.

Canon VIII: If anyone says that grace is not conferred by the said sacraments of the new law through the act performed, but that faith alone in the divine promise is sufficient to obtain grace, let them be condemned.[1]

---

1. Ibid., 7.Canons.

The teaching on the sacrament of Penance builds on the concepts above that the original sin and guilt received from Adam is overcome by the grace of baptism and discusses this practice of the Church through the centuries to address sins committed after baptism.

> Penitence was indeed at all times necessary to attain to grace and justice for all who have defiled themselves by any mortal sin, even for those who begged to be washed by the sacrament of Baptism; this is so that their sin is renounced and amended, and they might detest this great offence against God with a hatred of sin and a godly sorrow of mind.
>
> Contrition, the most prominent of the aforesaid acts of the penitent, is a sorrow of the mind and a detestation for the sin committed, with the purpose of not sinning in the future. This movement of contrition was always necessary to obtain the pardon of sins. In one who has fallen after baptism, it then at length prepares for the forgiveness of sins, when it is united with confidence in the divine mercy and a desire to perform the other things that are required to rightly receive this sacrament. Therefore, the Holy Synod declares that this contrition contains not only a cessation of sin and the purpose and beginning of a new life, but also a hatred of the old life.[1]

The other sacrament with a clear passage integrating sin and grace is that of anointing the sick, which is explained as follows.

> The thing signified and the effect of this sacrament are explained in these words: 'And the prayer of faith shall save the sick person and the Lord shall raise them up, and if they are in sin these shall be forgiven them.' The thing signified here is the grace of the Holy Spirit, whose anointing cleanses away sins, if there are any still to be expiated, and also the remains of sins; the Spirit raises up and strengthens the soul of the sick person by exciting in them a great confidence in the divine mercy. As a result, the sick person is supported, bears more easily the inconveniences and pains of their sickness and more readily resists the temptations of the devil who lies in wait for his heel; at times, they obtain bodily health, when this is good for the welfare of the soul.[2]

---

1. Ibid., 16.1, 6.
2. Ibid., 16.9.

Conclusion

The work at the Council of Trent becomes defining for much later Catholic theology. In the sacraments, one can generally see a very constructive approach being taken because, while the Protestant groups agreed on few aspects even of Baptism and the Lord's Supper, they were generally critical of a high medieval sacramental theology and what this meant for individual believers. The result at Trent was a reaffirmation and clarification of Catholic teaching. In terms of sin and justification, things were far more complex, firstly, because of the breadth of Catholic thought, which affirmed Augustine *and* Anselm *and* Bernard *and* Aquinas, and many others besides; and, secondly, because the different reforming voices emphasised different elements that were present in that Catholic spectrum, while all denied other elements. The Session on Justification thus seems to have been left with too great a task, either to state the Catholic position concisely, or to respond to Protestant views, concerning which there were clearly some misconceptions in any case.

The Canons of the Council of Trent are readily available online through a simple search and take very little time to read through. Be aware when accessing the theological sessions (as opposed to those opening and closing the Council) that the first part contains the theological material and the second part a set of reforms of the Church practice.

Conclusion

The European world changed massively between the end of the eleventh century and the middle of the sixteenth century, the period covered by this book. One of the biggest changes for the Church was the range of tools available to study the Christian faith. Anselm of Canterbury had the Scriptures (in Latin), many of the Church Fathers (principally Augustine) and some philosophical tools (mostly Plato) to work with the revelation of God. One of the most impressive aspects of Anselm's work is the type of thought that he was able to produce with so little, most notably in the *Cur Deus Homo* in which he highlighted substitutionary atonement more prominently than any thinker before him. Although he had access to few other ancient works beyond the Church Fathers and a bit of Plato, Anselm sounds almost modern in much of his writing and he balances concepts well, as this volume shows, in his work harmonising foreknowledge, predestination and grace with free will.

In the centuries that followed, many more ways of thinking were opened up to Christian scholars in the rediscovery of Aristotle, the influence of Jewish and Islamic thought coming in from the East and some scientific progress. Whenever we discuss Christian thought and doctrine, we must recognise that we do not do this in a neutral sense, but are using the philosophical and epistemological tools available to us and this affects our creation of concepts, our use of language and our appreciation (or not) of others using different methods.

Aquinas clearly stands out in this regard in the influence that Aristotle had on his thought and for which he is often criticised. Nevertheless, his writing on the nature of the will and the many aspects of the human consciousness that surround it can help us to think more deeply about a simple-sounding idea like 'free will', than if we understand this to encompass everything from our mind's initial concept through to the actions that we take. Luther and Zwingli, in particular, took exception to many of the Aristotelian models of Christian thought that they had been taught. However, we should not take their ideas as being independent of their context – Luther was a Renaissance humanist, while Zwingli has been better described as a Biblical humanist, and the methods associated with both these movements affect how they deal with Scripture and the Christian faith.

The result is a set of thinkers who take different approaches to the topics of sin, grace and free will, none of which matches exactly with how we might think about these ideas today, but in each of which we can find fellow Christians wrestling with what the Bible's teaching on these mean for the Church, if we seek to understand them rather than sit in judgement on them. This is a key method behind this series: the fact that what I find in these sources doesn't agree with how I would express these ideas should not lead me to exalt myself above them but rather to reflect on how they have come to their conclusions and to examine what informs my way of thinking for good or bad.

Around 1,500 years of Christian thought has now been surveyed in the first two volumes of this series on sin, grace and free will, with one more volume to come. That will begin towards the end of the sixteenth century with the thought of De Molina, particularly regarding free will, and will make its way through the modern world into the twentieth century, bringing this journey to its close.

Primary Sources

One of the main intentions behind these volumes, as has been stated on many occasions, is to encourage the reader to look at the primary sources from which these quotes have been pulled to explore the context in which ideas have been expressed. Below are the most accessible versions of the various works referenced in this book, and there may therefore be some slight changes of language from the translations found here but the references should help you quickly find the correct place.

Anselm of Canterbury:

De Libertate Arbitrii [On Free Will], tr. J. Hopkins and H. Richardson. Minneapolis: The Arthur J. Benning Press, 2000. Available at: http://www.jasper-hopkins. info/DeLibertate.pdf.

De Casu Diaboli [On the Fall of the Devil], tr. J. Hopkins and H. Richardson. Minneapolis: The Arthur J. Benning Press, 2000. Available at: http://www. jasper-hopkins.info/DeCasu.pdf.

De Conceptu Virginali [On Virgin Conception], tr. J. Hopkins and H. Richardson. Minneapolis: The Arthur J. Benning Press, 2000. Available at: http://www. jasper-hopkins.info/DeConceptu.pdf.

De Concordia [On Harmony], tr. J. Hopkins and H. Richardson. Minneapolis: The Arthur J. Benning Press, 2000. Available at: http://www.jasper-hopkins.info/ DeConcordia.pdf.

Bernard of Clairvaux:

On Grace and Free Choice, tr. D. O'Donovan. Kalamazoo, Michigan: Cistercian Publications, 1988.

Peter Lombard:

The Sentences, tr. G. Silano. Toronto: University of Toronto, 2007-2010.

Thomas Aquinas:

Summa Theologica, tr. Fathers of the English Dominican Province. Benziger Bros. edition, 1947. Available at: http://www.ccel.org/ccel/aquinas/summa.

Martin Luther

The Bondage of the Will, tr. H. Cole. London: Hamilton, 1823. Available at: http:// www.ccel.org/ccel/luther/bondage.pdf.

Table Talk, tr. W. Hazlitt. Philadelphia: Lutheran Publication Society, 1821. Available at: http://www.ccel.org/ccel/luther/tabletalk.pdf.

'The Heidelberg Disputation', in *The Book of Concord: Confessions of the Lutheran Church*. Available at: http://bookofconcord.org/.heidelberg.php

'Disputation Against Scholastic Theology' in *Luther's Works, Vol. 31: Career of the Reformer I* (ed. H. Grimm and H. Lehmann). Philadelphia: Fortress Press, 1957.

'Explanation of the 95 Theses' in *Luther's Works, Vol. 31: Career of the Reformer I* (ed. H. Grimm and H. Lehmann). Philadelphia: Fortress Press, 1957. Available at: http://www.oocities.org/united_in_christ_3in1/95explained.pdf.

'Concerning the Sacrament of Penance' in *First Principles of the Reformation or The Ninety-Five Theses and the Three Primary Works of Dr. Martin Luther* (ed. H. Wace and C. Buchheim). London: John Murray, 1883. Available at: http://www.ccel.org/ccel/luther/first_prin.pdf.

'The Blessed Sacrament of the Holy and True Body of Christ, and the Brotherhoods' in *Luther's Works, Vol. 35: Word and Sacrament I* (ed. E. Bachmann and H. Lehmann). Philadelphia: Fortress Press, 1960.

'Treatise on Baptism' (tr. C. Jacobs) in *Works of Martin Luther Volume 1*. Philadelphia: A.J. Holman, 1915.

'Treatise On Good Works' (tr. W. Lambert) in *Works of Martin Luther Volume 1*. Philadelphia: A.J. Holman, 1915. Reu translation available at: http://www.ccel.org/ccel/luther/good_works.pdf.

'On Christian Freedom' in Henry Wace and C. A. Buchheim (eds.), *First Principles of the Reformation*. London: John Murray, 1883. Available at: http://www.ccel.org/ccel/luther/christianliberty.txt.

'Concerning Rebaptism' in *Luther's Works, Vol. 40: Church and Ministry II* (ed. C. Bergendoff and H. Lehmann). Philadelphia: Fortress Press, 1958.

'Disputation Concerning Justification' in *Luther's Works, Vol. 34: Career of the Reformer IV* (ed. L. Spitz and H. Lehmann). Philadelphia: Fortress Press, 1960. Available at: https://www.uni-due.de/collcart/es/sem/s6/txt10_3.htm.

Ulrich Zwingli:

On Providence and Other Essays Durham, ed. S. Jackson. NC: The Labyrinth Press, 1922. Available at: https://ia600204.us.archive.org/31/items/OnProvidence/OnProvidence.pdf.

Commentary on True and False Religion, ed. S. Jackson. Durham, NC: The Labyrinth Press, 1923.

Huldrych Zwingli Writings, tr. E.J. Furcha. Allison Park, PA: Pickwick Publications, 1984.

John Calvin:

Institutes of the Christian Religion, tr. H. Beveridge. Available at: http://www.ccel.org/ccel/calvin/institutes.pdf.

On the Bondage and Liberation of the Will, tr. Graham Davies, ed. Tony Lane. Grand Rapids: Baker Books, 1996.

Council of Trent:

The canons and decrees of the sacred and oecumenical Council of Trent, tr. J. Waterworth. London: Dolman, 1848. Available at: http://www.documentacatholicaomnia.eu/03d/1545-1545,_Concilium_Tridentinum,_Canons_And_Decrees,_EN.pdf.

Index